UNLOCKING
the POWERS of
FAITH

UNLOCKING
the POWERS *of*
FAITH

GARTH L. ALLRED

Covenant Communications, Inc.

Cover art from *Pool of Bethesda* by Carl Heinrich Bloch. © Bethesda Danske Entre Mission, Copenhagen, Denmark. Used by permission.

Published by Covenant Communications, Inc.
American Fork, Utah

Printed in Canada
First Printing: October 1993

13 12 11 10 09 08 07   10 9 8 7 6 5 4 3 2

ISBN 1–55503–584–1
Library of Congress Catalog Card Number: 93-73457

To my many friends
who have helped me
write this book.

CONTENTS

PREFACE

Welcome, my friend! Welcome to the exciting and wonderful world of learning—learning how to develop your faith in the Lord Jesus Christ so that you can be healed of your pain, loneliness, confusion, and sorrow. Whether your problems are emotional, spiritual, or physical, you will find within this text important healing truths that can strengthen your faith and help you tap your own deep reservoirs of power.

Some people contend that the language of faith cannot be translated into the words of a book, that faith is simply something they feel, something they either have or don't have. To intellectualize faith, they say, destroys the enjoyment of it. Yet these same people would never suggest that those who most enjoy a football game know nothing about the rules of the game.

Few among us have plumbed the depths of this first principle of the gospel, "faith in the Lord Jesus Christ." While some elements of faith are difficult or impossible to convey through the written word, you can *learn* other, important aspects. These facets of faith will empower you with greater peace and freedom from pain. These learnable qualities of faith are the focus of this book.

Certainly we all can benefit by a closer look at the power level of faith—especially in this premillennial era when the prophets have repeatedly warned that for those who are unprepared, pain, sorrow, and suffering will dramatically increase.

However, while pain and suffering will be greatest among the unbelieving, the faithful are promised deliverance, as Nephi reminds us: "Behold, I, Nephi, will show unto you that the tender mercies of the Lord are over all those whom he hath chosen, because of their faith, to make them mighty even unto the power of deliverance" (1 Ne. 1:20).

For me, the quest for greater power in faith has been a life-long search. I have been a seminary, institute, or religion teacher within the educational system of The Church of Jesus Christ of Latter-day Saints for over a quarter of a century. I was also a professor of Bible Studies at the Jerusalem Center for Near Eastern Studies. Presently, as a professor of religion at the Brigham Young University—Hawaii Campus, I teach students enrolled in scripture and marriage classes. I also maintain a private practice in marriage, family, and individual psychotherapy in the Mormon community of Laie, Hawaii.

As an LDS religion professor and as a psychotherapist, I earnestly try to incorporate the gospel into my teachings of mental health principles. Especially interesting to me are those aspects of mental health that relate to the scriptures; for example, "For as he thinketh in his heart, so is he" (Prov. 23:7). I have come to appreciate how strongly our thoughts, beliefs, and actions affect our moods and physical health, and have come to profoundly know that the Holy Ghost is the fountainhead of all truth. The Holy Spirit leads us beside still waters and brings all things to our remembrance. It will eventually reveal to us all truth.

The Holy Spirit has led me to healing springs of truth, both in my professional studies and in my gospel studies. Many of these principles I share with the objective of helping you develop stronger faith to be healed.

In this text I have brought together two powerful sources of truth to help heal your pain: (1) faith in the Lord Jesus Christ and (2) faith in your own divine nature. It is in the balance of God's grace and your own properly focused thoughts that you will experience miracles in your life. To be healed by faith, you need to gain a more correct knowledge of your Heavenly Father's eternal plan for your happiness as well as greater knowledge about what you can do, exercising your God-given agency, to invite his healing power.

I have observed that many times people who are suffering pain, depression, sorrow, or pending death are "locked in" to a false belief about God's will for them and about their own ability to find relief. In their mistaken notions of reality, they believe that God is either testing them, Satan is tempting them, or other people are persecuting them.

Because they lack hope, their minds are darkened like a black hole. One sister told me she even felt as though she herself had become a black hole. Her persistent depression ultimately influenced her physically, sucking away her energy and vitality. She lost weight. Her eyes became sunken and lusterless.[1] When people are hurting like this they give up hope and do not see themselves in the proper light. They lack God's point of view about themselves. They see no roses in the garden of life, only weeds—darkness and destruction.

This book is a course in learning to work by faith in order to pull up the weeds and plant the roses in the garden of your thoughts, and thus your life.

Pulling weeds is learning to eliminate those nonproductive thoughts and mental images that keep you from the vision of things as they really are. Planting roses is receiving light and knowledge from the heavens which empower you with the Lord's view of things. However, faith helps you to see colors in more vivid hues—your perceptions of people, nature, and of yourself become more joyful and exciting. God's way is health and happiness. Your faith empowers you with hope for the future and fills your mind and heart with charity, the pure love of Christ, for yourself and others.

I do not wish to give the impression that a resolution of your pain and conflict is easy. It will take time and experience to learn how to give up your false beliefs and accept what is revealed to you. The Lord has promised, "Ask, and it shall be given you; seek, and ye shall find; knock, and it shall be opened unto you" (Matt. 7:7). However, remember to be careful about what you ask for. James warned, "Ye ask, and receive not, because ye ask amiss" (James 4:3). I trust that the words of this book will be true and faithful and thereby help you so that you do not ask amiss.

The ideas and principles presented in this work are valid, but they are not designed to be an exhaustive study of faith healing. They are not meant to take the place of psychotherapeutic treatment or medical care. This book is a primer describing basic, essential steps you must take to begin bringing about healing power in your life. It is to be used in conjunction with whatever course of treatment your doctor or health-care provider prescribes. If you have a life-threatening illness, you must take some life-supporting actions, which naturally include proper medical attention.

In a book like this, it is virtually impossible for me to make personal applications for you of all the principles discussed. Nor can I completely qualify every principle that I present, although I will try to address the most important ones. Reading this book is not the same as having personal contact with the author. Biblio-therapy (book therapy) is not the same as personal counseling. I am limited in my efforts to help you when I do not see you face to face. The human element is missing with just the written word. I cannot reach out and touch your hand or smile when you need reassurance. But in my words, I trust you will be able to find many true principles and a feeling of love that will help you move toward the light of health and peace of mind. Much of what you get out of this book will be a result of your own quiet reflection as you seek direction from the Holy Spirit.

We are promised that there will come a time when anything we ask will be given us—even in the moment we ask (D&C 24:6; 101:27). In the meantime, however, we must gradually grow in our faith and righteousness; we must progressively learn how to draw on the powers of heaven to be healed. This book is my gift to you to help you stop hurting and start healing and begin experiencing the power that comes through healing faith in the Lord Jesus Christ and in your own divine nature.

Although the ideas presented here are not to be taken as authoritative Church doctrine, I believe them to be true and have tried earnestly to ground each principle in the scriptures, statements made by latter-day prophets, or gospel-compatible mental health principles.

As you discover and learn how to use the healing power of faith, use it with joy for your own healing and the blessing of others. You are much more powerful than you have dreamed. You have a divine nature about you that is wonderful, marvelous, and Godlike. You have the power within you, when properly directed, to reach out and tap the wonderful healing powers of the heavens. May the Lord bless you in this challenging and rewarding quest.

NOTE

1. By emphasizing the effect of thoughts on one's physical health, I do not deny medical causes as well, but the emphasis of this book will be on the effect one's thoughts have on one's health. I affirm the latter but do not deny the former.

ACKNOWLEDGMENTS

This book is lovingly dedicated to Mary and Noriko, and to my children: Scott, Darron, Angela, David, JoEll, Michael, Amber, and Marc. I trust that my patients who have been in therapy with me will understand and forgive my enthusiasm when, in the course of their treatment, we discovered important healing principles that just had to be jotted down for use in this book. So many people have contributed so much.

I am especially grateful to Mary Ellen Smith Taylor for her encouragement and helpful editing of the early stages of this manuscript. Without her infectious enthusiasm for gospel-centered affirmations and visualizations, this book would never have been written.

I am particularly and deeply indebted to the late Marguerite DeLong, a majestic soul who mastered in her life the healing powers of faith. Having been born with spina bifida, she had never been without physical affliction. She underwent over twenty major surgeries during her two decades of life. In spite of her diminutive physical height, she had developed the qualities of a true spiritual giant. Through her untiring editing skills and sweet, trusting communion with the Spirit, she assisted me repeatedly in breaking down the walls of discouragement that would have otherwise blocked the completion of this work. Her sacred peek (and peak) experiences regarding her own divine nature, which she shared with me from time to time, provided a special spiritual dimension to this book that would be missing otherwise. Thank you, Marguerite.

I

Faith in the Lord Jesus Christ

Our Savior, Jesus Christ, is in and through all things. It is through his power that the worlds are and were created and all things are maintained. It is through him that all things have their being. He is the Light and the Life of the world. He is God's Almighty Son. He has descended below all things so that he might comprehend all things. He is the vine; we are the branches. Even as a branch is able to bear fruit because it is connected to and receives nourishment through the vine, even so you can be healed of your loneliness, pain, sorrow, or crippled body through the power of Jesus Christ, the true vine of our Heavenly Father.

1

The Search for Healing Faith

Whatsoever thing ye shall ask the Father in my name, which is good, in faith believing that ye shall receive, behold, it shall be done unto you.

—MORONI 7:26

I had to struggle to maintain my composure as I looked up from my desk. Donna,[1] a patient, had cut off all her hair with no attempt to style it. Without even looking in a mirror, she had wildly grabbed handfuls of hair and whacked them off.

This frantic action was Donna's way of crying out for help—an act of sheer frustration. She had shuffled into my office with her eyes staring at the floor, her clothes wrinkled, and her socks sagging. My first comment to her was simply, "You really must be hurting!" With that simple expression, Donna's emotional floodgates opened, and a surge of anger, frustration, bitterness, and pain came bursting out. For the first time in many months, she vented her festering pain and pent-up emotions.

Finally there followed a calmness in her voice and spirit. When her heart had become sufficiently contrite and she could listen, we were able to reflect upon the voice of the Good Shepherd: "My [daughter], peace be unto thy soul; thine adversity and thine afflictions shall be but a small moment; and then, if thou endure it well, God shall exalt thee on high; thou shalt triumph over all thy foes" (D&C 121:7–8). We went on to: "If the heavens gather blackness, and all the elements combine to hedge up the way; and above all, if the very jaws of hell shall gape open the mouth wide after thee, know thou, my [daughter], that all these things shall give thee experience, and shall be for thy good. The Son of Man hath descended below them all. Art thou greater than he? (D&C 122:7–8), and "Therefore, dearly beloved . . . let us cheerfully do all things that lie in our power; and then may we stand still, with the utmost assurance, to see the salvation of God, and for his arm to be revealed" (D&C 123:17).

For Donna, a fresh start came from our Savior through his holy scriptures. As she worked to change her thoughts and her focus, her despairing moods gradually changed.

What were the causes of Donna's intense emotional pain? Many medical scientists would assume that her deep depression and emotional outbursts were simply the results of hormonal and chemical dysfunction. Many psychologists would hold that her moods and outbursts were the consequence of pent-up negative thoughts, beliefs, and actions. Others would point to her neglectful husband and rebellious children as main contributors to her pain and suffering. Donna herself frequently voiced to me that her pains were her "just deserts." "God is punishing me," she often said, "for my past sins." Then she would quote Lord Byron, "The thorns which I have reap'd are of the tree I planted."

I believe that all of these factors are involved and to some extent contributed to Donna's pain. But I believe that the number one cause of her emotional and relationship problems was the insecurity she created by her own thought patterns! I agree with George S. Pransky when he points out the role of mind-sets and thought systems as they contribute to our insecurity:

> Many marriage counselors say the past—its unexpressed emotions and habit patterns—and poor communication are the "bad guys" that cause mental and relationship distress. These are the symptoms of relationship distress, not the cause. The cause, the real bad guy, is *insecurity*. Painful memories, negative emotions, habit patterns and bad communication are all *symptoms* of insecurity.
>
> If you want to understand why people do as they do and feel the way they feel, you need only to understand the role of insecurity in life. Insecurity is the source of distress and all counterproductive behavior.[2]

I believe that the greatest mind-set we can master has to do with who we really are as sons and daughters of God. The greatest thought system we can learn involves a knowledge of our Savior, Jesus Christ—a knowledge of his person, character and attributes, and his principles of salvation. Knowing about him and what he taught will bring peace in this world and eternal life in the world to come. The power of the scripture, "Know the truth and the truth will make you free" (John 8:32), lies in the fact that as we learn the truth about Christ's healing powers, we are no longer subject to insecurity!

Donna's mind-sets and thought systems were, for a time, devoid of a correct faith in Christ and his healing powers. She had forgotten that she was a daughter of God, that there can be peace in spite of difficulties, that there is growth potential in adversity. She had forgotten—or had never known—that she need not be victimized by the negative influences around her. As her thoughts changed, her moods changed. When her moods were low, she became caught up in self-defeating thoughts and actions. Persistent distress had affected her general health. When her thoughts changed and her moods were high, everything was different. She saw herself differently. She saw her husband differently. Even the world seemed a nicer place to live.

Have you experienced a belief similar to Donna's, that you are locked in a mortal prison of emotional or physical pain as long as you live or until the Second Coming, when Jesus will heal all disease and wipe away all tears? Do you think you are suffering because your faith is lacking in some way? Do you find yourself, in times of your despair, looking toward heaven and crying out, "Please help me, I'm hurting!"

As you pray for help, I trust that this work will help you find the peace you are seeking through new mind-sets and new thought systems that are centered in Christ and your own divine nature. I hope that I can help you get a fresh start by changing your thought patterns into faith-power, the true healing agent, the balm of Gilead!

UNITING THE SACRED AND THE SECULAR

Faith is a gospel principle referring to a strong belief or trust in the Lord Jesus Christ. Active faith can be emotionally healing, as in Donna's case, but also spiritually and physically healing. The healing power of faith involves learning how to apply faith, the first principle of the gospel, as a healing power. To understand this process it is necessary that you become acquainted with principles from both secular and spiritual sources.

We don't want to become extremists—either depending too much on the "arm of flesh," the learning and wisdom of men, or expecting divine intervention in matters where competent medical help is available and appropriate.

As a psychotherapist, I recognize, as the medical community does, that the biochemical conditions that exist in our bodies have a strong impact on our thoughts and moods; but I also know that our choice of thoughts has a powerful effect on our emotions and physical conditions. Before I begin sessions with my patients, I suggest they have a good physical checkup (to rule out any biochemical problems), and get a priesthood blessing from their husband, father, or bishop. Then I am in a good position to help them find the peace that comes through the healing power of faith. We need to take into account every aspect of our lives because they are all interdependent.

The early Saints who settled the Mormon community of Laie, Hawaii, recognized the need to join the academic and the spiritual elements of their lives. These pioneers of the Pacific laid out two of their city streets to show such union. The street running directly from the Temple toward the ocean is called Hale Laa, or "House of Light." The street running from BYU-Hawaii (formerly known as Church College of Hawaii) is named Kulanui, meaning "Big House." The joining of these streets forms a large circle near Temple Beach. From the air, the streets are seen as a giant V, or a huge compass, attached at the bottom by a large circle. This unusual mapping of streets appears strange to outsiders, but the symbolism is quite obvious to practicing Latter-day Saints. For the Saints, all truths are compatible and will blend perfectly whether they are from sacred temples or from secular universities, or even from what we might consider foreign cultures.

I believe that as distant doors are opened to the missionaries and as Israel is gathered from all nations—as we become more and more an international church—"They [who are gathered into the Church] shall bring forth their rich treasures unto the children of Ephraim, my servants" (D&C 133:30). Could it be that as East meets West there will be a complementariness of knowledge? Our highly technological culture has much to learn from those nations and cultures who realize the importance of mind and spirit healing connected with healing of the body.

When we from the western cultures pick up injured people off the highways of life, we hook them up to diagnostic computer systems and intravenous drip drugs—but we too often forget to talk to them, to comfort them, to ask about their family and faith. Other cultures are more sensitive about such things. While my family and I were in the Middle East, we visited Arab hospitals. There are no restrictions there. Families and friends all come to the hospital not just to visit but to almost move in with the patient. They hang pictures from home on the hospital walls. Food is cooked at home and brought to the patient. Extended families and neighbors all rally around the patient and provide wonderful support and healing comfort.

There is much that we can learn from these brothers and sisters. "For behold, the Lord doth grant unto all nations, of their own nation and tongue, to teach his word, yea, in wisdom, all that he seeth fit that they should have; therefore we see that the Lord doth counsel in wisdom, according to that which is just and true" (Alma 29:8). Since Israel has been scattered among all nations, it should not surprise us to find important healing truths from among all nations.

It would be naive to think that our western culture alone has the edge on truth—healing truths or otherwise. Of course, caution must be encouraged as we seek for proper healing principles and practices for our spirits, minds, and bodies. The spirit of discernment and wisdom is vital as we sift and sort through new ideas and techniques for healing.

THE SEARCH FOR PROPER HEALING PRACTICES

For as long as I can remember, I have been interested in the relationship of the spirit, mind, and body. I remember taking physiology classes that ignored our important Latter-day Saint knowledge of premortal intelligence and spirit. In more secular classes, the mind is regarded as simply electrical discharges of the brain. Accordingly, they believe that when the mind is sick, what is really sick is the functioning of the brain. By this logic, the classical mental disorders—depression, schizophrenia, and psychosis—are actually *brain* disorders and have no relationship to thought choices. This logic has obvious inadequacies: it is like saying that all car wrecks should be blamed on automobiles. The question is, do negative thoughts actually affect the brain, or does the brain cause the negative thoughts? Of course it works both ways, but our western culture and western science has had a tendency to stress the latter almost to the exclusion of the former.

Because the brain is a physical organ that can be weighed and dissected, medical scientists feel more secure in working with the biological brain than with the mind. The mind has proved impossible to define scientifically, even after many centuries of introspection and analysis. This lopsided emphasis on biology has contributed to the emphasis on technology and chemical prescriptions for treatment. It has also promoted, perhaps unwittingly, the pervasive atheistic or agnostic view that when the brain dies, the mind ceases to exist.

I do not want to downplay the importance of modern medicine. As a general statement in their favor, they are right in many of the things they affirm. But as a limitation, they are wrong if they deny or choose to ignore the role of the mind and spirit in the healing process. As time passes, I detect that modern medicine is gradually opening its doors to more holistic approaches to healing—doors that provide a view of the interconnection of the human spirit, mind, families, religion, and culture.

Norman Cousins, the famous editor and author, was an early pioneer in exploring mind and body healing. He fell gravely ill with a rare disease, and his extraordinary experiences as a patient became the subject of his best-selling book *Anatomy of an Illness*. He has generously shared what he has learned about emotions and health, laughter and medicine, mind and body. He became perhaps the country's best-known and most informed layman about these matters, approaching them, as one of his friends said, "with the discerning eye of a research scientist and the unabashed excitement of a child. He was a convert. He had a vision."[3]

In 1980, Norman Cousins suffered a severe heart attack. Again, he turned his harrowing recovery into a book, *The Healing Heart: Antidotes to Panic and Helplessness*. The University of California at Los Angeles invited him to become an adjunct professor of psychiatry and behavioral science; and until his death in 1990, he was the unofficial but enormously influential catalyst for the rapidly growing field of mind/body medicine. Books and articles are proliferating in this exciting area of discovery.[4]

It is refreshing to see these advances in mind/body research as they are being applied on a day-to-day level in the hurried and technology-driven world of modern medicine. From neonatal care to geriatrics, from same-day surgery to the treatment of chronic illness, medical professionals are finding that when they practice the "new medicine," their patients heal faster, leave the hospital sooner, and do better once they get home.

As we explore mind/body medicine, the questions that are always before us are: How do our emotions translate into chemicals in our bodies? How do thoughts and feelings influence health? How can we collaborate with our bodies to encourage healing? And as Latter-day Saints, we ask the all-important questions: How can we increase our faith in Christ to promote healing? How can we exercise faith to be healed in body, mind, and spirit and still say, "Thy will be done"? These are some of the issues addressed in this book.

SPIRITUAL LAWS THAT PROMOTE HEALING

We are governed by many different laws—spiritual laws, physical laws, and universal laws—most of which we do not yet recognize nor fully understand. These laws were created to fulfill a purpose, and they all complement each other. As we recognize these laws and learn how to use their positive and negative forces, we begin to have access to power beyond our comprehension. We are responsible for our own bodies, and everything from within our spirits is manifested in our flesh.

It is our goal to bring the mind, body, and spirit into total harmony, which is only possible when the spirit is in control and Christlike love prevails.

The scriptures reveal many laws that are health-related. In the New Testament, James gives us a pattern for blessing the sick: "Is any sick among you? let him call for the elders of the church; and let them pray over him, anointing him with oil in the name of the Lord: And the prayer of faith shall save the sick, and the Lord shall raise him up" (James 5:14–15). This same principle of giving priesthood blessings was affirmed in latter-day revelation, with the Lord's addition: "And whosoever among you are sick, and have not faith to be healed, but believe, shall be nourished with all tenderness, with herbs and mild food, and that not by the hand of an enemy" (D&C 42:43). In other words, when our faith is not sufficient to be healed, we are admonished to seek other remedies which may include medical and psychological help—but not by the hand of the enemy.

Though there has been impressive progress made in medical technology and in the mental health fields (psychology, psychiatry, psychotherapy, etc.), the Saints need to be wary of the hand of the enemy—man-made doctrines—that may be harmful or even destructive because they are contrary to the true order of heaven. Within these disciplines I have sometimes found polluted waters—assumptions and postulates that are false. I have discovered President Benson's warning to be true that an advanced degree in the social sciences "may be tantamount to a major investment in error."[5]

Someone once said, "If you are a hammer, everything looks like a nail." In other words, if you are a surgeon, surgery is the first treatment you think of; if you are a mental health practitioner, then psychotherapy is the first order of treatment considered. Professional humility and balance are greatly needed in the healing arts. The filtering of the secular waters through the gospel net is a great challenge, but the effort is rewarding in those moments when we find springs of healing waters.

The Apostle Paul instructed us to "prove all things; hold fast [to] that which is good" (1 Thes. 5:21). The Lord declared: "Cursed is he that putteth his trust in man, or maketh flesh his arm, or shall hearken unto the precepts of men, save their precepts shall be given by the power of the Holy Ghost" (2 Ne. 28:31). Important truths can be learned from the secular world. The scriptures charge us to learn

> Of things both in heaven and in the earth, and under the earth; things which have been, things which are, things which must shortly come to pass; things which are at home, things which are abroad; the wars and the perplexities of the nations, and the judgments which are on the land; and a knowledge also of countries and of kingdoms. (D&C 88:79)

Yet, sadly, I find people in the Church who reject medical and psychological help simply because this help lies outside the framework of the Church. Many times the process of healing takes in a combination of many different sources of help, working together to heal the whole person.

THE PROMISE OF PEACE THROUGH FAITH

When our efforts are properly directed toward Christ and his teachings, the result is peace—even in the midst of problems. (See

D&C 59:23.) Our minds and spirits can be healed even when the body is infirm or diseased. We are promised that if we properly exercise faith in the Savior, regardless of adversity, the Lord will bless us with peace. The Apostle Paul testified of his peace in spite of a "thorn in the flesh" that plagued him.

> For this thing I besought the Lord thrice, that it might depart from me. And he said unto me, My grace is sufficient for thee: for my strength is made perfect in weakness. Most gladly therefore will I rather glory in my infirmities, that the power of Christ may rest upon me. Therefore I take pleasure in infirmities, in reproaches, in necessities, in persecutions, in distresses for Christ's sake: for when I am weak, then am I strong. (2 Cor. 12:7–10)

Some problems may not be overcome or cured, such as Paul's thorn in the flesh. Others may not be overcome quickly. The road to recovery may be long for you, too; however, faith empowers you to experience peace in spite of adversity. This healing of the spirit, this holy peace comes through your mental and spiritual efforts to follow the promptings of the Holy Ghost, to search out correct principles, and to cheerfully do all that lies within your power. Faith allows you to stand still, "with the utmost assurance, to see the salvation of God, and for his arm to be revealed" (D&C 123:17).

Of her own tempered impatience, one Latter-day Saint woman wrote:

> I was feeling really sad and frustrated so I talked to a friend. After he left, I felt sad and lonely. I cried and I prayed "Father, what should I do?"
>
> His answer: "Cheerfully do all things that lie within your power and then wait. It will come. Be still and know that I am God." That really hit me. "Be still and know that I am God." This impression from the Lord connected with something my friend had told me. He said I didn't need to push or struggle for the promises and blessings—I was just to wait and nourish my faith and I then I will blossom as a rose. The blessings will come; the promises will be fulfilled. I know of my Father's love for me and of his Godhood.
>
> That assurance has come to me in quiet moments as I watch and pray and listen. When I am still, trust in him, and listen, he reveals himself to me in quiet, simple ways. I know he loves me. I know I'm not alone. He *is* aware of me and he *will* help me.

FAITH—A PRINCIPLE OF POWER

In our gospel conversations, we often define faith as strong belief plus action, trust, assurance, etc. Our fourth Article of Faith identifies faith as the first principle of the gospel. Paul defined faith as "the substance of things hoped for, the evidence of things not seen" (Heb. 11:1). To clarify its importance, Paul stated that "without faith it is impossible to please him: for he that cometh to God must believe that he is, and that he is a rewarder of them that diligently seek him" (Heb. 11:6). The Lectures on Faith elaborate on Paul's statement:

> If it should be asked—Why is it impossible to please God without faith? The answer would be—Because without faith it is impossible for men to be saved; and as God desires the salvation of men, he must, of course, desire that they should have faith; and he could not be pleased unless they had, or else he could be pleased with their destruction.[6]

Since faith is the first principle of the gospel, we may think that we will soon grow out of the need for faith and that we need to get on with greater and more important aspects of the gospel. In actual fact, faith is a pervasive, all-encompassing principle. In my own gospel study, I have come back again and again to the fact that faith is not only the first principle of the gospel, but also the underlying principle of all truth and power. Elder Vaughn J. Featherstone explains the importance of faith:

> What a great thing it is if we understand what faith is. What is faith? How does it work? Do you have total faith? . . . I doubt we will ever really get through an understanding and complete knowledge of faith in a lifetime. I don't care how intellectual you are, or how long you study, I doubt you will ever come to an end of the study of faith, the first principle of the gospel. The gospel is so simple that a fool will not err therein, but it is so beautiful and so sophisticated that I believe that the greatest intellectual can make a study of faith and never come to an end of understanding.[7]

In the *Lectures on Faith*, faith is described as a principle of action and power:

> Faith is not only a principle of action, but of power also, in all intelligent beings, whether in heaven or on earth. Thus says the author of the epistle to the Hebrews (11:3):
> "Through faith we understand that the worlds were framed by the word of God, so that things which are seen were not made of things which do appear."

By this we understand that the principle of power which existed in the bosom of God, by which the worlds were framed, was faith; and that it is by reason of this principle of power existing in the Deity, that all created things exist; so that all things in heaven, on earth, or under the earth exist by reason of faith as it existed in HIM.

Had it not been for the principle of faith the worlds would never have been framed, neither would man have been formed of the dust. It is the principle by which Jehovah works, and through which he exercises power over all temporal as well as eternal things. Take this principle or attribute—for it is an attribute—from Deity, and he would cease to exist.

Who cannot see, that if God framed the worlds by faith, that it is by faith that he exercises power over them, and that faith is the principle of power? And if the principle of power, it must be so in man as well as in the Deity? This is the testimony of all the sacred writers, and the lesson which they have been endeavoring to teach to man.[8]

This passage is teaching us *faith-power*. The scriptures are filled with examples of faith as a principle of power. In the Doctrine and Covenants we read that "the rights of the priesthood are inseparably connected with the powers of heaven, and that the powers of heaven cannot be controlled nor handled only upon the principles of righteousness" (D&C 121:36). Examples of such power in faith include Enoch speaking the word of the Lord, when the earth trembled and the mountains fled. (See Moses 7:13.) Joshua commanded, "Sun, stand thou still," and the sun obeyed (Josh. 10:12–13). Moses was promised that he would be made "stronger than many waters; for they shall obey thy command as if thou wert God" (Moses 1:25). The Nephites during the days of Jacob increased their faith until they could "command in the name of Jesus and the very trees obey us, or the mountains, or the waves of the sea" (Jacob 4:6). Peter, spying a lame man near a gate of the temple who had been unable to walk for the forty years of his life, simply said, "In the name of Jesus Christ of Nazareth rise up and walk." The result? "He leaping up stood, and walked, and entered with them into the temple, walking, and leaping, and praising God" (Acts 3:1–10).

Although faith is a principle of sublime power, for your faith to be healing you must have a correct knowledge of Christ and his teachings; otherwise you have no focus for your faith. Before you can exercise sufficient faith in Christ to be healed, you must learn of him, his character and his attributes. You must first know that a loving and kind Father in Heaven lives and that there is sufficient power reserved in the Atonement to cleanse you from sin, heal you, justify you, and even sanctify you. Before we can exercise faith sufficient for health and well being, we must have an awareness of the eternal principles involved in health and happiness.

The knowledge of truth makes us free (John 8:32). All blessings are predicated upon eternal laws. We read from the Doctrine and Covenants that "There is a law, irrevocably decreed in heaven before the foundations of this world, upon which all blessings are predicated—And when we obtain any blessing from God, it is by obedience to that law upon which it is predicated" (D&C 130:20–21). So it is with the faith to be healed—we must obey the law by which faith operates if we are to receive our desired blessing.

There are certain doors associated with our health and happiness which can be unlocked as we come to more fully know of the Savior and the correct principles he and his prophets have taught. How, then, does one discern correct healing principles from false ones in our search for healing principles? There are many false voices calling, "Come unto me and be healed—and bring your money!" How are you to know how to best strengthen your faith without being misled?

MEASURING THINGS OF THE SPIRIT

Spiritual experiences may be hard to communicate to others. Healings through faith are difficult, if not impossible, to measure with traditional medical instruments. A person may be wracked with physical pain and still be full of joyful anticipation of promised blessings. Physical healings through faith-power seem to manifest themselves in full strength only outside the framework of scientific observation, and seem to diminish progressively as their study becomes more and more scientific.[9] Traditionally, science has been associated with quantitative (numbers) measurement ever since Galileo banned quality (values) from the sphere of scientific knowledge, and most scientists today still take this view. Yet, a science concerned only with numbers and based exclusively on measurement is inherently unable to deal with experience, quality, values, or things of the spirit. The more scientists insist on quantitative statements, the less they are able to describe the nature of the spirit and the mind of people.

Robert Matthews, former dean of religious instruction at Brigham Young University, explained that the theology of the Latter-day Saints makes us quite different from the rest of the world in our search for truth:

> We are teaching a doctrine and philosophy that came from another world, from a more advanced culture, and is out of sync with the wisdom of this world. Gifts of the spirit, without which the true gospel cannot exist, are not a function of the natural world. We are dealing with a celestial law in the midst of a telestial world of natural law. Conflict, or at least incongruity [between traditional science and LDS theology], is inevitable.[10]

How, then, can we know if a suggested healing principle is true and good? The Book of Mormon provides a powerful test to help us in this regard. Alma compared the word of God (truth) to a seed. He explained that any seed that does not (1) swell within our breast, (2) enlarge our soul, (3) enlighten our mind, or (4) become delicious to us is not a true seed and should be cast out. (See Alma 32:28.)

In my formal schooling, in reading, in conferences I have attended, and in my private practice, I have encountered treatment programs that to me have been quite offensive. I find it comforting and reassuring to remember that the Lord is my true Shepherd. He, through his Holy Spirit, guides me into truth (Moro. 10:5). It is he who causes "me to lie down in green pastures: he leadeth me beside the still waters. He restoreth my soul: he leadeth me in the paths of righteousness for his name's sake. Yea, though I walk through the valley of the shadow of death, I will fear no evil: for thou art with me" (Ps. 23:2–4).

In your search for true healing principles, the Good Shepherd will lead you as you earnestly seek to follow him. The Prophet Joseph Smith taught that "a man is saved no faster than he gets knowledge."[11] Similarly, you can only gain mastery of your emotions and avoid false therapies as you gain an understanding of gospel principles and correct medical practices—seeds of truth from two sources that can be both helpful and healing. In your discovery of good seeds, you will find that healing faith-power will grant you a fresh start and that you will enjoy a wonderful road to recovery.

NOTES

1. All names have been changed to protect the identity of those mentioned.
2. George S. Pransky, *Divorce Is Not the Answer: A Change of Heart Will Save Your Marriage* (Bradenton, Florida: Tab Books, 1990), xii.

3. Norman Cousins, *Anatomy of an Illness* as quoted in Bill Moyers, *Healing and the Mind* (New York: Doubleday, 1993), xi.

4. The following books deal with mind/body medicine: Deepak Chopra, *Quantum Healing: Exploring the Frontiers of Mind/Body Medicine* (New York: Bantam, 1990); Paul Davies, *God and the New Physics* (New York: Simon and Schuster, 1984); Larry Dossey, *Space, Time, and Medicine* (Boston: Shambhala, 1982); Rene Dubos, *Man, Medicine, and Environment* (New York: Praeger, 1968); Jon Franklin, *Molecules of the Mind* (New York: Bantam, 1987); Stephen M. Hawking, *A Brief History of Time* (New York: Bantam, 1988.); Michio Kaku and Jennifer Trainer, *Beyond Einstein* (New York: Bantam, 1987); Stephen Locke and Douglas Colligan, *The Healer Within* (New York: Dutton, 1986); Bill Moyers, *Healing and the Mind* (New York: Doubleday, 1993); Mahesh Maharishi, *On the Bhagavad-Gita* (London: Penguin, 1967); Mahesh Maharishi, *Science of Being and Art of Living* (Boston: Houghton Mifflin, 1978); Anthony Smith, *The Body* (New York: Viking, 1986); and Ken Wilber, ed., *Quantum Questions* (Boston, Shambhala, 1984).

5. Ezra Taft Benson, *Conference Report,* April 1969, 12.

6. *Lectures on Faith* 7:7.

7. Vaughn J. Featherstone, "As If they Would Ask Him to Tarry a Little Longer," in *Speeches of the Year,* 1975 (Provo, Utah: Brigham Young University Press, 1976), 375.

8. *Lectures on Faith* 1:13–17, emphasis added.

9. Fritjof Capra, "Can Science Explain Psychic Phenomena?" *Re-Vision* (Winter/Spring).

10. Robert J. Matthews, "What is a Religious Education?" address given at a meeting of full time religious education faculty of Brigham Young University, Park City, Utah, 31 August 1989.

11. Joseph Smith, Jr., *Teachings of the Prophet Joseph Smith,* sel. Joseph Fielding Smith (Salt Lake City: Deseret Book, 1976), 217, 357 (hereafter cited as *Teachings*).

2

Faith and Mental Exertion

When a man works by faith he works by mental exertion instead of physical force.
—LECTURES ON FAITH 7:3

The power of faith is one of the gifts of the Spirit that you can draw upon to help heal your emotional, spiritual, and physical wounds. Faith brings salvation; miracles are wrought by faith; by faith the worlds were made. God is God because faith dwells in him independently; and faith is power, the very power of God himself. We read in the *Lectures on Faith* that faith in the broad, universal sense, outside the realm of religion "is the moving cause of all action . . . in all intelligent beings. . . . Who cannot see, that if God framed the worlds by faith, that it is by faith that he exercises power over them, and that faith is the principle of power? And if the principle of power, it must be so in man as well as in the Deity?"[1] As you investigate healing faith-power, you will find that it is more involved than just positive thinking, as the following story illustrates.

Some years ago I was able to establish a relationship of trust with a sick and suffering student. Wracked with depression associated with a particular birth defect which had plagued her for twenty years, Kathy was contemplating suicide. The physical pain and the social rejection were more than she felt she could bear. Although she had grown up in the Church and had been taught the gospel, Kathy had never really captured the image of her eternal worth, her true spirit identity, and the assurance of God's justice—that in time she would have a perfect body. As I visited with her, I told her of the Prophet Joseph Smith's promise that all the injustices experienced in this life will be made up in the resurrection provided we continue faithfully.[2] After days and weeks of counseling and encouragement, prayer and renewed faith, Kathy was able to make a change, a complete turnaround in the way she thought and felt about herself and her condition. Her physical defect did not change, but her emotional pain concerning it was healed. In time she completed a mission, where she served cheerfully and successfully.

Kathy's growth is not exceptional. You too can develop this kind of faith-power. As you seek to keep the commandments of the Lord, you will find important healing treasures that can bless your life and the lives of others.

The Lord has given us the promise that those who walk "in obedience to the commandments, shall receive health in their navel and marrow to their bones; And shall find wisdom and great treasures of knowledge, even hidden treasures; And shall run and not be weary, and shall walk and not faint" (D&C 89:18–20). There are powers associated with faith, when your mind and spirit are in harmony with the Holy Ghost, that have scarcely even been considered. The last frontier may not be the ocean, nor even space, but your own mind—when it operates in unity with truths revealed by the Spirit of the Lord. As you progressively bring your thoughts, feelings, and actions into harmony with the Lord, you will increase in the degree of power you will have with the heavens. Though the powers of the heavens are readily available at all times, their accessibility is dependent upon your ability to exercise your faith—through your own mental exertion.

FAITH IS MENTAL EXERTION

The word *faith,* all by itself, seems a little passive. Some popular writers have used the word *faithing*—a verb—to more fully describe the active nature and power of healing faith.

> Faithing is trusting that everything will work out for the highest good of all concerned. Beyond that, faithing is realizing that everything already

is working out for the highest good of all concerned. We may not like it that way, but with faith we realize that our opinions and desires about how we think it should be aren't necessarily the way it will work out best.

Faithing is actively setting aside our personal shoulds, musts, opinions and beliefs and moving into the flow of what's actually happening. With faithing, we put acceptance above opinion.[3]

The *Lectures on Faith* stress the same idea, although with much greater understanding. Faith as a principle of power is not just something we have; it is something that we do. It is mental exertion focused on eternal verities.

> Let us here offer some explanation in relation to faith, that our meaning may be clearly comprehended. We ask, then, what are we to understand by a man's working by faith? We answer—we understand that when a man works by faith he works by mental exertion instead of physical force. It is by words, instead of exerting his physical powers, with which every being works when he works by faith.[4]

When you work by faith, you exert yourself mentally. You exert yourself to focus your thoughts, words, attitudes, and beliefs on true principles.

There are four steps involved in active faith.

1. Messengers give you information about particular healing procedures and truths. These messengers may be teachers, prophets, scriptures, writers of books, and the Holy Ghost who prompts you with ideas and feelings that empower you to be healed. "And by the power of the Holy Ghost ye may know the truth of all things" (Moro. 10:5).

2. When you give credence to this information—the testimonies of others—when you do not cast it out because of unbelief, you are led to marvelous discoveries.

> We have now clearly set forth how it is, and how it was, that God became an object of faith for rational beings; and also, upon what foundation the testimony was based which excited the inquiry and diligent search of the ancient saints to seek after and obtain a knowledge of the glory of God; and we have seen that it was human testimony, and human testimony only, that excited this inquiry, in the first instance, in their minds. It was the credence they gave to the testimony of their fathers, this testimony having aroused their minds to inquire after the knowledge of God; the inquiry frequently terminated, indeed always terminated when rightly pursued, in the most glorious discoveries and eternal certainty.[5]

3. Once you receive information and testimony from others, you must exert yourself to action; you must focus your thoughts and attitudes on these truths.

4. As you walk in obedience to the commandments, your efforts are rewarded. You "shall receive health in [your] navel and marrow to [your] bones; . . . and shall run and not be weary, and shall walk and not faint" (D&C 89:18, 20). Thus, you are empowered to draw upon the healing influences of the heavens. Figure 1 shows the process involved in this kind of faith-power.

We are bombarded, of course, with information from many different sources. Television, newspapers, videos, speakers, and advertisements all seem to demand our attention, our thoughts, and our faith with the promise of life-styles like the rich and famous. We have to be so careful about the kind of information we choose to value so we are not misled.

FOCUS YOUR THOUGHTS

The prophets have warned of the importance of guarding our thoughts. Solomon declared, "For as [a man] thinketh in his heart, so is he" (Prov. 23:7). Christ stressed the power of our thoughts when he contrasted the law of Moses with his higher law. In the Old Testament, Moses emphasized right actions: "Thou shalt not kill" and "Thou shalt not commit adultery" (Ex. 20:13–14); but in the New Testament, the Lord accentuated right thoughts: "Thou shalt not be angry," and "Thou shalt not lust." (See Matt. 5:22, 28.)

Your choice of thoughts will affect your feelings and your body. Your body (soma) reflects what your mind (psyche) dwells upon. Hospital beds are full of people who have psychosomatic illnesses. This does not mean that their pain is not real. It simply means that their thoughts play a major part in their illness and in their ability to get better. Similarly, the content of your thoughts—how you mentally exert yourself—will promote either healing or destructive processes in your spirit and body.

Nephi's experiences give a scriptural example of this. As he sat pondering the things his father taught him about the tree of life, his choice of thoughts were positive and active. Nephi's efforts were rewarded, and he was caught away by the Spirit and learned of marvelous things past, present, and future. (See 1 Ne. 11:11–14.) It was Nephi's faith that prepared and empowered him to be taught by the Spirit.

Messenger → **Information** → **Faith** → **Power**

A messenger loves you and introduces you to heavenly powers and healing principles.	Possessing information, you have an object upon which to focus your faith.	You exert yourself mentally by focusing your thoughts on the trust you have received.	You are thus empowered to draw upon the healing influences of the heavens.

Figure 1. The four steps of active faith.

As rays of the sun can be focused through a lens and concentrated to produce energy to cause things to burn, so can your mental energies be focused on Christ and united with his Holy Spirit to the point that miracles are wrought. "And there were great and marvelous works wrought by the disciples of Jesus, insomuch that they did heal the sick . . . and all manner of miracles did they work among the children of men; and in nothing did they work miracles save it were in the name of Jesus" (4 Ne. 1:5).

Your thoughts have a powerful impact on your health. Thoughts of gratitude and love for the Lord energize your spirit and body. The healing power of faith means that we learn to direct our mental energy—our thoughts, attitudes, beliefs—toward Christ and his healing power. Our faith-power is increased as we remember Jesus' suffering—that through his atonement, power has been provided to make us whole. Jesus Christ descended below all things that he might comprehend all things (D&C 88:6). "And all things are before him, and all things are round about him; and he is above all things, and in all things, and is through all things, and is round about all things; and all things are by him, and of him, even God, forever and ever" (D&C 88:41). Amazing! How many of us really realize that Jesus can heal our pain?

Stephen E. Robinson has suggested a comparison that helps us understand how Christ's power can enter and bless our lives.

> In mortality, perfection [including faith to be healed] comes to us only through the Atonement of Christ. We cannot generate our own. We must become one with him, with this perfect being. There is a merger. Some of my students who are studying business understand this concept better if I talk in business terms. You take a small, bankrupt firm that's about ready to go under and merge it with a corporate giant. What happens? Their assets and liabilities flow together, and the new entity that is created is solvent.[6]

Through Jesus' atonement, we have the power to merge with him. Jesus' love is sufficient to heal broken hearts and crippled bodies. He can make all things right. Jesus is "the way, the truth, and the life" (John 14:6). Learning of the Lord and his powers to heal will bring you greater peace. The time will come when "they shall not hurt nor destroy in all my holy mountain, for the earth shall be full of the knowledge of the Lord, as the waters cover the sea" (2 Ne. 21:9).

To have faith in Jesus Christ is not merely to believe that he is who he says he is, or to believe *in* Christ. Healing faith requires that you believe what he says, that he can save you. Of course, you must believe in his identity, that he is the Christ; but you must also believe that through him you can be cleansed, purified, and saved from all your enemies, including emotional, spiritual, and physical illness.

People who are in pain or who are suffering some kind of handicap are often fearful of bothering others. They sometimes believe they are bothering the Lord by taking their problems to him—that in some way they weary him. This is simply not true. He is so very approachable. In fact, the Lord has explained, "I am the vine, ye are the branches: He that abideth in me, and I in him, the same bringeth forth much fruit: for without me ye can do nothing" (John 15:5). Here, the branches—that is, you—cannot bring forth fruit unless you are attached to the vine—Jesus Christ—from which healing moisture and nutrients are obtained. Jesus is rooted in his Father, the source of all power and healing energy. From him are all good gifts received.

The gift to be healed is one of the gifts of the Spirit. (See D&C 42:48; 46:19.) To be healed you must learn about Christ, the Atonement, the consequences of sin, how the laws of justice and mercy operate, why you must be baptized, and how you can come to God through the companionship of the Holy Spirit. But this learning must be childlike, simple, trusting, unencumbered by the intellectual embroidery that is so common in our day and time. The Lord taught the Nephites his doctrine that all people "must repent, be baptized . . . [receive the Holy Ghost,] and become as a little child, or they can in nowise inherit the kingdom of God" (3 Ne. 11:37–38). Childlike trusting and believing are prerequisites to the healing power of the Lord.

Partaking of the sacrament can help you focus your thoughts in childlike ways. When you partake of the sacrament, you use the words and music of the sacramental hymns to help you focus your thoughts on the atoning sacrifice of the Savior and thereby experience the emotions of love and gratitude that the service evokes. The bread and water help you visualize his suffering in Gethsemane and on the cross as acts of love to heal and help you. Through the shedding of his blood, "ye are bought with a price" (1 Cor. 6:20). Robert L. Millet wrote: "The cumulative weight of all mortal sins, somehow, past, present, and future, pressed upon that perfect, sinless, and sensitive soul! All infirmities and sicknesses were part, too, of the awful arithmetic of the Atonement."[7]

As I think of Christ's atonement, I am filled with appreciation for all that has been done for me. I am filled with desire to focus my thoughts on the Savior and his will for me. As I do his will, I will be empowered to be healed and blessed. I know, too, that much is expected of me. I must do as much as I can to receive my desired blessing.

STUDYING IT OUT IN YOUR MIND

As gracious as the Lord is in his love for us, he also expects us to learn through our own efforts too. As a good parent, he does not answer our petitions until we have exerted ourselves significantly to show our sincerity. Perhaps Oliver Cowdery's experiences were recorded for us to learn this important lesson:

> Assuredly as the Lord liveth, . . . even so surely shall you receive a knowledge of whatsoever things you shall ask in faith, with an honest heart, believing that you shall receive. . . . I will tell you in your mind and in your heart, by the Holy Ghost. . . .
>
> Remember that without faith you can do nothing; therefore ask in faith. Trifle not with these things; do not ask for that which you ought not. . . . And according to your faith shall it be done unto you. (D&C 8:1–2, 10–11)

Sometimes you may receive answers to your prayers but not recognize the hand of the Lord in what has transpired. You may not recognize the Lord's miracle until well after it has happened to you. When you receive impressions in your heart, you can use your mind either to rationalize them away or you can acknowledge them as having come from the Lord and prepare to act upon them. It is well to remember the Lord's counsel, "And in nothing doth man offend God, or against none is his wrath kindled, save those who confess not his hand in all things, and obey not his commandments" (D&C 59:21). You and I need to be careful what we do with impressions from the Lord.

Many times when we rationalize impressions away, it reflects a lack of faith in what the Lord is telling us. To ask in proper faith means that we ask with confidence, utilizing all of our efforts to understand what God is trying to tell us. Oliver Cowdery, while attempting to translate the golden plates from which we got the Book of Mormon, did not ask with this kind of exertion. He was gently but clearly reproved by the Lord for not putting forth sufficient mental effort to translate, save it were to ask God the meaning of the ancient characters. The Lord explained:

> You have not understood; you have supposed that I would give it unto you, when you took no thought save it was to ask me. But, behold, I say unto you, that you must study it out in your mind; then you must ask me if it be right, and if it is right I will cause that your bosom shall burn within you; therefore, you shall feel that it is right. But if it be not right you shall have no such feelings, but you shall have a stupor of thought that shall cause you to forget the thing which is wrong. (D&C 9:7–9)

So it is with the faith to be healed. The Lord expects you to study things out in your mind—to visualize and reflect upon the desired blessing with a proper healing hope in Christ, believing that you shall receive. Learning to think of faith as "mental exertion" will become one of your most effective tools in overcoming your sufferings, loneliness, and addictions. The important point for you to know now, however, is that you are free to choose your thoughts and are limited only by an inadequate supply of principles upon which to focus your thoughts.

YOU ARE FREE TO CHOOSE, FREE TO ACT

You have the freedom to control your thoughts. President Ezra Taft Benson said,

> You are the stage manager. You are the one who decides which thoughts will occupy the stage. Remember, the Lord wants you to have a fulness of joy like his. The devil wants all men to be miserable like unto himself. You are the one who must decide what thoughts you will entertain. You are free to choose, but you are not free to alter the consequences of those choices. You will reach whatever you dwell upon—what you consistently allow to occupy the stage of your mind.[8]

You have your free agency.

In the Church we use the term "free agency" in reference to what others call "free will." Certain disciplines in psychology have suggested that man does not have free will, but that we are simply reactors to our physical heredity or our social conditioning. The scriptures, however, affirm that we do have our agency. (See 2 Ne. 2:27; D&C 93:30.) I remember one time trying to prove to a group of classmates at a state university that we have free will. With almost each point I made about my ability to exercise agency, to make choices, they would counter with, "The choice you made was a result of previous conditioning, not a result of free will." It is really quite hard, if not impossible, to prove to the secular world that we have free will. To me, faith assures me that we do, indeed, have free will.

Heredity and environment do influence you to some extent, but still your mind is free—within limits—to rationally interpret your heredity and your environment and to decide what kind of impact each will have on you. Many sociologists argue this point, but the word of the Lord, especially in the Book of Mormon, is clear that you are free to choose and free to act, and that you are responsible for each choice and action.

Father Lehi explained to his son, Jacob, that in the creation, God created some things to be acted upon and other things to act for themselves. (See 2 Ne. 2:14.)

> Wherefore, men are free according to the flesh; and all things are given them which are expedient unto man. And they are free to choose liberty and eternal life, through the great Mediator of all men, or to choose captivity and death, according to the captivity and power of the devil; for he seeketh that all men might be miserable like unto himself. (2 Ne. 2:27)

One of the big lies Satan promotes in the world is that you are simply acted upon, that you have no free will. This belief leads many to helplessly accept their negative thoughts and external conditions as beyond their ability to control.

The knowledge that you are a free agent helps you to dispel the common belief among many Christians that all good comes from God and all evil comes from Satan. Joseph Smith taught that there are three independent agents: "the Spirit of God, the spirit of man, and the spirit of the devil. All men have power to resist the devil."[9] You have the power to choose good or evil independent of God and Satan.

If you choose to follow the light of correct principles, you will approach the righteousness and power of God. Should you choose to follow the darkness of ignorance and error, you approach the evil and weakness of Satan. Either direction you go will affect your health—for good or for ill. You are free to choose; the power is within you.

THE POWER AND LIMITATIONS OF THOUGHTS

Thoughts are powerful creative forces. Everything in the room in which you are now sitting was first someone's idea, whether it be a pencil, a table, or a window. Even plant and animal life existed first as an idea in the mind of God. All the good, fine, and noble creative acts of humanity were conceived as a spark in someone's mind: the Constitution of the United States, the Statue of Liberty, the works of great literature. Emerson said, "Great men are they who see that spiritual is stronger than any material force, that thoughts rule the world."[10]

You have the power to choose who and what you are by the thoughts you think. Where you are in life is a consequence of all of your previous thoughts—positive and negative—which includes even your thoughts dating back into the premortal life. If you wonder what your previous thoughts have been, just take a look at where you are now. If you are not pleased with some parts of your life, then you need to take a look at the thoughts that got you there. If you do not like where you are, the good news is that thoughts can be changed, rechanneled into more constructive patterns with more positive results. Some changes require considerable time and energy, while others require less. The point is that thoughts make you what you are—that is how powerful they are.

Your choice of thoughts affects your attitudes about the physical world. For instance, when you choose to view a bucket of water as either half full or half empty, your thoughts do not change the nature of the bucket in the least, but they do affect your mood—whether you are pleased or saddened about the amount of water in your bucket. However, there will come a time when you will understand more about the power of faith, when righteous thoughts can dramatically affect the physical nature of things. Jesus turned the water to wine; he calmed the sea of Galilee with the power of his thoughts coupled with priesthood power.

Even now, your thoughts affect your physical world in powerful ways. If you persist in thoughts about wealth, you will probably think of ways and means to obtain money, houses, boats, and campers. Just as you develop physical skills and habits through repetition (like typing, automobile driving, piano playing, etc.), you form habits and patterns in your thinking. As an example, when parents repeatedly respond negatively to rainy days, saying, "I hate it when it rains," their children pick up these attitude habits themselves: "Yes, I hate it when it rains, too!" One mother checked under her little girls' bed every night to make sure there was no "evil man" there. You can imagine the kind of fears the little girls formed through this repeated suggestion.

Through repetition you form mental habits that can hurt you or help you. You can form positive habits in your thinking by attending church meetings, visiting with uplifting friends, reading good books, and studying the scriptures. A friend of mine found a scripture about "mount[ing] up with wings as eagles" (Isa. 40:31). When she was in pain, she would visualize herself astride a giant eagle whose mighty power carried her to lofty heights, high above the mundane world. In her words, "the visualization did not take the pain out of me, but it took me out of the pain." She and her eagle are becoming very good friends. She is focusing on the positive amid the negative.

You can do it, too. If you have a pain in your left foot, you can think how grateful you are that the pain is not in your jaw. Think of all your bodily functions that *are* working well, that you take for granted: digestion, circulation, respiration, assimilation. Really, it is a great blessing to be able to choose your thoughts in this way.

There are limitations, however, to the power of your thoughts. To focus on the positive is not to deny that evil exists. War, disease, abuse and Satan are all very real. Those people who believe that evil and corruption exist only in your mind exhibit a form of denial that is destructive to both mental health and relationships. Roberto Rossellini said, "I am not a pessimist; to perceive evil where it exists is, in my opinion, a form of optimism."[11] Knowledge of evil is also a form of intelligence.

Although we have great power and freedom to focus our thoughts, there are certain limitations to what we can do with them. Thoughts are not all-powerful. When some people first discover how powerful thoughts are, they begin worshiping the human mind as though it were God. But some people get weird ideas and carry correct principles to an extreme that God never intended. You cannot, for instance, pull up to an intersection and with your mind cause a red light to turn green.

Some secular religions are founded upon this idea—that if you develop your mind you can subordinate all physical things. They, through meditation and chanting (and some through drug-induced hallucinations), seek to alter their conscious awareness, so as to become oblivious to their physical surroundings. They seek to enter a state of non-consciousness, non-awareness. This creates a separation between the participant and the physical world. This separation can be the cause of disorientation, confusion, and, eventually, illness. We Latter-day Saints, on the other hand, view the physical creation as a crowning blessing (we were "added upon" by obtaining physical bodies). (See Abr. 3:26.) Our heaven is not a non-existence or a non-awareness of evil or any physical reality. Rather it is a fulness of existence, including the abundance and dominion of the physical world.

There is another way in which thoughts can be destructive. Some people use "positive thinking" as a form of denial of adversity and evil in their lives. They believe incorrectly that all problems can be eliminated right now through strong faith and positive thinking. If you don't happen to agree with their timetable, they accuse you of lacking faith. They may even believe that your lack of faith neutralizes their faith.

These people often come across in a holier-than-thou fashion. If they experience some adversity in their life, for instance, if their child develops a life-threatening illness, and their positive thinking does not cure the child, these people tend to blame their spouse for not thinking positively enough—or not having enough faith. They believe they are true and faithful but their spouse is weak in the faith, and that is why the child is not healed. Beware of holier-than-thou or extreme or fanatical thought patterns in yourself and in others.

If you have a miraculous healing, wonderful! If you have a slow, progressive recovery, great! If you have the usual series of ups and downs that people with afflictions and illnesses generally go through, find something to be grateful for every day, every hour, every minute. You can develop an attitude of gratitude. There is great power in the life of one who "yields to the enticings of the Holy Spirit, and putteth off the natural man . . . and becometh as a child, submissive, meek, humble, patient, full of love, willing to submit to all things which the Lord seeth fit to inflict upon [us], even as a child doth submit to his father" (Mosiah 3:19).

VIRTUE AND CHARITY—KEYS TO KNOWLEDGE AND POWER

It is a totally new concept to some people that they can choose virtuous and charitable thoughts. They believe that thoughts just come and go with no real decision on their part. The Lord explained our ability to choose virtue and charity when he exhorted,

> Let thy bowels also be full of charity towards all men . . . and let virtue garnish thy thoughts unceasingly; . . . and the doctrine of the priesthood shall distil upon thy soul as the dews from heaven. The Holy Ghost shall be thy constant companion, . . . and thy dominion shall be an everlasting dominion, and without compulsory means it shall flow unto thee forever and ever. (D&C 121:45–46)

"Virtue" in this scripture is more than sexual morality. Virtuous thoughts include contemplations of all things that are lovely, beautiful, uplifting, ennobling, and true. So, by focusing your thoughts on uplifting things, you reap certain powers of the Holy Spirit.

Whatever you focus your thoughts on is what you get in return. If you dwell on things carnal, sensual, and devilish, that is what you receive. When you focus on the words of eternal life, you receive joy and power into your life. Paul reminds us that "our gospel came not unto you in word only, but also in power, and in the Holy Ghost, and in much assurance" (1 Thes. 1:5).

LEARNING TO THINK AND FEEL BETTER

Just as with the half-full or half-empty buckets, you can learn to see the buckets of the world as being half full; you can learn to see the positive in spite of the negative. You may not always change your physical pain, but there have been many cases reported in which dramatic physical changes have occurred through changes in thought patterns. Tens of thousands of cancer patients, whose cancers have been in "spontaneous remission" for years, know why. They changed their thinking, and their thinking changed the course of the cancer. It is possible for thoughts to have an impact for good over any life-threatening illness, infection, or pain you can name.

You can learn to more effectively focus your thoughts, draw upon holy healing power, and experience greater enjoyment in this life. The Prophet Joseph Smith reminds us that learning to be healed is a progressive thing:

We consider that God has created man with a mind capable of instruction, and a faculty which may be enlarged in proportion to the heed and diligence given to the light communicated from heaven to the intellect; and that the nearer man approaches perfection, the clearer are his views, and the greater his enjoyments, till he has overcome the evils of his life and lost every desire for sin; . . . But we consider that this is a station to which no man ever arrived in a moment: he must have been instructed in the government and laws of that kingdom by proper degrees, until his mind is capable in some measure of comprehending the propriety, justice, equality, and consistency of the same.[12]

Since we progressively learn how to use the healing powers of the Lord, this book will help you with valuable insights into how you can focus your thoughts and draw upon these heavenly healing powers. Your Savior Jesus Christ has the power to heal your loneliness and your pain, but you have to learn of him and trust that he can help you. Jesus must become the center of all that you think, feel, and do. When you learn to trust the Lord in this manner, you can rejoice with Nephi of old who happily declared, "We talk of Christ, we rejoice in Christ, we preach of Christ, we prophesy of Christ, and we write according to our prophecies, that our children may know to what source they may look for a remission of their sins" (2 Ne. 25:26). Jesus is the power of our salvation.

Remember, when you work by faith, you work by mental exertion. You exert yourself to develop powerful, healing, and joyful thought patterns centered on the source of all truth—Jesus Christ.

The power is within you to reach out to the Lord. He will show you the way to do constructive thinking to counteract destructive thought patterns. This book is the voice of a friend calling you to commune with personages and powers in heaven that will help you overcome your problems and experience peace in spite of adversity. Study this course as a road map—a plan showing you how to reach out to the Good Shepherd, how to exert yourself in faith to obtain his help to heal your pain and loneliness.

NOTES

1. *Lectures on Faith* 1:12–17.

2. *Teachings,* 296.

3. John-Roger and Peter McWilliams, *You Can't Afford the Luxury of a Negative Thought,* (Los Angeles: Prelude Press, 1991), 239.

4. Lectures on Faith, 7:3.

5. Lectures on Faith 2:56; emphasis added.

6. Stephen E. Robinson, "Believing Christ: A Practical Approach to the Atonement," *BYU Today* 44, (November 1990): 29.

7. Robert L. Millet, "Joseph Smith and the New Testament," *Ensign,* December 1986, 26. Also see Alma 7:11–13; Isa., 53:3–5; Matt. 8:17.

8. Ezra Taft Benson, "Think on Christ," *Ensign,* April 1984, 11.

9. *Teachings,* 189.

10. As quoted in McWilliams, *Negative Thought,* 50.

11. As quoted in McWilliams, *Negative Thought,* 126.

12. *Teachings,* 51.

3

Obtaining Help from the Lord

And ye shall know the truth, and the truth shall make you free.
—John 8:32

Did you know that worrying is a form of atheism? You cannot exert your faith to be healed if you indulge in excessive worrying, since to be healed is to be made happy. But how does one avoid worrying? How can we be healed and made happy in such a confusing and fallen world?

The answer is that we must learn *how* to be healed. There are powers in the heavens and in your own mind that you have not yet learned to fully tap. As C. W. Leadbeater observed, "It is the commonest of mistakes to consider that the limit of our power of perception is also the limit of all there is to perceive."[1]

God knows ways and means to bring about healing power that many are not yet aware of: "For my thoughts are not your thoughts, neither are your ways my ways, saith the Lord. For as the heavens are higher than the earth, so are my ways higher than your ways, and my thoughts than your thoughts" (Isa. 55:8–9). Life in today's world appears so complicated and the challenges so overwhelming as to be beyond our individual capacity to resolve them or even see how God could possibly resolve them. We all need help from powers beyond our perception. The problem is that we don't always know how to receive help; we do not know how to draw on the powers of heaven to obtain divine assistance.[2]

How can it be that we sometimes feel our urgent pleas for help have gone unattended when the Lord himself has said, "Ask, and ye shall receive; knock, and it shall be opened unto you" (D&C 4:7)?

When you do not seem to receive your desired blessings, the reason is that you either are not following the spiritual laws for receiving help—either by ignorance or refusal—or you are simply not recognizing the help as it comes. Evidently, the Lord intends that we do our part. But what, specifically, are we to do? One important principle in receiving blessings is that we bind the Lord by keeping his commandments. Expressing gratitude for blessings already received is another.

Years ago, a woman asked Spencer W. Kimball for a blessing to combat a crippling disease. For some time Elder Kimball prepared himself spiritually; then, fasting, he was prompted to bless her to be healed. Some weeks later she returned, angry and complaining that she was "fed up" with waiting for the Lord to give the promised relief. He responded, "Now I understand why you have not been blessed. You must be patient, do your part, and express gratitude for the smallest improvement noted."[3]

Elder Richard G. Scott points out that

> help from the Lord generally comes in increments. . . . He can immediately cure serious illnesses or disabilities, or even allow the dead to be raised. But the general pattern is that improvement comes in sequential steps. That plan gives us an opportunity to discover what the Lord expects us to learn. It requires our patience to recognize his timetable. It provides growth from our efforts and trust in him and the opportunity to express gratitude for the help given.[4]

Elder Scott then summarized what we need to do to receive help from the Lord:

1. Ask the Father in the name of Christ.
2. Diligently keep his commandments.
3. Ask with faith in Christ.
4. Ask for that which is right.
5. Express gratitude.[5]

As you earnestly conform to the will of the Lord, your prayers will be answered. Not all of your prayers will be answered as you *wish;* but when you ask in faith, they will always be answered in a way that you *need.* It is not always easy to know why the Lord blesses you or requires your patience in the way that he does, yet still there are some things of which you can be certain. The Lord will never ask you to endure anything that is not completely in harmony with his plan for your ultimate happiness.

Remember, though, that you cannot expect his help if you are immoral or otherwise deliberately disobedient—unless you sincerely repent.

Sometimes you may need help in keeping the commandments so you can receive blessings. One young man I have been visiting with has been working on a personal problem for many years. He has received innumerable priesthood blessings but the problem still persists. He recognizes that he must keep the commandments to receive help, but the help he needs is in keeping the commandments! What can he do?

First, he needs to do some major restructuring of his thoughts. He needs to change the image he has of himself and the image he has of his relationship with Christ. He is learning that he can change his poor self-image by learning to see himself as the Lord sees and loves him. As he acquires a more positive self-image, he also gains a more courageous heart, as well as a broken heart and a contrite spirit before the Lord. This improved self-image and new humility before the Lord is part of what constitutes the "mighty change" of heart of which Alma spoke (Alma 5:14). Although we are all unworthy before our Savior, we are nevertheless commanded to call upon him for deliverance. (See 2 Ne. 4:18; Ether 3:2.)

You, too, can learn this pattern of healing, which is a prerequisite to drawing on the powers of heaven. The specific steps involved will be discussed in subsequent chapters. Generally, most of your present problems are tightly linked with a low self-image, feelings of unworthiness, and a false view of how God sees you. Once you learn to bring your self-image in harmony with the Lord's view of you, you will be empowered to change your negative emotions and eventually your negative behaviors. You will be unburdened, set free as if you are soaring to new heights.

In order to obtain help from the Lord, your thoughts must be focused on truth—especially the truth about who you really are and about the promises your Heavenly Father offers you. One of the greatest truths that you will ever learn is that the gospel of Jesus Christ is the Lord's plan for your happiness. To gain unshakable faith in Jesus Christ is to flood your mind and life with the brilliant light of gospel truths. He stands at the door and knocks, but you must open the door and allow him in (Rev. 3:20). When you allow him to enter your life, you will no longer be left to struggle alone with challenges you know you cannot resolve or control yourself. Jesus can be your Savior each and every day of your life.

The restored gospel of Jesus Christ teaches that you are literally a child of God. This fact, coupled with your eternal intelligence, gives you boundless value and power when it is properly understood. If you were simply an evolved animal or a creation of men, you would have limited value. Only when you come to understand that you are literally a child of God and that your being is eternal and therefore has eternal value, will you gain a sense of belonging to something greater than that given through the experiences of living on this fallen earth. You have a value that is incomprehensible and unimaginable. When you begin to understand, feel, and picture the reality of this principle, then you need not be overwhelmed nor have your sense of self-worth shattered in the face of adversity when it comes along. You need not be overburdened by the confused voices so prevalent in our world, voices that would have you believe you are much less than you are. Among all who would persuade you, one voice stands out—the voice of the Good Shepherd declaring your salvation. His voice alone is needful.

ONE THING IS NEEDFUL

Patricia T. Holland recounts events surrounding one of her trips to the Holy Land. She said:

> My health was going downhill. I was losing weight steadily, and I wasn't sleeping well. . . . I didn't have any reserve to call on. My tank was on empty, and I wasn't sure there was a filling station anywhere in sight.
>
> It was just a few weeks later that my husband had the assignment in Jerusalem . . . and the Brethren traveling on the assignment requested that I accompany him. "Come on," he said. "You can recuperate in the Savior's land of living water and bread of life." As weary as I was, I packed my bags, believing—or, at the very least, hoping—that the time there would be a healing respite.

On a pristinely clear and beautifully bright day, I sat overlooking the Sea of Galilee and reread the tenth chapter of Luke. But instead of the words on the page, I thought I saw with my mind and heard with my heart these words: "[Pat, Pat, Pat], thou art careful and troubled about many things." Then the power of pure and personal revelation seized me as I read, "But one thing [only one thing] is [truly] needful." (Luke 10:41–42)

After describing the beautiful May sun at Gibeon, where the sun stood still for Joshua (see Josh. 10:12), Sister Holland explained:

Our loving Father in Heaven seemed to be whispering to me, "You don't have to worry over so many things. The one thing that is needful— the *only* thing that is truly needful—is to keep your eyes toward the sun— my Son." Suddenly I had true peace. I knew that my life had always been in his hand—from the very beginning! The sea lying peacefully before my eyes had been tempest-tossed and dangerous—many, many times. All I needed to do was to renew my faith, and get a firm grasp on his hand— and *together* we could walk on water."[6]

How true Sister Holland's revelation is for all of us. The Lord has said, "Look unto me in every thought" (D&C 6:36). We are partners with the Lord; when we look unto him with an eye single to his glory, he can unburden us.

YOUR EYE SINGLE TO THE GLORY OF GOD

President Ezra Taft Benson has reminded us, "If thoughts make us what we are and if we are to be like Christ, we must think Christlike thoughts."[7] Having Christlike thoughts is the same thing as having your eye single to the glory of God. "And faith, hope, charity and love, with an eye single to the glory of God, qualify him for the work" (D&C 4:5). Christ did only what his Father commanded him to do; his thoughts were centered on the glory of his Father.

For this reason, as you increase in Christlike thoughts, you will receive Christlike power. From the Doctrine and Covenants we read of this promise:

And [Jesus] received all power, both in heaven and on earth, and the glory of the Father was with him, for he dwelt in him. . . . I give unto you these sayings that you may understand . . . and in due time receive of his fullness. For if you keep my commandments you shall receive of his fullness. (D&C 93:17, 19–20)

As mentioned earlier, the power to overcome pain and problems is not restricted to the limitations of our mortal abilities. Elder Russell M. Nelson reminded us that it is possible to achieve what seems to be impossible.

> Learn and obey the teaching of God. From the holy scriptures, heaven-sent lift will be found for heaven-sent duties. . . . Faith is nurtured through knowledge of God. It comes from prayer and feasting upon the words of Christ through diligent study of the scriptures. . . .
>
> Imagine, if you will, a pair of powerful binoculars. Two separate optical systems are joined together with a gear to focus two independent images into one three-dimensional view. To apply this analogy, let the scene on the left side of your binocular represent your perception of your task. Let the picture on the right side represent the Lord's perspective of your task—the portion of his plan he has entrusted to you. Now, connect your system to his. By mental adjustment, fuse your focus. Something wonderful happens. Your vision and his are now the same. You have developed an "eye single to the glory of God" (D&C 4:5; see also Morm. 8:15). With that perspective, look upward—above and beyond mundane things about you. The Lord said, "Look unto me in every thought" (D&C 6:36). That special vision will also help clarify your wishes when they may be a bit fuzzy and out of focus with God's hopes for your divine destiny. Indeed, the precise challenge you regard now as "impossible" may be the very refinement you need, in his eye.[8]

We all battle the enemies of discouragement, feelings of unworthiness, death, physical pain, loneliness, and sin. When you yield your life and love to Christ and the principles he has brought forth, you can declare with Ammon, "I know that I am nothing; as to my strength I am weak; therefore I will not boast of myself, but I will boast of my God, for in his strength I can do all things" (Alma 26:12). The Lord has promised the faithful Saints, "I will fight your battles" (D&C 105:14).

KNOWLEDGE AND FAITH—THE POWER OF DELIVERANCE

Many non-LDS Christians believe that Christ saves them because he is good—not because they can do any good thing of themselves. Latter-day Saints know that the Lord saves us, not *in* our sins but *from* our sins and from their effects. Through the power of our Heavenly Father and his Almighty Son, we can be healed, saved, and sanctified. But only through the Lord Jesus Christ can we be *truly* healed and helped.

Steven Cramer has suggested that, "Trying to alter deep-seated . . . habits with willpower and human behavioral techniques alone is about as effective as shooting at a battleship with a BB gun." He continues by explaining, "No one can change the carnal nature of the heart and disposition by 'iron-jawed willpower,' or by behavioral techniques and self-improvement programs alone. We may do much good in controlling our behavior, but until we allow Jesus Christ to alter our hearts and desires, we will suffer a continual struggle between the desires of the flesh and the will of the spirit."[9]

Jesus has power to save us from our sins, but we must first reach out for his healing grace. To be saved from our sins and from the pain we suffer, we must believe, as the power of faith and belief is connected with our ability to see in our mind the desired outcome.

In science, seeing is believing. In matters of faith, believing is seeing. A wheat farmer visualizes beforehand his positive results. He determines that the seed is good before he purchases and plants. He trusts that the seed will have life in it. He anticipates the harvest in his mind. He expects a harvest. He plants the seed, nourishes it and in due season reaps a harvest of golden grain. This is all a positive process of faith.

So it is with the healing power of faith. You must trust that the Lord can heal you; you must see in your mind the desired blessing; you must anticipate a harvest of a sound mind, stable emotions, and good health; and you must nourish your mind with virtuous thoughts and your body with healthful foods in order to reap in abundance.

The brother of Jared followed this pattern when he found answers to his problems. The Lord asked him: "Believest thou the words which I shall speak? And he answered: Yea, Lord, I know that thou speakest the truth, for thou art a God of truth, and canst not lie" (Ether 3:11–12). Because the brother of Jared believed, he was shown, not only the spirit body of Jesus, but also "all the inhabitants of the earth which had been, and also all that would be . . . even unto the ends of the earth" (Ether 3:25). Because of his faith he saw with his own eyes those things which before he had seen only with an eye of faith. (See Ether 12:19.) So it is with all of us. We see first in our minds the blessing of deliverance from sin and suffering, we obey the commandments, we ask in righteousness, and eventually we are delivered from bondage according to God's will and wisdom (Mosiah 7:33).

Can you see why it is necessary to have knowledge of the Savior before you can have faith in him for deliverance? Faith cannot exist in a vacuum. You have to focus your faith on the Savior and his power to heal you. Before you can do this you must know about him—his character, his attributes, his powers, his intense love for you. It was necessary for prophets in every dispensation to teach the true nature of God. Otherwise their children could not exercise their faith in the true God to be healed:

> The thought was first suggested to their minds that there was a God, which laid the foundation for the exercise of their faith.
>
> The extent of their knowledge respecting [God's] character and glory [and thus the quality of their faith] will depend upon their diligence and faithfulness in seeking after him, until, like Enoch, the brother of Jared, and Moses, they obtained faith in God, and power with him to behold him face to face. . . .
>
> It was human testimony, and human testimony only [from the prophets], that excited this inquiry, in the first instance, in their minds. It was the credence they gave to the testimony of their fathers, this testimony having aroused their minds to inquire after the knowledge of God; the inquiry frequently terminated, indeed always terminated when rightly pursued, in the most glorious discoveries and eternal certainty.[10]

Among the glorious discoveries and eternal certainties that you can discover is that through faith the power of the Lord can deliver you from your sin and suffering. The pattern to follow is clear: First, you must know the truth about your Heavenly Father, his character, attributes, and his powers to heal and bless you. Then you must be diligent and faithful in seeking after him. When properly executed, this search will result in glorious discoveries, including deliverance from spiritual and physical bondage as well as answers to your righteous prayers.

Christ is the center of all truth and power. As the 1969–70 Gospel Doctrine manual emphasizes, "Only in him can any man find the strength, the power and the ability to live a godly life. Only in Christ is there power to transform the human mind and the human heart."[11]

THE LIGHT AND POWER OF CHRIST IN ALL THINGS

The transforming power of Christ is infused in all things above, in, and below the earth "to fill the immensity of space" (D&C 88:12).

A friend of mine spent many hours with me as a coworker in an LDS temple. In that sacred setting, he and I shared our thoughts and feelings about the gospel. Some years later he experienced a stroke, which made it virtually impossible for him to speak. As months went by, he struggled to communicate with me about his illness. In labored, halted speech he explained that during the worst part of his sickness he was caught, as it were, between two worlds—the spirit world and mortality. During the time he was too sick to communicate with his family and friends, at the times of greatest pain, he could pray to the Lord in his mind and immediately the pain would be taken away.

During his recovery, he learned that Christ was the center of all things, that through the power and the light of Christ all things are held together—the rocks, the trees, the mountains, and the waves of the sea. My friend struggled to find the words that described the spiritual knowledge he had gained. He said he loved to watch grass, trees, plants, and children. He knew that the light of Christ held all things in their place—and that this same light enlightens our understanding of things.

As my friend spoke, I reflected on certain passages in the Doctrine and Covenants that teach that the light of Christ is truly in and through all things: "Which light proceedeth forth from the presence of God to fill the immensity of space—The light which is in all things, which giveth life to all things, which is the law by which all things are governed, even the power of God who sitteth upon his throne, who is in the bosom of eternity, who is in the midst of all things" (D&C 88:12–13). Furthermore, Jesus Christ himself "ascended up on high, as also he descended below all things, in that he comprehended all things, that he might be in all and through all things, the light of truth; Which truth shineth. This is the light of Christ" (D&C 88:6–7).

While among the Nephites, the resurrected Lord "did heal them every one as they were brought forth unto him. And they did all, both they who had been healed and they who were whole, bow down at his feet, and did worship him; and as many as could come for the multitude did kiss his feet, insomuch that they did bathe his feet with their tears" (3 Ne. 17:9–10). Because Jesus Christ is in and through all things, each of us is personally offered redemptive power that can heal and help us, strengthen us and empower us, to gain control over our emotional and physical diseases.

You can look forward to a similar day of healing, although you need not wait until the Second Coming to be blessed by the Lord.

Through newly discovered medical technology and through an increased understanding of faith, you can experience better health now. Actually, you have several major healing powers available to you: the priesthood, the gifts of the Spirit, the power that lies within your own mind, and angels. All of these sources of healing power are empowered by the light of Christ. Medical science and all the natural healing arts of the ages can also be empowered by the light of Christ. Mormon, in writing to his son Moroni, explained that angels are sent to the sons and daughters of God so they can exercise sufficient faith and lay hold on every good thing—from whatever source. (See Moro. 7:21–26.) Angels can show you the way, directing your thoughts and your faith to the therapeutic powers of the Spirit or the technology of medical science. Christ will direct you to the true source of healing: "And ye shall know the truth, and the truth shall make you free" (John 8:32).

BEING IN HARMONY WITH HEAVEN

The faith to be healed is a process based on truth, which can bring the power of Christ into your life. It is not simply the power of positive thinking. Unlocking the healing power of faith involves learning to make intelligent choices in your thoughts, feelings, and actions; choices that are in harmony with the Spirit of the Lord and enable you to draw upon the powers of heaven to be blessed.

Elder McConkie has pointed out that working by faith is "not the mere speaking of a few well chosen words." He continues by saying:

> Only persons who are in tune with the Infinite can exercise the spiritual forces and powers that come from him.
>
> Those who work by faith must first have faith; no one can use a power that he does not possess, and the faith or power must be gained by obedience to those laws upon which its receipt is predicated. . . . Those who work by faith must believe in the Lord Jesus Christ and in his Father. They must accept at face value what the revealed word teaches as to the character, attributes, and perfections of the Father and the Son. They must then work the works of righteousness until they know within themselves that their way of life conforms to the divine will, and they must be willing to lay their all on the altar of the Almighty.
>
> And then, when the day is at hand and the hour has arrived for the miracle to be wrought, then they must be in tune with the Holy Spirit of God. He who is the Author of faith, he whose power faith is, he whose works are the embodiment of justice and judgment and wisdom and all

good things, even he must approve the use of his power in the case at hand. Faith cannot be exercised contrary to the order of heaven or contrary to the will and purposes of him whose power it is. Men work by faith when they are in tune with the Spirit and when what they seek to do by mental exertion and by the spoken word is the mind and will of the Lord.[12]

In short, Elder McConkie outlined the process by which you can acquire the faith to overcome your pain. He pointed out that you must have faith in order to acquire faith. But this can be discouraging if you do not understand the point he is making. You receive faith for exercising faith. You receive mercy for mercy, grace for grace. In other words, faith is a gift you receive from the Holy Spirit as you exert your mind to reach out to the Lord. As you reach out to God, he will respond to you with double measure. He will enlarge your faith, and you will feel his Holy Spirit encircle you and magnify you until the perfect day.

UNLOCKING THE HEALING GIFTS OF THE SPIRIT

You have to be open to the promptings of the Spirit in order to draw upon healing powers. Sometimes I work with Church members who are very closed to suggestions from others. They are active in attending their Sunday meetings but still have serious problems and they wonder why. One reason is that in spite of their activity, they lack the humility that unlocks the windows of heaven. Their minds are closed to new ideas and to new problem-solving approaches, and they persistently think that other people need to change so they themselves can be happy.

Thoughts and ideas born of the Spirit can have a great healing impact upon you, but you have to have the humility of a child and be open to suggestion or heaven remains locked and you cannot receive the desired blessing. A broken heart and a contrite spirit qualify you to receive. If you remain self-assured, proud, and defiant you cannot receive. Or in contrast, some cannot receive because they are the exact opposite; they feel unworthy, unwanted, ashamed, guilty, and rejected by the Lord and others, so they cannot exercise sufficient faith to be healed.

The Holy Ghost does not usually shout his exhortations. Most often the Spirit whispers in a still, small voice, through sudden strokes of ideas and feelings. When heeded, such promptings can lead you to better health and happiness. If you ask in faith and humility, you will receive. If you do not ask in faith and humility, you will not receive.

To achieve healing, you need to understand these cause-and-effect realities as they relate to your health, happiness, and relationships with others. You also need to decide now that your Heavenly Father loves you, that he is merciful, kind, and benevolent. Sometimes it takes a desperate situation to wake us up to our dependency on the Lord. This is especially true regarding health and emotional pain and healing.

Your Heavenly Father knows you better than you know yourself. He also knows what you need to do in order to overcome your adversity and return to him. The Holy Ghost can be a light to your feet, a guide to your path, and can bring all things to your remembrance—including those things you need to do to unlock the healing gifts of the Spirit. (See Ps. 119:105.)

THE SPIRIT WHISPERS JOY AND PEACE

You can always tell the true Spirit of the Lord because it will whisper peace to your soul. Several months after Joseph Smith was martyred, he appeared to Brigham Young at Winter Quarters. President Young asked him to speak to the Saints one more time. The Prophet explained that his mission in mortality was over and that President Young must now do the speaking. Brigham Young then asked for a message to deliver to the Saints. The Prophet replied:

> Tell the people to get the Spirit of the Lord and it will lead them right. . . . They can tell the Spirit of the Lord from all other spirits; it will whisper peace and joy to their souls; it will take malice, hatred, strife and all evil from their hearts; and their whole desire will be to do good, bring forth righteousness and build up the kingdom of God. Tell the brethren if they will follow the Spirit of the Lord, they will go right. Be sure to tell the people to keep the Spirit of the Lord."[13]

The keys and powers that emanate from the Holy Ghost are a free gift to those with whom the Lord is pleased, those who choose to have faith in him. But they are never given to those with whom he is not pleased, who choose things that are carnal, sensual, and devilish. Elder Parley P. Pratt beautifully described the peace and joy the Holy Ghost radiates:

> The gift of the Holy Ghost adapts itself to all [our bodily] organs or attributes. It quickens all the intellectual faculties, increases, enlarges,

expands and purifies all the natural passions and affections, and adapts them, by the gift of wisdom, to their lawful use. It inspires, develops, cultivates and matures all the fine toned sympathies, joys, tastes, kindred feelings and affections of our nature. It inspires virtue, kindness, goodness, tenderness, gentleness and charity. It develops beauty of person, form and features. It tends to health, vigor, animation and social feelings. It invigorates all the faculties of the physical and intellectual man. It strengthens and gives tone to the nerves. In short, it is, as it were, marrow to the bone, joy to the heart, light to the eyes, music to the ears, and life to the whole.[14]

"In the presence of such persons," Elder Pratt explained, "one feels to enjoy the light of their countenances, as the genial rays of a sunbeam." This mutual attraction is consistent with latter-day revelation that states: "For intelligence cleaveth unto intelligence; wisdom receiveth wisdom; truth embraceth truth; virtue loveth virtue; light cleaveth unto light; mercy hath compassion on mercy and claimeth her own; justice continueth its course and claimeth its own" (D&C 88:40). When you meet others who love the Lord as you do, you feel a spiritual synergy in which the relationship's power is greater than the sum of the two separate parts because the Holy Spirit is present and lends its blessing. "He that receiveth the word by the Spirit of truth receiveth it as it is preached by the Spirit of truth. Wherefore, he that preacheth and he that receiveth, understand one another, and both are edified and rejoice together" (D&C 50:21–22). The specific manifestation of such relationships has been described by Elder Pratt:

> Their very atmosphere diffuses a thrill, a warm glow of pure gladness and sympathy, to the heart and nerves of others who have kindred feelings, or sympathy of spirit. No matter if the parties are strangers, entirely unknown to each other in person or character; no matter if they have never spoken to each other, each will be apt to remark in his own mind, and perhaps exclaim, when referring to the interview, "O what an atmosphere encircles that stranger! How my heart thrilled with pure and holy feelings in his presence! What confidence and sympathy he inspired! His countenance and spirit gave me more assurance than a thousand written recommendations or introductory letters."[15]

The true Spirit of the Lord—the spirit of love, joy and peace—can sanctify all your relationships, and heal your mind, heart, and body.

SPEAKING SPIRIT TO SPIRIT

Joseph Smith explained that when God reveals things through the Holy Ghost, he reveals them "to our spirits precisely as though we had no bodies at all; and those revelations which will save our spirits will save our bodies."[16] In other words, direction from the Spirit of the Lord does not necessarily come through your five senses. A modern revelation explains that it is a process that takes place inside of you: "Behold, I will tell you in your mind and in your heart, by the Holy Ghost, which shall come upon you and which shall dwell in your heart. Now, behold, this is the spirit of revelation; behold, this is the spirit by which Moses brought the children of Israel through the Red Sea on dry ground" (D&C 8:2–3). Here the Spirit of the Lord acts as a feeling as well as enlightenment. Nephi told his wayward brothers that they could get no direction from the Lord because they were "past feeling" (1 Ne. 17:45).

Your Heavenly Father loves you, but he expects you to cooperate by loving yourself. He is reaching out to you and giving you light this very moment as you read these words. You can get through any dark situation with his help. You, like an engineer on a night train, are expected to go as far as you can see down the track. When you get farther down the track, you will be able to see farther. Your Heavenly Father is working with you in a fallen world. You can reach out and receive of his saving grace. You can make choices that will allow his Holy Spirit to empower your life.

Elder Boyd K. Packer affirmed that the Holy Ghost can help you find answers to your problems. He explained that

> If we lose the spirit and power of individual revelation, we have lost much in this Church. You have great and powerful resources. You, through prayer, can solve your problems without endlessly going to those who are trying so hard to help others. . . . I know that he is close, that we can go to him and appeal, and then, if we will be obedient and listen and use every resource, we will have an answer to our prayers.[17]

The Spirit of the Lord can enlighten you, and you will find your own way through your pain in a way that will work best for you. You can face your fears of losing control. You and the Spirit of the Lord can accomplish anything that is necessary. Be true to yourself. Honor your righteous desires to do what is right. Acknowledge to yourself, to others, and to the Lord that you choose to do what is good and true and beautiful. Offer to the Lord a broken heart and a contrite spirit— the sacrifice required of the Latter-day Saints. This habit of humility is the key to all learning, including learning how to deal with pain and suffering. Let your humility show in all your relationships, and the Holy Ghost will speak to your spirit and heal you.

YIELDING TO THE ENTICINGS OF THE HOLY GHOST

When we are humble, the Lord can reveal knowledge to us. Knowledge of correct healing principles is fundamental to improving your health and well being; the influence and gift of the Holy Ghost is not limited to convincing you that the gospel is true. The Holy Ghost will guide you into all truth, including ways to find peace and healing power in spite of adversity. (See Moro. 10:5.)

A former patient of mine experienced the tragic consequences of not following the promptings of the Holy Spirit—adversity she had brought upon herself. When I first met Bonnie, she had broken the law of chastity and had been excommunicated. She complained of depression, inability to make decisions, and TMJ (a severe pain in her jaw that had not been relieved through dental therapy). Bonnie had been divorced but was still living with Richard, the father of her young child. Richard, though friendly with me, was bitterly antagonistic toward the Church for excommunicating her.

Bonnie came to me for help in making a decision. She was not sure if she should pursue her relationship with Richard and remarry, or reclaim another love relationship with a former high school sweetheart who was presently married but who might give up his marriage if Bonnie were to show interest. Bonnie told me that her parents were very active in the Church and that her father was a branch president. I received a letter from her at Christmas time that told of her healing. It read:

> Thank you for helping us come to the truth. Thank you for helping me mature my views of love and for Rich. We have great news. Rich was baptized . . . and has received the Aaronic priesthood as a priest. I was rebaptized . . . [and] that has brought great joy to me, my family, and my friends.
>
> Looking back, I can see how the devil had a firm hold on me and how I had allowed my thoughts to be poisoned. My life was crumbling into a pile of dashed hopes and broken dreams until a certain experience opened my eyes.
>
> It came in a dream. A dark, menacing presence was forcing its will upon me, weighing me down so as to paralyze my body and captivate my soul. I literally fought for my life, using all my strength and will, but was getting nowhere. Just when I thought I was doomed because I could fight

no more, my mind flashed upon the words, "In the name of Jesus Christ, I order you to leave." No sooner had I thought these words than the presence drew back. With that release, I regained control of my limbs, sat up, now realizing I was fully awake, spoke the words aloud, and watched as it withdrew and vanished. How perilously close I had come to destruction, to complete captivation of my soul! How blessed I am for the knowledge of my Savior and the Atonement.

Once I had put God and Christ back at the head of my life, everything turned around. We have moved . . . and live with my parents. Rich and I are remarrying . . . with a temple marriage planned for next Christmas time. We also have a beautiful baby girl . . . "a gift from God."

Bonnie's story illustrates how Satan can have great power over us if we do not follow the promptings of the Holy Ghost. The scriptures teach us that Satan is miserable and seeks the misery of all mankind. However, we have a promise that Satan can have no power over us unless we ignore the enticings of the Holy Spirit; if we do, we are vulnerable to his influence. Joseph Smith explained: "All beings who have bodies have power over those who have not. The devil has no power over us only as we permit him. The moment we revolt at anything which comes from God, the devil takes power."[18]

Let's look at the process that empowered Satan to poison Bonnie's thoughts, bringing such sadness into her life.

1. She had received a knowledge of the gospel in her home, but, for whatever reason, chose neither to exert herself nor to focus her thoughts on the principles she had been taught. She did not place her trust in these principles. She did not exert faith.

2. She chose to ignore the enticings of the Holy Spirit. Progressively her negative self took control.

3. She allowed other people to influence her thinking. They poisoned her mind with thoughts that were contrary to the Lord's plan of happiness.

4. Her thoughts influenced her feelings and she became despondent and depressed.

5. She withdrew from her family and friends and reacted bitterly when they reached out to help her.

6. Her health deteriorated and she experienced stress-related disorders.

7. While in her negative state, she was not willing to accept accountability for what was happening to her. She blamed others and

circumstances for what was happening, even though she had allowed it all to happen.

Lacking trust in the Lord's plan for happiness, Bonnie allowed herself to be lured by negative influences. Not until after she experienced pain and sorrow was she finally able to draw upon her knowledge of the truth and yield to the enticings of the Holy Ghost. She reached out to the protection and healing power of Jesus Christ. Then she was empowered to make different choices that were sufficient to reduce her distress, bringing about her return to health and spiritual vitality.

ACCOUNTABILITY FOR CHOICES

Bonnie was accountable for her choices. She had chosen her thoughts, feelings, and actions—the natural consequences of which resulted in her pain and sorrow.

As I worked with her, I explained that my role as a therapist was like a tutor, a mentor, a teacher. She would have to do most of the work. My job as a therapist was to give her support and teach her healing principles. If she would consider and apply them, they would enable her to find the peace she so desperately wanted. I explained that in no way could I impose these principles and ideas upon her. I would be a supportive friend that could show her the way, the pathway of the gospel that always leads to peace and a greater sense of well-being.

You, too, are accountable for the choices you make. You must not believe principles that are suggested to you by others unless the principles "ring true" to you according to the definition of a good seed given by Alma, to "enlarge [your] soul; yea, it beginneth to enlighten [your] understanding" (Alma 32:28). When you exert faith in healing principles and act upon them, the restorative blessings you receive will be your own. On the other hand, if you choose to follow the fad therapies and false spirits that are abroad in the land, you are responsible for the consequences as you are accountable for your choices. When you follow the counsel of the prophets, the scriptures, and the Holy Spirit, all of which may also direct you to the appropriate medical care, you will find the promised blessings that come to the faithful.

BALANCING GOD'S GRACE AND YOUR EFFORTS

Not everyone is healed in the same way or at the specific time they would like. Why is it that some receive immediate answers to their prayers while others do not—especially when it seems that they exert themselves equally in keeping the commandments? What makes the difference?

When one is not healed, is it because of something lacking in the individual? Is there a principle that is being violated or not applied? If so, what is that principle? Since there is a law upon which all blessings are predicated, what is the law upon which healing power can be received into one's life? How does the statement about not being able to be saved any faster than one gains knowledge apply to being healed?

I don't have answers to all these questions, but there are more answers available than we usually take advantage of. The Lord said, "For as the heavens are higher than the earth, so are my ways higher than your ways" (Isa. 55:9). When I am at a loss to explain what seems to be injustice, like Nephi of old, I exclaim, "Nevertheless, I know in whom I have trusted" (2 Ne. 4:19).

Neither present-day medical practitioners nor gospel sources have complete answers to these questions. There are, however, significant insights and practical helps that can be gained from the fields of medicine and psychology, as well as gospel sources—the scriptures, the writings of inspired leaders, and the promptings of the Holy Spirit.

It has been said that "man's extremity is God's opportunity," and to support this statement a passage from the Book of Mormon is often quoted by Latter-day Saints: "It is by grace that we are saved, *after all we can do*" (2 Ne. 25:23; emphasis added). The *grace* here is God's love and kindness shown to us, especially through the Atonement of his Son, Jesus Christ.

A continual challenge for you will be to balance the role of God's grace and your own personal effort in working through problems. How many of us have ever done *all* we can do? You may say, "Must we first do everything that lies within our own power before the Lord will assist us? How dismal! How disheartening! Who can ever do it?" We often feel like we are unworthy to receive his blessings because we have never done *all* that lies within our power.

As Robert Millet has pointed out, "Some may conclude [erroneously] that the Lord's grace can be extended to us only after (meaning following or subsequent to) my doing all I can do. This notion is incorrect. The fact is . . . the Lord's enabling power comes to us *all along the way.* I feel that 'after all we can do' means instead 'above and beyond all we can do, it is by the grace of God that we are saved.'"[19]

Stephen E. Robinson explained how this principle worked in his family. He tells of a time when his wife experienced an emotional breakdown.

> My wife and I were living in Pennsylvania. Things were going pretty well; I'd been promoted. It was a good year for us as a family, though a trying year for Janet personally. That year she had our fourth child, graduated from college, passed the CPA exam, and was made Relief Society president. We had temple recommends, and we held family home evening. I was serving in the bishopric. I thought we were headed for "LDS yuppiehood." Then one night the lights went out. Something happened in my wife that I can only describe as "dying spiritually." She wouldn't talk about it or tell me what was wrong. That was the worst part. For a couple of weeks she did not wish to participate in spiritual things, and she asked to be released from her callings.
>
> Finally, after about two weeks, one night I made her mad, and then it came out. She said, "All right. You want to know what's wrong? I'll tell you what's wrong. I can't do it anymore. I can't lift it. I can't get up at 5:30 in the morning and bake bread and sew clothes and help my kids with their homework and do my own homework and do my Relief Society stuff and get my genealogy done and write the congressman and go to the PTA meetings and write the missionaries . . ." And she just started naming off one brick after another that had been laid on her, explaining all the things she could not do—a catalog of her flaws and imperfections. She said, "I don't have the talent that Sister Morrell has. I can't do what Sister Childs does. I try not to yell at the kids, but I lose control, and I do. I've just finally admitted that I'm not perfect, and I'm not ever going to be perfect. I'm not going to make it to the celestial kingdom. I'm not 'Molly Mormon,' and I can't pretend I am, so I've given up. Why break my back trying to do what I can't?"
>
> Well, we started to talk, and it was a long night. I asked her, "Janet, do you have a testimony?"
>
> She said, "Of course I do! That's what so terrible. I know it's true. I just can't do it."
>
> "Have you kept the covenants you made when you were baptized?"
>
> She said, "I've tried and I've tried, but I cannot keep all the commandments all the time."
>
> Then I rejoiced because I could see that there was light at the end of the tunnel.
>
> . . . It is possible to be an active member of the Church, to have a testimony of its truthfulness, to hold leadership positions, and still to lose

track of the "good news" at the gospel's core. This is what happened here. Janet was trying to save herself. . . . She did not understand why [Jesus] is called the Savior.

Janet was trying to save herself with Jesus as an advisor. But we can't do that. No one is perfect. . . . We must not only believe IN Christ, we must *believe* Christ when he says, "I can cleanse you and make you celestial. . . ."

Of course we fail at the celestial level. That's why we need a savior, and why we are commanded to approach God and to call upon him so we may receive according to our desires. In the New Testament the Savior says, "Blessed are they which do hunger and thirst after righteousness: for they shall be filled" (Matt. 5:6). We misinterpret this scripture frequently. We think it says, "Blessed are the righteous," but it does not. When are you hungry? When are you thirsty? When you don't have the object of your desire. Blessed are those who hunger and thirst after the righteousness that God has, after the righteousness of the celestial kingdom, because as that becomes the desire of their hearts, they can achieve it—they will be filled. We receive "according to our desires."[20]

Through her ordeal, Sister Robinson learned to depend more upon the Lord's grace and less upon her own frantic efforts to be perfect. We all live in a fallen world, and none of us are "good" in the sense that we can be perfect in earning our salvation. The brother of Jared, too, recognized that because of the Fall, he was alienated from God; nevertheless he was obedient and called upon the Lord.

> Now behold, O Lord, and do not be angry with thy servant because of his weakness before thee; for we know that thou art holy and dwellest in the heavens, and that we are unworthy before thee; because of the fall our natures have become evil continually; nevertheless, O Lord, thou hast given us a commandment that we must call upon thee, that from thee we may receive according to our desires. (Ether 3:2)

Notice that he starts his prayer with an apology for being an imperfect man approaching a perfect God. We do *not* have to be perfect in order for the Savior to bless us. But we must petition him with sincerity of heart, trusting in his ability to save us from all our enemies: pain, persecution, disease, and even death. "Therefore, dearly beloved brethren, let us cheerfully do all things that lie in our power; and then may we stand still, with the utmost assurance, to see the salvation of God, and for his arm to be revealed" (D&C 123:17). We do all we can with hope in our heart that we might receive the desired blessings.

I counsel my family to hurry but not to rush, to move quickly to accomplish what needs to be done, but not to panic. We all need to be about our Father's business and trust that his help will sustain us, but "it is not requisite that a man should run faster than he has strength" (Mosiah 4:27). When you learn to balance your efforts and the Lord's saving and healing grace, then the Holy Ghost can teach you in the things you need to know and do in order to draw upon divine healing powers.

SUDDEN STROKES OF IDEAS

You may not know, presently, what you need to do to overcome your negative thinking, your pain and your suffering. But with time and practice—in balancing your own efforts and the Lord's healing grace—you will find that the Holy Ghost will direct you into paths and avenues leading to your desired blessing.

Direction often comes to the faithful in the form of inspiration from the Holy Ghost. You will experience sudden strokes of ideas and feelings that will provide you with information, then direction, and then peace. As Joseph Smith explained,

> A person may profit by noticing the first intimation of the spirit of revelation; for instance, when you feel pure intelligence flowing into you, it may give you sudden strokes of ideas, so that by noticing it, you may find it fulfilled the same day or soon; (i.e.) those things that were presented unto your minds by the Spirit of God, will come to pass; and thus by learning the Spirit of God and understanding it, you may grow into the principle of revelation, until you become perfect in Christ Jesus.[21]

Sudden strokes of ideas may prompt you to seek a particular physician or counselor, a certain remedy, a special blessing under the hands of a priesthood holder who possesses the gift of healing, or the Spirit may direct you to do a number of other things.

Miracles happen when you learn to follow promptings from the Lord. President Ezra Taft Benson is one who has not hesitated to act upon sudden strokes of ideas. While on a speaking tour as U.S. Secretary of Agriculture, he

> had been warned to expect hostile crowds in Austin, Texas, but before leaving the area, he felt impressed to suggest to the governor that he declare a day of fasting and prayer, and assured him that rain would be forthcoming. Three days later San Antonio had two inches of rain. A local paper reported, "Secretary of Agriculture Ezra Taft Benson apparently has contacts that are literally out of this world. When Benson left San Antonio on

Sunday he promised south Texas farmers and ranchers immediate drouth
aid. Less than 24 hours later it rained for the first time in months."[22]

These kinds of strokes of ideas can happen frequently. A lady I
know has been plagued by chronic arthritic pain; medication is of
only sporadic benefit. Frequently, because of the pain, it is difficult for
her to sleep. She recently reported to me that during one restless,
painful night, as she prayed for relief, the voice of the Spirit whispered,
raise your arms above your head and rest them on the pillow. She did
so and the pain immediately left for the rest of the night and she was
able to sleep.

You probably have heard many other Saints bear testimony about
how they have been able to draw upon the powers of heaven and
receive healing grace. These testimonies probably arouse within you a
desire to receive healing direction in your own behalf. As you receive
sudden strokes of ideas and direction from the Holy Spirit, it is important that you strengthen others with your increased faith so that they
may benefit as you have. The specific idea may be to benefit you
alone, but the increased faith can be shared to benefit anyone.

You should not impose your knowledge and faith on others, but
when they are seeking and asking, you ought to freely and wisely share
your testimony of healing truth. Such is the purpose of this book. I
want to share with you sacred treasures of knowledge that have been
given to me—knowledge and faith that can both heal and bless.

As you receive direction from other people and through sudden
strokes of ideas, you will want to follow the counsel of Paul to "Prove
all things; hold fast [to] that which is good" (1 Thes. 5:21). With time
and experience, you will learn the patterns by which the Lord blesses
and protects those who love and serve him.

A PATTERN FOR HEALING GRACE

Just as there are physical laws that govern our physical world, there
are laws that govern things spiritual. With experience in a physical
world—running, jumping, bouncing a ball, or sending a rocket to the
moon—we perceive laws, rules, and patterns that help us make connections and applications that give us control in our physical universe.
Through experience with spiritual things we learn control, too. There
are laws "upon which all blessings are predicated" (D&C 130:20). The

Lord is bound when we do what he says, but the Lord also warns, "When ye do not what I say, ye have no promise" (D&C 82:10). Seeing physical patterns helps us understand spiritual patterns that lead to promised blessings.

In a conference talk, Sister Janette C. Hales described her attempts to make a sport coat for her husband by following a commercial pattern. She saw parallels between following physical patterns and following spiritual patterns in order to reach our goals.

> As awareness of [the importance of] patterns has continued, I have become very appreciative of the Lord's patterns. Patterns for his handiwork are detailed in the scriptures. They describe the building of a tabernacle, an ark, an altar, and temples. The materials are important; the purpose is grand. Then comes that most important pattern of righteousness set by Jesus Christ, "a pattern to them which should hereafter believe on him to life everlasting" (1 Tim. 1:16). In every imaginable setting from ancient times to modern days, we see this pattern repeated—faith in the Lord Jesus Christ, repentance, baptism, the gift of the Holy Ghost. Patterns are meant to be repeated.[23]

The Lord has given us a pattern by which we may know if we are acceptable to him and are eligible for his blessings. "And again, I will give unto you a pattern in all things, that ye may not be deceived . . . Wherefore he that prayeth, whose spirit is contrite, the same is accepted of me if he obey mine ordinances" (D&C 52:14–15).

You have every right to draw upon the healing powers of heaven if you are humble and have received the ordinances of the gospel. Once again, you do not have to be perfect to be blessed. If you are seeking to keep the commandments, the gifts of the Spirit are available to you. The Lord promises that the gifts of the Spirit are for those who "keep all my commandments, and him that seeketh so to do" (D&C 46:9).

The healing powers that may come to you through promptings of the Holy Ghost may not always take the pain out of you, but the Spirit of the Lord will always take you out of the pain. When you have the Spirit with you, you may feel uncomfortable in your pain, but you can still have peace. The gospel promises deliverance for those who are faithful. (See 1 Ne. 1:20.) If all pain and suffering were immediately eliminated, one of the major purposes of this world would be violated—learning pleasure by experiencing pain and appreciating the sweet by tasting the bitter. The importance of adversity in this learning process is the subject of the next chapter.

NOTES

1. As quoted in McWilliams, *Negative Thought,* 418.
2. For excellent reading on this topic, see Grant Von Harrison, *Drawing on the Powers of Heaven* (Orem: Keepsake Paperbacks, 1979).
3. Told by Richard G. Scott, "Obtaining Help from the Lord," *Ensign,* November 1991, 85.
4. Scott, "Obtaining Help from the Lord," 85.
5. Scott, "Obtaining Help from the Lord," 84.
6. Patricia T. Holland, "One Thing Needful," *Ensign,* October 1987, 26.
7. Ezra Taft Benson, "Think on Christ," *Ensign,* April 1984, 11.
8. Russell M. Nelson, "With God, Nothing Should Be Impossible," *Ensign,* May 1988, 34.
9. Steven A. Cramer, *Conquering Your Own Goliaths* (Salt Lake City: Deseret Book, 1988), 14.
10. *Lectures on Faith* 2:31, 55–56.
11. *In His Footsteps Today* (Salt Lake City: Deseret Sunday School Union, 1969), 4.
12. Bruce R. McConkie, *A New Witness for the Articles of Faith* (Salt Lake City: Deseret Book, 1985), 191–92.
13. Journal History, 23 February 1847.
14. Parley P. Pratt, *Key to Theology,* 10th ed. (Salt Lake City: Deseret Book, 1973) 100–101.
15. Pratt, *Key to Theology,* 101, 102.
16. *Teachings,* 355.
17. Boyd K. Packer, "Self-Reliance," *Ensign,* August 1975, 89.
18. *Teachings,* 181.
19. Robert Millet, book review of *The Broken Heart: Applying the Atonement to Life's Experiences,* by Bruce Hafen, *BYU Studies* 30 (Fall 1990): 59.
20. Robinson, *Believing Christ,* 27, 29.
21. *Teachings,* 151.
22. Sheri Dew, *Ezra Taft Benson, A Biography* (Salt Lake City: Deseret Book, 1987), 280–81.
23. Janette C. Hales, "A Pattern of Righteousness," *Ensign,* May 1991, 83.

4

The Purpose of Adversity

For it must needs be, that there is an opposition in all things. If not so, . . . righteousness could not be brought to pass, neither wickedness, neither holiness nor misery, neither good nor bad.

—2 Nephi 2:11

This life is provided for us to gain intelligence and for us to learn truths by encountering opposition and opposites. Adam and Eve did not fully appreciate the peace of Eden until their eyes were opened after their transgression. It was only after sweating and laboring while hauling hay during the hot summer months in Canada, that I learned the glory of ice-water and bologna sandwiches. The Prophet Joseph Smith explained that "by proving contraries, truth is made manifest."[1] We must learn through opposition and adversity; there is no other way to appreciate the sweet without knowing the bitter, the pure without knowing the evil, the pleasurable without knowing the painful. But in spite of pain, the righteous are promised *peace*. (See D&C 59:23.)

Things have to go wrong sometimes so that you will be able to tell the difference when things go right. Ever since the Fall, mankind has been subjected to all manner of adverse circumstances: rejection, disappointment, sorrow, disease, and death. In our fallen world, illness, aging, and pain are inevitable. The only group we are aware of that escaped these adversities were the inhabitants of the city of Enoch.[2]

The aim of gospel covenants and medical therapy is to overcome the problems of pain, sickness, and suffering. The Prophet Joseph Smith said,

> Salvation is nothing more nor less than to triumph over all our ene-mies and put them under our feet. And when we have power to put all ene-mies under our feet in this world, and a knowledge to triumph over all evil spirits in the world to come, then we are saved, as in the case of Jesus, who was to reign until He had put all enemies under His feet, and the last enemy was death.[3]

We have come to this fallen world to learn good from evil, but we do not actively seek opposition just for the learning experience. We don't go to the Las Vegas Strip, for example, just to see how much evil we can resist. Neither do we deliberately seek suffering. The Lord has said that "sufficient unto the day is the evil thereof" (Matt. 6:34). In other words, you encounter enough opposition day by day without deliberately searching for it. It would not be in keeping with the Lord's plan for you to accept your pain and suffering without trying to over-come it. Rather, from the beginning Adam was commanded to sub-due the earth and have dominion over it (Gen. 1:28).

Although we all experience adversity, the Lord expects us to do the best we can to take charge of our own health and happiness. You are responsible for the maintenance of your own health. You are expected to do all that you can to be physically and emotionally fit so that you can enjoy life and good health, so you can bless the lives of others and serve in the Lord's kingdom wherever he needs you. Don't be among the crowd who turn responsibility for their health and well-being over to health professionals. Doctors and therapists may assist you in the process of recovery, but the primary responsibility for preventing dis-ease, relieving distress in your life, and establishing your own well-being rests with you as an individual.

STRESS AND DISTRESS

Illness can teach you to appreciate your health. Adversity can motivate you to achieve higher levels of health. Spiritual growth is often concealed in your pain and your distress.

It is important that we discuss *distress* as one of the common adversarial elements of life. Some kinds of stress are not unhealthy; positive stress motivates us to eat when we are hungry, to sleep when we are tired, to change positions in a chair to rest our body, to work for a living, to achieve in school, etc. However, the kind of stress that takes the form of continual, unrelieved frustration, hostility, or resentment is called *distress* and is the most accurate predictor of heart attacks and other health and behavioral problems.[4]

Prolonged distress suppresses your body's immune system that provides natural defenses against infections and other diseases. This is a key element in helping you to understand the link between distress and your illness.[5]

Distress and peace are mutually exclusive—they cannot coexist. Although you may not achieve a stress-free state in this life, you can strive for a distress-free life—which is a state of inner peace. We are promised that "he who doeth the works of righteousness shall receive his reward, even peace in this world and eternal life in the world to come" (D&C 59:23).

Your Heavenly Father, through his Holy Spirit, can guide your efforts as you learn to manage those everyday stressful situations. Through faith, you will be able to prevent them from boiling over to a condition of distress in which you conclude that all your conflicts are unresolvable and you are consigned to a life of pain and suffering. As you learn to handle your everyday stress through faith, you will be strengthened to handle death, the greatest stressor of all—the death of loved ones and, eventually, your own.

DEALING WITH DEATH

Through faith, you need not fear death any more. You may mourn the separation of a loved one who passes away; but when it happens, you will have peace, a peace born of faith in the Lord Jesus Christ. You will experience the reality of the Comforter.

Learning to mourn properly is a challenge for even the most faithful Latter-day Saints. This is a lifetime of good-byes. Upon graduation from high school, you leave behind your dear friends. If you have been on a mission for the Church, you have met and left behind loved ones when you return home. From time to time you have met certain people whose friendships seem to spark eternal memories—as though you have known them before. You move from place to place and wonder through misty eyes if you will meet these loved ones again.

We all face the aging process; we say good-bye to our youthful bodies, our prized hair. Through fire, theft, moth, or rust we see things pass away which played an important part in our lives. Eventually, we will say good-bye to it all with our own deaths. Learning to mourn, to grieve, to say good-bye in a constructive way that strengthens instead of weakens is an invaluable tool. "Blessed are they that mourn," the Lord has promised, "for they shall be comforted" (Matt. 5:4).

Latter-day Saints know that death is part of the merciful plan of God. (See 2 Ne. 9:6.) It is the escape hatch from a fallen and lonely world into a much better life where the righteous move with the rapidity of lightning. The faithful in the spirit world enjoy the presence of God and association with dear family and friends. But your knowledge of things as they will be does not minimize your sense of loss in the present.

When someone dear to us dies, our minds, bodies, and emotions go through a process that is as natural and as healing as that required for a physical wound. Please know that your feelings of loss, sadness, hurt, anger, and fear at good-byes are a natural part of the healing process for all of us.

Research shows that we human beings recover from loss in three distinct but overlapping phases. The first is shock/denial; the second, anger/depression; the third, understanding/acceptance. No matter what the loss may be—from the loss of the car keys to the death of a loved one—we all go through these phases. The only difference is the time it takes to go through them and the intensity of the feelings that we pass through at each point. Grieving must be done in its own time. We should not try to rush through the stages.

In the first stage, shock/denial, we can't believe the news. We say, "It can't be true. He was too young to die," or, "There must be some mistake in the diagnosis. This illness cannot be terminal." We go numb. This ability to numb and deny is a blessing. Serious, catastrophic losses are too hard to take all at once, so the Lord provides this phase of denial for us to experience the shock more slowly.

In the next stage, anger/depression, we may want to shake our fist at the Lord and say angrily, "Why is this happening to me?" Or depression causes us to say to ourselves or others, "I just don't want to go on. I can't cope any longer!" I am not suggesting that you should seek and promote feelings of anger and depression. But know that these feelings over the loss of a loved one (or even over your own impending death) are a natural human process. It is a natural stage of recovery you must pass through. To get through this stage, think of yourself slowly floating through the current of your grief. Do not resist it. Pass through it, but do not allow yourself to remain in a "problem dwelling" state of mind.

In the final stage of mourning, understanding/acceptance, you accept the inevitable and understand that God's hand is in your life and will strengthen you through this trial. This area of mourning is the golden stage. You are supported by the Holy Ghost, the Comforter. You reflect on the promises of the Lord and they not only comfort you, but they enlighten your mind, enlarge your soul, and become delicious to you (Alma 32:28). In anticipation of a glorious resurrection after an inevitable death, you are led to sing with Lehi, "Oh how great the goodness of our God, who prepareth a way for our escape from the grasp of this awful monster; yea, that monster, death" (2 Ne. 9:10). The blessings of the gospel covenant truly provide for peace in this world and eternal life in the world to come (D&C 59:23).

ALL THESE THINGS WILL GIVE YOU EXPERIENCE

In spite of the promised peace through gospel living, in our weakness we sometimes grow weary of the struggle. We have been taught that mortality is a place of learning, a place for experience, but sometimes we feel exhausted, tired, frustrated, and just plain worn out.

President Gordon B. Hinckley recounts the story of an attractive and competent young woman. She was divorced and was the mother of seven children then ranging in ages from five to sixteen. One evening she went across the street to deliver something to a neighbor. She recounts her experience:

> As I turned around to walk back home, I could see my house lighted up. I could hear echoes of my children's voices as I had walked out of the door a few minutes earlier: "Mom, what are we going to have for dinner?" "Can you take me to the library?" "I have to get some poster paper tonight." Tired and weary, I looked at that house and saw the light on in each of the rooms. I thought of all of those children who were home wait-

ing for me to come and meet their needs. My burdens felt very heavy on my shoulders.

I remembered looking through tears toward the sky, and I said, "Oh, my Father, I just can't do it tonight. I'm too tired. I can't face it. I can't go home and take care of all those children alone. Could I just come to you and stay with you for just one night? I'll come back in the morning."

I didn't really hear the words of reply, but I heard them in my mind. The answer was, "No, little one, you can't come to me now. You would never wish to come back. But I can come to you."

President Hinckley pointed out that

There are so many, so very, very many, like that young mother. She recognizes a divine power available to her. She is fortunate enough to have some around to love her and help her, but very many do not have such help. In loneliness and desperation, watching their children drift toward drugs and crime and helpless to stop that drift, they weep and pray. There is a remedy for all of this. . . . It is found in the gospel of the Son of God."[6]

Although you will be called upon to struggle, the Lord kindly urges you not to be "weary in well doing" nor to "charge God foolishly" (Job 1:22; Gal. 6:9; 2 Thes. 3:13; Alma 37:34). There may be times when, to be loving, Heavenly Father will chasten you. Even when you are rebuked by your Heavenly Father, you need not lose faith, for in the chastisement is a renewing of his love: "My son, despise not thou the chastening of the Lord, nor faint when thou are rebuked of him: For whom the Lord loveth he chasteneth" (Heb. 12:5–6).

President Wilford Woodruff counseled that mercy is inherent in adversity: "The chastisements we have had from time to time have been for our good, and are essential to learn wisdom, and carry us through a school of experience we never could have passed through without."[7] Your challenge is to endure whatever the Lord sees fit to inflict upon you for your good (Mosiah 3:19). The Lord customizes your life's experiences to bring about your greatest joy. On one of those rare occasions when the voice of the Father was heard, he said, "Yea, the words of my Beloved are true and faithful. He that endureth to the end, the same shall be saved" (2 Ne. 31:15). When we consider all the things that the Father could have said, why was it he mentioned *endurance*? One reason is that the Lord would structure your mortality for your learning experience. (See Abr. 3:25; Mosiah 23:21.) Peter said that your "fiery trial" should not be thought of as "some strange thing" (1 Pet. 4:12).

You may think and feel that there are so many things to be endured: illness, injustice, insensitivity, poverty, loneliness, rejection, depression, ignorance. Paul reminds us that even the son of God, though the Lord of the universe, "endured such contradiction of sinners against himself" (Heb. 12:3). Paul observed, "Now no chastening for the present seemeth to be joyous, but grievous: nevertheless afterward it yieldeth the peaceable fruit of righteousness" (Heb. 12:11).

Elder Neal A. Maxwell has pointed out that

> "peaceable fruit" comes only in the appointed season thereof, after the blossoms and the buds. Otherwise, if certain mortal experiences were cut short, it would be like pulling up a flower to see how the roots are doing. Put another way, too many anxious openings of the oven door, and the cake falls instead of rising. Moreover, enforced change usually does not last, while productive enduring can ingrain permanent change. (See Alma 32:13.)[8]

As soon as we reach the required level of righteousness by suffering our afflictions with great patience and faith, the Lord will deliver us from our pain and suffering. (See Mosiah 24:16.)

A young student driver, a former student of mine, was once involved in an automobile accident in which her best friend, who was a passenger in the car, was killed. After missing seminary for three or four days after the accident, she finally returned to her classes, but sat despondent and saddened on the back row of the classroom. In an attempt to help her understand and work through the pain and anguish she was experiencing, I read with her the following passages from the Doctrine and Covenants:

> And if thou shouldst be cast into the pit, or into the hands of murderers, and the sentence of death passed upon thee; if thou be cast into the deep; if the billowing surge conspire against thee; if fierce winds become thine enemy; if the heavens gather blackness, and all the elements combine to hedge up the way; and above all, if the very jaws of hell shall gape open the mouth wide after thee, know thou, my son, that all these things shall give thee experience, and shall be for thy good.
>
> The Son of Man hath descended below them all. Art thou greater than he? (D&C 122:7–8)

Although these passages did not bring immediate relief, the young student was able to reflect on an important gospel principle—that dreadful experiences can be turned to our learning and our good.

Those who are unduly impatient with the Lord, who want immediate deliverance from suffering, suggest that they have greater faith in their own timetable than in his. Heavenly Father does not require you to suffer longer than is needful. However, some people continue to suffer much longer than necessary simply because they do not know that there are healing principles that can free them from the pain.

The way to rid your life of unnecessary suffering is clearly defined in the scriptures and by living prophets.

1. You have a *desire* to be healed. (Some people hang on to their suffering to meet some illegitimate need for power and attention.)

2. You *learn* practices and principles relating to the healing process (the purpose of this book).

3. You learn to *trust* in these principles.

4. You *apply* the principles.

5. You *acknowledge* the hand of the Lord in your healing. Expressing gratitude to your Heavenly Father places you in a position to receive even greater blessings under his hand.

NEVER CONSIDER SUICIDE

You must never consider suicide as a way of ridding yourself of pain, heartache, or disappointment. Death does not change feelings, moods or your spiritual make-up. Only the scenery changes. You may lose all that you have in taking your own life, and your burden will be increased. The peril of suicide far outweighs any perils here. It should comfort those who have contemplated suicide to remember that only God is the judge of each soul and the severity of the trials each person faces. All it takes is to see hope in one positive act to be able to see a glimmer of light that you had missed before. Despair is never justified, because God rules the universe and will, in the end, make all things right. In the meantime, we are here to learn from our mistakes. Because God knows our weaknesses and loves us anyway, we don't need to judge ourselves harshly. If we take life one step at a time, we won't worry about how others may judge us, or use others' opinions as measuring sticks to beat ourselves up with. We will instead forgive ourselves and be grateful for the things that help us grow. We need to remember that our most severe challenges may one day reveal themselves to be our greatest teachers.

To have faith in our God is to trust that he is fair. In the end you will find many happy surprises. Even though you may be called to experience great pain and suffering in this life—to travel through the valley of the shadow of death—the Lord gives his promised blessing of deliverance. Never, never, never give up. The time will come when you will "be received into the kingdom of the Father to go no more out" (3 Ne. 28:40).

Although you will have to pass through adversity while in this life, the Lord in his kindness has provided his church upon the earth to bless your life and provide a bulwark against the fiery darts of the adversary. As you live the gospel of Jesus Christ, Christ himself becomes the focus of your faith. The way our membership in the Church can help us achieve that focus is the subject of the next chapter.

NOTES

1. Joseph Smith, *History of the Church*, 6 vols., 2d ed. (Salt Lake City: Deseret Book Company, 1973), 6:428.
2. See Moses 7:21; *Teachings of the Prophet Joseph Smith*, p. 170–71.
3. *Teachings*, 297.
4. For an informative discussion of the nature of stress and its role in various illnesses, see Kenneth R. Pelletier, *Mind as Healer, Mind as Slayer* (New York: Delta, 1977); also Peter G. Hanson, *Stress for Success* (New York: Doubleday, 1989).
5. All the details of this relationship are not yet fully known, but the general connection has been verified by numerous studies. Full recognition of distress and its connection with the immune system will bring about a major shift in medical research. Such a shift is now urgently needed, since stress-related chronic and degenerative diseases that are characteristic of our time constitute the major causes of death and disability.
6. Gordon B. Hinkley, "What God Hath Joined Together," *Ensign*, May 1991, 73.
7. *Journal of Discourses*, 2:198.
8. Neal A. Maxwell, "Endure It Well," *Ensign*, May 1990, 33.

5

Church Membership and Gospel Faith

Behold, you have not understood; you have supposed that I would give it unto you, when you took no thought save it was to ask me.

—D&C 9:7

Your membership in the Church alone will not resolve all your problems. I recall one middle-aged sister who was experiencing severe anxiety that seemed to be a result of her "mental diet," that is, her choice of thoughts. Her priesthood leaders had referred her to me for counseling. She had a history of drug and alcohol abuse before she joined the Church, but now she recognized that these substances were no longer an option for her when she needed a calming influence. As she sat there before me, desperately trying to gain some composure, her eyes red from hours of weeping, she asked, "Why do I hurt so much? Things are so much better since I joined the Church a year ago, but I still have periods when I am terribly depressed."

As I listened to this sister vent her frustrations, I noted that she had serious misconceptions about what membership in the Church should do for her. In effect, she believed that because she had joined the true church, she should automatically have gained the solutions to all her emotional problems. She believed that her depression should have been taken away at the moment she was baptized and was given the gift of the Holy Ghost.

I tried to explain to her that membership in the Church does not provide immediate answers to all our problems. Spiritual growth and knowledge come gradually, line upon line, precept upon precept, here a little and there a little. (See Isa. 28:9–10; 2 Ne. 28:30–31.) I also explained to her that certain kinds of depression and emotional problems can be caused by physical disorders unrelated to one's mental diet. When they are physically induced, they need to be treated by medical professionals. When they are a result of mental diet, the teachings of the Church can assist immensely. But here again, just being a member of the Church does not mean we automatically know how to control our thoughts. Growth in mastery over our thoughts and learning how to cope is gradual as the Spirit leads each of us to healing truths.

Joining the Church and being an active member is not enough for your salvation, although it is an important first step. Baptism alone will not change your life or cure your physical or emotional problems. You must learn to walk by faith if you expect to find deliverance from your pain and obtain your desired blessing. This process of walking by faith is not just a pleasant option. It is a divine imperative! You must "press forward with a steadfastness in Christ, having a perfect brightness of hope, and a love of God and of all men. Wherefore, if ye shall press forward, feasting upon the word of Christ, and endure to the end, behold, thus saith the Father: Ye shall have eternal life" (2 Ne. 31:20).

What is required in your "pressing forward" is exposure to correct principles upon which you can focus your faith. Additionally, you are required to be obedient to the other principles of the gospel such as temperance, patience, brotherly kindness, humility, diligence, charity, devotion to God, wisdom in following the counsel of priesthood leaders, and following other promptings of the Spirit. (See D&C 4; 2 Pet. 1:1–10.) Incorporating these principles into your life is a gradual process, an upward-spiraling path that will lead you to even higher levels of knowledge as it confirms additional truths in your heart and mind.

Do not be discouraged as you look at the pathway before you. We do not perceive grass growing but, imperceptibly, it *is* growing. Since your changes toward healing will be gradual, they will require your sustained effort in the right direction even when you cannot recognize great progress. When you first begin to learn how faith works, you will be particularly vulnerable to discouragement. Sometimes you will become distracted and discouraged and lose sight of meaningful growth that has already taken place.

Three weeks after Michelangelo began sculpting his magnificent David, we can imagine him joyfully engaged in his work. His vision of the finished creation was indelibly stamped in his mind and heart. As he worked, he did not see the remaining rough edges and unsmoothed curves as evidence of failure. He saw and built only on his previous day's progress. Likewise, your changes will require a sustained effort. Distractions and discouragements can cause you to lose sight of meaningful growth. On the other hand, your successes in one area will sustain you in another. Consider your goals to be an exciting adventure—one in which you can take pleasure along the way.

Alma explained how you can grow in your faith until you reap the desired blessing:

> And now, behold, because ye have tried the experiment, and planted the seed, and it swelleth and sprouteth, and beginneth to grow, ye must needs know that the seed is good.
>
> And now, behold, is your knowledge perfect? Yea, your knowledge is perfect in that thing, and your faith is dormant; and this because you know, for ye know that the word hath swelled your souls, and ye also know that it hath sprouted up, that your understanding doth begin to be enlightened, and your mind doth begin to expand.
>
> O then, is not this real? . . .
>
> If you will nourish the word, yea, nourish the tree as it beginneth to grow, by your faith with great diligence, and with patience, looking forward to the fruit thereof, it shall take root; and behold it shall be a tree springing up unto everlasting life.
>
> And because of your diligence and your faith and your patience with the word in nourishing it, that it may take root in you, behold, by and by ye shall pluck the fruit thereof, which is most precious, which is sweet above all that is sweet, and which is white above all that is white, yea, and pure above all that is pure; and ye shall feast upon this fruit even until ye are filled, that ye hunger not, neither shall ye thirst.
>
> Then, my brethren, ye shall reap the rewards of your faith, and your diligence, and patience, and long-suffering, waiting for the tree to bring forth fruit unto you. (Alma 32:33–35, 41–43)

Your physical, spiritual, and emotional growth will be a gradual process. In a revelation given to the Prophet Joseph Smith in May of

1833, we learn that during Jesus' mortal ministry, even he did not receive a fulness of the Father's power all at once. "He received not of the fulness at first, but continued from grace to grace, until he received a fulness" (D&C 93:13). John bore record that after Jesus' baptism, "He received a fulness of the glory of the Father; And he received all power, both in heaven and on earth, and the glory of the Father was with him, for he dwelt in him" (D&C 93:16–17). And then, to emphasize the pattern of Christ's empowerment as an example for us, we read,

> I give unto you these sayings that you may understand and know how to worship, and know what you worship, that you may come unto the Father in my name, and in due time receive of his fulness. For if you keep my commandments you shall receive of his fulness, and be glorified in me as I am in the Father; therefore, I say unto you, you shall receive grace for grace. (D&C 93:19–20)

Your divine nature will grow gradually. As it grows, it is important that you associate with others who are growing too. The Church is intended to provide this kind of wholesome atmosphere—for the perfecting of the Saints.

In the Church, as in our families, we are taught to live in harmony one with another and are given opportunities to practice Zion-like traits such as cooperation, patience, humility, service, and love. But remember, the conditions in Zion —such as unity of mind and heart, righteousness, and economics that will allow the abundant gifts of the Spirit to bless and heal to be manifest (Moses 7:18; 4 Ne. 1:3; D&C 70:14)— do not come about overnight. In the King Follett discourse, the Prophet Joseph Smith affirmed that gospel growing is a gradual process.

> Here, then, is eternal life—to know the only wise and true God; and you have got to learn how to be Gods yourselves, and to be kings and priests to God, the same as all Gods have done before you, namely, by going from one small degree to another, and from a small capacity to a great one; from grace to grace, from exaltation to exaltation, until you attain to the resurrection of the dead, and are able to dwell in everlasting burnings, and to sit in glory, as do those who sit enthroned in everlasting power.[1]

When you join the Church, you become a citizen of the Kingdom of God with all the rights, privileges, powers, and blessings belonging to spiritually begotten sons and daughters of Jesus Christ. You must remember that as a member, you are an heir of all the promised blessings including the marvelous gift of the Holy Ghost, which will guide you into all truth. You will grow gradually in the gospel toward exaltation, and you will grow gradually in your faith to be healed. The programs of the Church can assist you on your journey. However, the Lord is your shepherd, your teacher, and your healer. You are responsible for learning of his ways through his Holy Spirit. Your immediate Church leaders, bishops, and teachers will assist you as they are able. Inspired materials such as books, media, and the scriptures will also assist you.

In your continued spiritual growth you will seek and find the gifts of the Spirit such as diligence, faith, and patience. You must not mistake your slow movement for lack of progress. As a reminder of your progress, compare what you know now to where you were only a few months, even weeks, ago.

GAINING BY GIVING

You should view your membership in the Church as a means to an end—a means by which you can be taught by word, deed, precept, and power how to make changes. These positive changes in your thinking, feeling, and acting will lead not only to better health, but also to greater peace, and eventually to eternal life. The gospel of Jesus Christ leads you to salvation. The Church is the means of spreading the gospel of Jesus Christ. Dean L. May points out the importance of Church activity as a means of gaining more spiritual power through selfless service.

> Any activity that causes us to think less about our own situations and to work together to achieve common ends is helping us to live in a manner consistent with Enoch's Zion. As Joseph A. Young, Brigham's son, expressed it to the Saints of the Richfield United Order in 1874, "The feeling of 'mine' is the greatest feeling we have to combat."
>
> Perhaps most importantly, we should participate full[y] in the programs available in each Latter-day Saint ward. In my judgment the carping one often hears against the Church as opposed to the gospel is missing a vital point. The Church programs, even if they seem at times intrusive, repetitious, and tedious, are in essence a basic training course in communal values and practices. They throw us into daily interaction with persons of all ages and of different social, economic, and educational backgrounds. They hound us into visiting such people and participating in programs to

help them and receive help from them in a myriad of ways. They urge us out of our comfortable tendency to pursue only our own lives and in our own way. When we oppose and resist Church programs we need to ask if we are not succumbing to the siren call of the world, pulling us back into the great sin of our time where "every man walketh in his own way, and after the image of his own god, whose image is in the likeness of the world" (D&C 1:16).[2]

Sister Marguerite DeLong has explained that learning to serve is learning to lead in righteousness.

> To serve is to lead. True leaders serve the people they are called to lead. They lead by example. This is why the calling of women—as wives, mothers, nurturers, and teachers is so vital. In these roles I am to serve others and in so doing lead them to Christ. Service born of charity binds both parties together in a holy loving relationship. This is why unrighteous dominion is so very wrong. It sets up a vertical, power oriented relationship instead of a level, service oriented one. When I allow others to serve me I am giving them an opportunity to grow, too, through leadership.
>
> Priesthood leadership is always service oriented. Its power and authority cannot be maintained by force. It can only work by gentleness, meekness and love unfeigned which enlarges the soul without hypocrisy or guile. All of these traits are characteristics of true service which is pure leadership. True leaders say "Come fly with me!" The leader is on the level with those whom he/she leads. They are one. The real me is a leader in the Lord's army because as such I am a servant. I hold the sword of truth in my hand. Because I am a servant I am a beacon light to those with whom I come in contact throughout my life. My real self uses the sword of truth to protect and defend [my loved ones] from the influences of the adversary . . . I teach them truths which enable them to defend themselves. My sword is an instrument of life and deliverance instead of death and destruction.[3]

Next to your family, the Church is the most important place you can render the kind of service that will empower you to receive your desired blessings from the Lord. As you bless the lives of others, you are blessed; you receive grace for grace. For example, imparting knowledge as a teacher gives you knowledge. The temple experience is a perfect example of how this process works. As you perform vicarious ordinances for those who have died, you have renewed within your own mind and heart the promises you made with the Lord. You are empowered by his Spirit as you bless the lives of those who have gone beyond the veil.

THE CHURCH AND THE GOSPEL

The mission of The Church of Jesus Christ of Latter-day Saints, simply stated, is to proclaim the gospel, perfect the Saints, and redeem the dead, thus bringing the living and the dead to Christ. (See Eph. 4:11–12.) The Church has the responsibility of preaching the gospel of peace to every nation, kindred, tongue, and people. But the Church itself is not the gospel. It alone does not save us. The power that saves us comes from Christ, and we become recipients of that power by living the principles and receiving the ordinances of the gospel. The ordinances are the authorized channels through which the blessings of peace and salvation flow.

Put another way, the Church is the outward vehicle that carries the inward power of salvation of the gospel into our lives. The healing power of faith, on the other hand, works from the *inside* out. In order to receive the healing power of Christ in your life, you make choices that lead to faith and repentance. Faith and repentance are the gospel-centered treatment programs for people in pain.

Can you see why, in this respect, it is helpful to differentiate between the Church and the gospel? If we do not understand this distinction, we may be distracted in our priorities. As a bishop I sometimes heard young people say they know the Church is true—and well they should. One young girl reported that, when she was faced with temptation, she asked herself, "What would the Church think if I were to do this?" I was glad she checked herself by reflecting upon the Church, but she could make a higher appeal still—to check herself by what the Savior would think. I want my children, my ward members, and my students to make their decisions based upon the gospel of Jesus Christ, as prompted by the Spirit, and as modeled by Christ's own thoughts and actions.

Some may think this is a distinction without a difference, but I am convinced that an appeal to inward promptings is more lasting than outward exhortations. I want people to know that the Church is true, to take advantage of the cooperative principles it teaches and the opportunities it offers to practice them. But since the Church organization is carried out by imperfect mortals, these imperfect people can let us down. The gospel truths will never let us down. The ultimate power of the gospel rests in the Atonement of Jesus Christ that empowers us to overcome sin, temptation, and disease. It is our ultimate goal to put on the full armor of God—the power of the restored gospel of Jesus Christ as it is taught within his true and living Church here upon the earth.

Too often we try to motivate others to do better without penetrating "the inner man" where the gospel must truly operate if it is to help and heal. When we finally internalize the gospel as we should, we will then enjoy its full blessings as Enoch's people did. Then our attempts will no longer be external, cosmetic, and superficial (as our attempts often are after listening to motivational speakers of the world). Shad Helmstetter has suggested that too often a meeting

> consists of an audience of anxious listeners, sitting enthralled while a dynamically enthusiastic speaker weaves for them a web of pure magic, the spun gold of [prosperity, i.e.,] riches and success.
>
> For an hour or two he will imbue his listeners with a new sense of destiny, a grand new vision of their unlimited selves, all of them capable of scaling the highest mountains of their imagination, if only they believe that they can. . . .
>
> Companies and groups of all sizes and descriptions rely on that kind of motivation to pep up their people, give a high point to their conventions and sales meetings, and send the troops away, ready to go out and fight dragons, close more sales, fix problems fast, and reach new heights of achievement. . . .
>
> Popular lecturers and speakers, dynamic orators, enlightening the faithful with the contagious zeal of the greatest Sunday morning sermons, captivate, charm, cajole, and convince their listeners of their ultimate potential. They fascinate, enrapture, entertain, and enchant. They do what they came there to do: they motivate.
>
> For the most part, these motivators do the best job they can. They get people thinking. They paint pictures, a gallery of suggested dreams, which show others what can be, what they *can* do. They are the pied pipers of success, leading the average would-be achiever toward something better. They stimulate minds, inspire new ideas, and reaffirm the resolve to get at it, get something done, accomplish something worthwhile, set some goals, tackle the problems, and move forward. But there is a problem with that kind of motivation: it is external and it does not last.[4]

All external motivation is temporary if it is not internalized. When the motivator is removed, the behavior soon dies out and the energy of change is dissipated. This is especially true when we are active in the Church but not active in the gospel. External motivation is like running a car on its battery. The battery is designed to get the car started, but then the car must run on its own. External exhortation in the

Church may stimulate interest to get things going, but it is not sufficient for solid gospel change, any more than the Law of Moses,[5] with its emphasis on external behavior, was sufficient to bring about an inward change in the minds and hearts of the Israelites. External motivation may influence you to make a change, but it cannot make the change for you.

The Church, by way of analogy, is like a coach who supports, encourages, invites, requires, and disciplines. But when the coach is gone, so is the support, the encouragement, the discipline, and the reward. The gospel, on the other hand, teaches us to take righteous initiative, which President Benson has said is the key to exaltation. Once you learn to follow the Spirit, you become a self-starter, a self-motivator, and self-maintainer; you become a free agent with the ability to make things happen on your own. Two examples illustrate this important principle.

I know a parent who explained to his young daughter, who was beginning early morning seminary for the first time, that if she wanted him to drive her to seminary each morning, she would have to awaken him. Each morning at 6:00 a.m. the girl would gently touch her father on his shoulder and say, "Dad, it's time to get up and take me to seminary." Here the motivation was internalized. The girl was going to seminary upon her own initiative, and the rewards and accomplishments that resulted were her own. Such should be the case with achievements in the Boy Scout and Young Women "Pursuit of Excellence" programs. The more the parents use external motivators, the less likely the values will be internalized in their children.

Another example involves a parent who wanted his two eldest sons to become Eagle Scouts. He built a signaling device so his sons could learn the Morse code and get the signaling merit badge. However, his boys were neither interested nor involved. Having learned his lesson, the father told a younger son that if he wanted to get his Eagle badge, he would have to take the initiative himself. The father said he would help if he were asked, but the initiative must be the boy's. This son became an Eagle just after he turned fourteen because he was motivated internally and took the initiative to accomplish the tasks required for each advancement.

In a similar way, the Lord invites you to follow him. He wants you to take the initiative. He will never force you to do righteous acts. There is no such thing as forced righteousness. The Lord uses magnets to draw you to him, not handcuffs. The Lord's drawing power is in his message and in his person. The Holy Ghost bears witness to you as one of the Lord's sheep, that you might hear his voice and follow him.

When you are willing in your heart to pay the price for true discipleship, you will follow the Lord because of your deep love for him. You are a part of the Latter-day covenant Israel, an heir to all the promised blessings. "This shall be the covenant that I will make with the house of Israel; After those days, saith the Lord, I will put my law in their inward parts, and write it in their hearts; and will be their God, and they shall be my people" (Jer. 31:33).

I know that great healing power can come into your life as you honestly reach out for the promises of our Lord and Savior, Jesus Christ. As you honor your covenants and seek to do his will, you can experience a comfort and a peace not of this world. The Lord has promised you that he will not leave you comfortless. He will come unto you. He promised, "Peace I leave with you, my peace I give unto you: not as the world giveth, give I unto you. Let not your heart be troubled, neither let it be afraid" (John 14:27). Jesus is your Lord, your Savior, your Great Deliverer. He has the power to move mountains, trees, and seas! He has the power to heal you of pain, suffering, and loneliness.

NOTES

1. Smith, *History of the Church,* 6:306.
2. Dean L. May, "The Economics of Zion: Plotting Zion Today Where There Is No Poor," *Sunstone* 14 (August 1990): 21.
3. Marguerite DeLong, personal correspondence with the author.
4. Shad Helmstetter, *What to Say When You Talk to Your Self,* (New York: Pocket Books, 1986), 91–92.
5. The Law of Moses was established with the purpose of focusing the people's mind on Christ. When the Israelites lost the meaning of the rituals, they lost their power to come unto Christ. What was left, eventually, was a system of dead rites and ceremonies because their focus was limited to the outward form and did not include the inward meaning.

II

Faith in Your Divine Nature

You have two natures: one worldly and carnal, the other spiritual and divine. These two natures are constantly at war with each other. Satan and his followers tempt you to be carnal, sensual, and devilish. Your Father and all the hosts of heaven encourage you to develop your divine nature and to increase in faith, hope, and charity. In the end, you choose which voice you will follow, but the consequences are inevitable: disease, death, and sorrow if you follow your carnal self or, on the other hand, health, life, and happiness if you follow your divine nature.

We live in the days just preceding the Millennium when Satan has frightening power and where we observe and experience increasing immorality, violence, fear, death, and disease. The only way to withstand this barrage of corruption is to rise above your carnal self, to determine within yourself that you will honor your covenants with the Lord. To do this, you must develop your divine nature—your real self—your inner self's ability to choose the right. Your real self is that part of your nature that was faithful and true to the cause of the Savior in the premortal existence.

Your real self is like a divining rod which even now responds to the light of Christ and the promptings of the Holy Ghost to bless and heal your body and soul. On the other hand, your carnal self—your false self—relies on the "arm of flesh" for healing power, and you become frustrated and disappointed because of these futile investments in error.

As you develop faith in your divine nature and suppress the demands of your carnal self, you will grow in your power with the Lord to be blessed and healed of every pain and sorrow.

6

Your Thoughts and Your Health

And he shall mount up in the imagination of his thoughts as upon eagles' wings.

—D&C 124:99

The faith to be healed of your pain and loneliness requires both faith in the Lord Jesus Christ and faith in your own divine nature. Whereas Part I of this book gives suggestions on how to develop your faith in the Lord, this part shows you how to develop faith in your own divine nature, your spiritual self, your real self.

The Lord Jesus Christ loves you and has suffered and died for your sins if you will but come unto him that he may help and heal you. You are precious in his sight. Your worth is much greater than your sins and your shortcomings. You have a divine nature that is sacred, holy, beautiful, lovely, sensitive to truth, and, oh, so loved by your Heavenly Father. You are a spark struck from the fires of his eternal blaze. There are things you can do that will fan that spark so that it becomes a powerful healing fire. The light within you, when merged with the powers of heaven, can purge the dross, refine, sanctify, bless, and heal you. Nothing is impossible to those who have a deep and abiding faith.

The Apostle Peter, speaking to members of the Church in his day, counseled them to develop their divine natures that they might receive the abundant blessings and escape the carnal world of lust.

> Simon Peter, a servant and an apostle of Jesus Christ, to them that have obtained like precious faith with us through the righteousness of God and our Saviour Jesus Christ: Grace and peace be multiplied unto you through the knowledge of God, and of Jesus our Lord, according as his divine power hath given unto us all things that pertain unto life and godliness, through the knowledge of him that hath called us to glory and virtue: whereby are given unto us exceeding great and precious promises: that by these ye might be partakers of the divine nature, having escaped the corruption that is in the world through lust. (2 Pet. 1:1–4)

Peter explained this process of holy empowerment—how we develop our divine nature and become fruitful in Christ as we develop Christlike traits of character, which are, in fact, gifts of the Holy Spirit:

> And beside this, giving all diligence, add to your faith virtue; and to virtue knowledge; and to knowledge temperance; and to temperance patience; and to patience godliness; and to godliness brotherly kindness; and to brotherly kindness charity. For if these things be in you, and abound, they make you that ye shall neither be barren nor unfruitful in the knowledge of our Lord Jesus Christ. (2 Pet. 1:5–8)

As you follow the promptings of the Holy Ghost, you receive the power of God in your life. For "as many as received him, to them gave he power to become the sons of God, even to them that believe on his name" (John 1:12). The Lord honors all his promises. He has declared, "I, the Lord, am bound when ye do what I say; but when ye do not what I say, ye have no promise" (D&C 82:10).

Among the commandments of the Lord that most effectively influence the development of your divine nature, is the command to guard and control your thoughts.

> Let virtue garnish thy thoughts unceasingly; then shall thy confidence wax strong in the presence of God; and the doctrine of the priesthood shall distil upon thy soul as the dews from heaven. The Holy Ghost shall be thy constant companion . . . and without compulsory means it shall flow unto thee forever and ever. (D&C 121:45–46)

THE POWER OF YOUR THOUGHTS

You may think that *thinking* is a small thing, but consider for a moment what has resulted from human thoughts. As you look around you—at a chair, a picture, a television, a house—everything you see was an idea first before it became a reality. One prominent writer said, "Thinking is an experimental dealing with small quantities of energy, just as a General moves miniature figures over a map before setting his troops in action."[1]

A simple thought involves a few microwatts of energy flowing through your brain, but it can have an enormous impact on your body. Sometimes the effect can be dramatic. Think of scratching your fingernails on a chalkboard. What kind of feelings do you experience? Or visualize cutting a lemon with a stainless steel knife. Squeeze a few drops of the lemon on the shiny knife blade and then touch your tongue on the lemon juice. What happens in your mouth? Do you begin to salivate? Your thoughts cause your body to react in certain ways. As you change your thoughts, you change your feelings. The mind and the body are like parallel universes. Anything that happens in the mental universe must leave tracks in the physical one.

The people who visit with me in my office may be laughing one moment and then crying the next—just because I changed the topic of our conversation. When a person does this, however, note that nothing was changed in the objective world; only thoughts were changed. Negative thoughts produce negative feelings; positive thoughts create positive feelings. Every good thought you think contributes its share to the totality of your well-being.[2]

Your thoughts have a great deal of influence over your immune system. Thoughts seem to be innocuous, almost ephemeral things. And yet, a thought—or, more accurately, a carefully orchestrated series of thoughts—has a significant impact on your mind, your body, your emotions, and the world around you. Harvard psychologist Mary Jaznowski took thirty healthy students and divided them into three groups. One group worked on crossword puzzles; the second was given relaxation training; and the third received relaxation training and visual imagery training—imagining their powerful and strong immune systems attacking weak flu and cold viruses. Group One showed no increase in immune cells. Group Two showed a slight increase. Group Three showed a significant increase in immune system activity after only one hour of training.[3]

You too can use your mind to teach yourself to relax, to visualize changes in your body, and to increase the probability of those changes actually occurring. If you pay more attention and give more time and energy to becoming aware of your mental processes, you will be much more effective in reaching your goals. The important thing to remember at this point is that you are free to choose your thoughts. Satan cannot force his influence upon you and God will not do so. You are independent and free to make your choices.

THREE INDEPENDENT AGENTS

The Prophet Joseph Smith taught a principle relative to our moral agency that is sometimes not understood by Church members: "There are three independent principles; the Spirit of God, the spirit of man, and the spirit of the devil. All men have the power to resist the devil."[4] Brigham Young taught the same idea when he said:

> God is the author of all good; and yet, if you rightly understood yourselves, you would not directly attribute every good act you perform to our Father in Heaven, nor to his son Jesus Christ, nor to the Holy Ghost; neither would you attribute every evil act of a man or woman to the devil or his spirits or influences; for man is organized by his Creator to act perfectly independently of all influences there are above or beneath. Those influences are always attending him, and are ready to dictate and direct—to lead him into truth or to lead him to destruction. But is he *always* guided by those influences in every act? He is not. It is ordained of God that we should act independently in and of ourselves, and the good is present when we need it. If we will ask for it, it is with us.[5]

The fact that you are independent is a powerful concept because it brings out the importance of taking initiative in bringing healing power into your life. God and Satan represent the two extremes. Whether you are thinking thoughts that lead to death and destruction or to life and healing, you are making the choice. You, however, must take initiative. Free agency is established in such a way that you must ask Heavenly Father, in the name of Jesus Christ, in order to draw on the powers of heaven. You will not find answers from above if you are always looking downward. In the healing process you must seek to unify your own efforts with those of the Father. If you ask, the Holy Ghost will lead and guide you. The Holy Spirit will show you how to draw on the healing power of Christ and how to develop the healing power of your own mind and spirit.

Sometimes it is difficult to know whether promptings that come are revelations from the Lord or from your own mind. Whether truth is given directly from God at a moment of need or whether a truth given to you earlier surfaces into your thought processes at a particular time, truth will always bring peace to your mind and heart. You are a child of God. You have the agency to innovate change, using your own mind as a source of power.

Many scriptural accounts give examples of healing power from the divine nature. During Jesus' mortal ministry a certain lady approached him: "For she said within herself, If I may but touch his garment, I shall be whole. . . . Jesus turned him about, and when he saw her, he said, Daughter, be of good comfort; thy faith hath made thee whole" (Matt. 9:21–22). From this account you can learn an important principle. Not only can Jesus heal you, but your own divine nature can be a source of healing power. The woman had taken the initiative to reach out to the Lord. She was a free agent. Jesus did not reach out to her; she reached out to him, and by the power of her own faith she was healed.

We are expected (1) to receive help from Christ, and (2) to develop healing faith within ourselves. Of the former charge, the Lord promises, "that as many as receive me, to them will I give power" (D&C 11:30). Of the latter we read, "Sanctify yourselves" (D&C 88:68. See also D&C 133:62; D&C 20:31). Furthermore, regarding the power of our own agency, the Lord has explained, "The power is in them, wherein they are agents unto themselves" (D&C 58:28).

Part of your test in mortality is to determine to what extent you will respond to truth when you hear it. President John Taylor has described the effects of truth upon receptive souls in these words:

> When truth shall touch the cords of your heart [including truth about your divine nature] they will vibrate; then intelligence shall illuminate your mind, and shed its luster in your soul, and you shall begin to understand the things you once knew, but which had gone from you; you shall begin to understand and know the object of your creation.[6]

When your mind, your spirit, your divine nature, comfortably blends with the righteousness of Christ and the Holy Spirit, you sense great joy. On the other hand, no pain is more severe than are the feelings of alienation when you are disobedient and are separated from the Spirit of the Lord. For instance, when Joseph Smith and Martin Harris lost the 116 pages of the Book of Mormon manuscript, the Spirit left Joseph, who then felt great anguish. During this time, the Lord commanded Joseph to repent: "Lest I humble you with my almighty power; . . . lest you suffer these punishments of which I have spoken, of which in the smallest, yea, even in the least degree you have tasted at the time I withdrew my Spirit" (D&C 19:20). Some people who have felt the withdrawal of the Lord's Spirit have said they felt like they had rocks in their chest—rocks that burned hotly and weighted them down heavily.

When the reverse is true, when you feel a union of your spirit with the Spirit of the Lord, you feel happiness, and this union generates great spiritual powers, including healing powers. When your mind and heart are linked together with the Lord and his purposes, you are truly blessed. You have the moral agency to choose, to control, the kinds of thoughts you dwell on and the results that will follow.

CHOOSING YOUR THOUGHTS

Someone once said, "That which gets your thoughts, gets you!" Although this statement is true, the tone implies that you do not have control of what comes into your mind. Your mind is not a passive receiver of positive and negative impressions around you. You are not simply acted upon. You control what gets into your thoughts and remains there. You may not always have the ability to control the ideas that initially come into your mind, but you and you alone choose what remains. In other words, you can't keep a bird from landing on your head, but you can keep it from building a nest there. Because an evil thought enters your mind, you need not think that you are an evil person—unless you choose to nourish the thought, feed it, and make it your own.

Did you know that Satan can talk to you in your mind using the tone of your own voice? When this happens, you may think that the thoughts and feelings you experience constitute the real you. Do not be misled. If you do not like a thought, refuse to own it. Replace it with a worthy thought. If necessary, borrow God's strength and power to resist negative thoughts and ask him to take them from you.

When you do not like your thoughts, you can choose either to ignore them or to change them. Your mind is like a television with all kinds of signals being received. You can change channels; you can choose the pictures that play on the screen of your mind. You have the God-given freedom to choose. Because you can choose your thoughts, you have control of your thoughts. This is the liberty wherewith you are made free (Mosiah 23:13).

The principle of free agency has no greater application than in connection with your thoughts—you *choose* what you think about and how you see things. While you cannot always choose your external environment, you can always choose what stays in your mind and how you choose to view your situation and your world. Furthermore—and this can be a blessing or a cursing—once you have chosen your thoughts, you are destined to experience their corresponding feelings. When you choose happy thoughts you will experience happy feelings; when you choose sad thoughts you will have sad feelings. More importantly, when you think sick thoughts, you get sick; but when you think healthy thoughts, you become healthier.

You rarely have feelings that were not preceded by a corresponding thought. For example, the death of your grandmother does not cause your remorse; the sadness comes from your thoughts about her death such as: "I will miss her," "She was not ready to go," "Grandpa cannot get along without her," etc. Your grandmother may have died two days before you learned about her passing. Her death did not cause your grief; it was your thoughts about her death—after you learned about it—that brought your sorrow.

The more your thoughts are centered on Christ, his teachings, and his power, the more free you are of unnecessary pain and grief. For instance, when you anticipate a resurrection and a happy reunion with your grandmother, you are free to think vastly different thoughts than the thoughts of people who know nothing about the spirit world and the eventual resurrection. With knowledge of the plan of salvation, you can focus your thoughts on more positive things. Thoughts are like seeds. What you plant is what you harvest.

As a mental gardener, if you plant thoughts such as "I have no friends," "I am dumb," "I am fat," "I am ugly," "I have an unhappy marriage," "I am not a good parent," " I hate life," what will you get? You have literally planted seeds of thought that can only give you an increase of their own kind—even an abundance. That is the opposite of what you want to get. As Carolyn Pearce Ringger pointed out, "Negative thoughts trigger faith into a backward motion."[7]

You are a mental gardener. You plant seeds daily in your life. In your backyard gardens, if you plant peas, you get peas; if you plant corn, you get corn; if you plant beans, you get beans. As you plant one kernel of corn, you do not get back only one kernel. You receive an abundance.

The more aware you are of your thoughts, the better you can control your feelings and your actions—and your health. Here, then, are the basic principles for unlocking the healing power of faith:

- Your feelings come from your thoughts.
- You can control your thoughts.
- Therefore, you can control your feelings.
- Your thoughts, feelings, and actions all affect your health.

You have awesome power to control your own life. But you and I should always be on guard, realizing that our choice of thoughts determines our feelings, actions and, to a large extent, our very health. (See Figure 2.) In order to make choices necessary for our growth, we must have options. Some LDS writers have suggested that within us are two natures—one that is a source of light and health, and another that is a source of darkness and disease.

YOUR REAL SELF AND YOUR FALSE SELF

As mentioned in the introduction to Part II, you have two natures within you—a carnal, worldly self and a divine, spiritual self. Sterling and Richard Ellsworth have labeled these natures your "false self" and your "real self." These descriptive terms relate to your negative and positive thought patterns. They state that "inside each one of us, the war in heaven is never over. Inside us, whether we are aware of it or not, there is a constant struggle between our real self and our substitute world self. All of our thoughts and actions reflect this battle."[8] (See Figure 3.) Your real self chooses thought patterns of faith, hope, charity and health. Your false self chooses thought patterns that reflect things carnal, sensual, and devilish and foster disease and death.

Your real self chooses light and truth patterns that are filled with happiness, cheerfulness, optimism, and a desire to serve others. Consequently you are filled with life, light, and power. Always choosing patterns of light and truth is one of the hallmarks of the real you. Your false self chooses patterns of darkness and you feel unhappy, depressed, argumentative, withdrawn, ornery, and selfish. Your false self responds to the influence of Satan and his hosts; your real self responds to the enticings of the Holy Ghost.

Your Feelings Come from Your Thoughts

Falsehood

What is happening
is making me
think the way I do.

Truth

I am free to choose my
thoughts about what is
happening to me.

THOUGHTS

What is happening
is making me feel
the way I do.

My feelings come from
my choice of thoughts.

FEELINGS

What is happening
is making me do
what I do.

I act the way I do
because of my feelings.

ACTIONS

You think other people or
outside circumstances
always determine your
thoughts, feelings, and
actions. If this were so,
you would always be acted
upon—no agency.

You know that your feel-
ings come from your
choice of thoughts. You
can choose your thoughts;
therefore you can choose
your feelings and actions—
free agency.

RESULTS

Figure 2. You have free agency and are in control of your thoughts, feelings, and actions. If you allow people and events to control your thoughts, you have no agency.

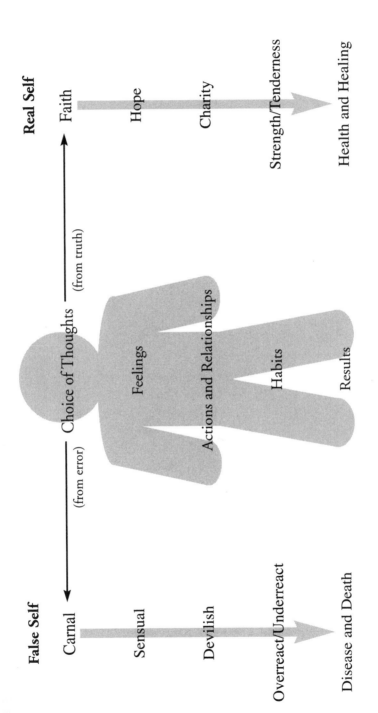

Choose a Thought, Choose the Result

Real Self

Faith

Hope

Charity

Strength/Tenderness

Health and Healing

Choice of Thoughts

(from truth)

(from error)

Feelings

Actions and Relationships

Habits

Results

False Self

Carnal

Sensual

Devilish

Overreact/Underreact

Disease and Death

Figure 3. Create the effects you want by choosing your thoughts.

It is helpful to think of your real self as your eternal spirit self—your true divine nature. It is innocent, ageless, powerful, lovable, and youthful. It comes from the past, experiences the present, and anticipates a magnificent future. It is against no one; it sees everything; it is not condemning; and it allows all men their free agency. Your real self is not selfish. It centers on "we and ours" instead of "me and mine." It is genuinely cooperative instead of confrontationally competitive in relationships.

Sometimes you may think that you do not have a real self or that the real you is a being of darkness—a weak, miserable creature that hides in a cave, and when it comes out at all, it is shy, withdrawn, inhibited, and weak, or even rude, crude, mean, and abusive. Don't you believe it! Don't be dismayed, thinking you have to invent, build, or otherwise labor to let your real self have ascendancy in your life.

You do not have to create your real self. You have only to let it come out. Your true spirit self came from the presence of your Heavenly Father. You came pure and holy. One of the purposes of this life is, with the help of the Holy Ghost, to give birth, growth, and power to your real self—to learn how your real self can gain ascendancy over your physical body. God, angels, prophets, along with good friends and family members eagerly await the emergence of your real self. Sadly, and unnecessarily, many people die before their real self is reborn. You need not be one of those people. Right now, even as you consider that you have a real self, you experience a twinge of hope. Let that hope grow as you learn how to give your real self more control.

When you choose to act from your real self, you are in harmony with the universe, "then shall thy confidence wax strong in the presence of God; and the doctrine of the priesthood [including that of healing truth] shall distil upon thy soul as the dews from heaven" (D&C 121:45).

You begin to discover your real self, your true divine nature, as you learn of your heavenly origins. President Marion G. Romney stated that the most important knowledge available to you as a mortal being is a knowledge that you are literally a child of God,

> a knowledge [that] is beyond the ken of the uninspired mind. . . . The only means by which such knowledge can be had is divine revelation. . . . The aspirations, desires, and motivations of one who accepts, believes, and by the power of the Holy Spirit obtains a witness of the truth that he is a begotten son or daughter unto God differs from the aspirations of him who believes otherwise, as the growing vine differs from the severed branch.[9]

While it is true that you are a child of God, it is important that you remember that you have the two natures, your real self and your false self. Ever since the fall of Adam and Eve, you and I, their children, have a part of us that is attracted to spiritual light from above and a part of us that is attracted to spiritual darkness from regions below. When we choose light, we are healed. When we choose darkness, we are weakened.

Recovery from pain requires discovery—finding your real self's ability to form an alliance with the powers of heaven to bring about healing changes. Discovering your real self enables you to more fully and appropriately love yourself and others. The real you doesn't react to other people who are angry by either becoming angry yourself or by giving in to them. When others are in their negative selves and are shooting angry arrows at you, your real self has the ability to be like a shadow that nothing can hurt. The arrows will pass right through and cause you no harm at all. Your real self will whisper at times, "It really doesn't matter."

Your real self is filled with positive energy: light, goodness, kindness, love, patience, charity, hope, and so on. Your negative self is filled with negative energy: darkness, hatred, fear, unkindness, intolerance, selfishness, despair, discouragement, and so on. Over time you become attracted to people who have similar "spiritual energy fields." "For intelligence cleaveth unto intelligence; wisdom receiveth wisdom; truth embraceth truth; virtue loveth virtue; light cleaveth unto light; mercy hath compassion on mercy and claimeth her own" (D&C 88:40).

Positives attract positives and negatives attract negatives. You begin to associate with others like you who have an impact upon you—and you upon them—for good or for evil. But you always have the agency to choose to live from your real self and affect others for good. A positive spiritual synergy can be established to the mutual benefit of everyone in your range of influence.

Your real self can always do things better than your negative self. It can reason better, solve problems better, relate with others better, sense the promptings of the Holy Ghost better, and acquire faith power better. Your real self does not take other people's actions and behaviors as a reflection of your own self-worth. The Apostle Paul, in his letter to the Galatians, expressed this clearly. He wrote:

Walk in the Spirit, and ye shall not fulfil the lust of the flesh. For the flesh lusteth against the Spirit, and the Spirit against the flesh: and these are contrary the one to the other. . . . Now the works of the flesh are manifest, which are these; Adultery, fornication, uncleanness, lasciviousness, idolatry, witchcraft, hatred, variance, emulations, wrath, strife, seditions, heresies, envyings, murders, drunkenness, revellings, and such like: of the which I tell you before, as I have also told you in time past, that they which do such things shall not inherit the kingdom of God. But the fruit of the Spirit is love, joy, peace, longsuffering, gentleness, goodness, faith, meekness, temperance. . . . If we live in the Spirit, let us also walk in the Spirit. (Gal. 5:16–25)

It seemed obvious to the Apostle Paul that if you desire to be happy, you must discern between the voice of your divine nature as the receiver of the Holy Spirit, and the subtle misleading voices of your false self, which can rightly be called your "lower nature." Your false self seeks after the carnal appetites and wants of the flesh—excessive pleasures that lie outside the limits described by the Lord for your happiness.

Your real self, on the other hand, seeks for a proper balance between things of this world and things of the spirit. Your real self defines any situation, mood, bad day, or problem as an important learning part of life. During periods of distress, your negative self wants to change and control others in order to reduce the tension, but your real self recognizes that the only person you can now or ever change or control is yourself. Your real self seeks the opportunity to influence others for good, but your false self will try to force others to change.

When you begin making changes in your world by starting with yourself, you will recognize that you are responsible for your own negative thoughts, feelings, and actions. They may have been whispered there by Satan, but it is your job to get rid of them.

By way of analogy, when you squeeze an orange, orange juice comes out—because that is what is inside. When you are in your false self and you are under pressure, it is like being squeezed. Anger, bitterness, and jealousies come out if that is what is inside of you. When the real you is under pressure, you remain calm, relaxed, tranquil, and in control—because that is what is inside of you. When others get hot, your real self gets cool. Wisdom, forbearance, tolerance, and a quiet firmness come out—because that is what your real self is like.

When the real you performs acts of kindness, you feel good about yourself and about what you are doing. You feel love and charity for the people you're serving. Your source of happiness is not tied up in the behaviors of other people. Happiness is inside you because you allow your real self to make the choices. You work from the inside out. Your self-esteem, therefore, is not conditioned by external things like clothes, power, beauty, position, riches, or status in the eyes of men. Those are all values that the false self seeks.

People who allow their false self to take control think they are unacceptable, even from birth. They may even think that through their agency in the premortal life, they made choices that make them unworthy in this life, and that is why they have so many problems. Your real self knows and accepts that Christ's atonement has made you clean from any sins you may have committed in the premortal world. As you came into this world you came sanctified, pure and holy (D&C 74:7). "Every spirit of man was innocent in the beginning; and God having redeemed man from the fall, men became again, in their infant state, innocent before God. And that wicked one cometh and taketh away light and truth, through disobedience, from the children of men, and because of the tradition of their fathers" (D&C 93:38–39). Disobedience and false traditions help develop your false self in this fallen world, but you did not come here with a burden of sin. Your tendency toward sin is a consequence of the Fall.

When King Benjamin referred to the "natural man," he was referring to our fallen natures. Since the time of the fall of Adam and Eve, we are prone to give power to our false selves.

> For the natural man is an enemy to God, and has been from the fall of Adam, and will be, forever and ever, unless he yields to the enticings of the Holy Spirit, and putteth off the natural man and becometh a saint through the atonement of Christ the Lord, and becometh as a child, submissive, meek, humble, patient, full of love, willing to submit to all things which the Lord seeth fit to inflict upon him, even as a child doth submit to his father. (Mosiah 3:19)

In the above scripture, the "natural man" is the false self. Your real self wants to yield to the enticings of the Spirit, to experience happiness and peace. When you yield yourself to the Spirit of the Lord, your physical surroundings may not always change, but the way you view them will reflect the comforting, peaceful aura of the Spirit. You feel authentic and whole. You get excited about these faith-power principles because they work. Your real self is familiar with and rejoices in these gifts from the Spirit of God.

When your real self makes decisions, you will be in tune with the Holy Ghost and in harmony with the will of God. Your real self is full of light and intelligence. Integrity, love, tenderness, assertiveness, consideration, modesty, and chastity are beautiful and dependable dimensions of your real self.

You are in a constant struggle to allow the real you to have ascendency in your life. When your false self takes control, the natural man in you responds to the siren call of your lower nature; your thoughts, feelings, and actions become carnal, sensual, and devilish.

You are free to make choices according to the promptings of the Holy Ghost or Satan. "Wherefore, the Lord God gave unto man that he should act for himself. Wherefore, man could not act for himself save it should be that he was enticed by the one or the other." (2 Ne. 2:16. See also 2 Ne. 2:11; D&C 29:39; D&C 58:28.)

The following example shows how you are free to choose patterns of light or patterns of darkness—liberty or captivity:

There once were two sons of an alcoholic father. One son became a Catholic priest, the other an alcoholic just like his father. Both sons were interviewed and asked why they had chosen their particular lifestyle. Both sons gave the same answer: "What would you expect, with a father like mine?" Both sons had enough good examples around that they could see that not everyone in the world was like their father. Each son made a choice. One chose to overcome the adversity of his situation; the other chose to succumb to it.

It is important that you master your false self choices now. Don't let more time pass without change. Don't die unprepared. We have an explicit warning that we should not procrastinate the day of our repentance. The thoughts, feelings, and actions you choose in this life will continue with you after you die. Book of Mormon prophets have explained that the same spirit that possesses your body in this life will have power over you in the eternal world (Alma 34:34). This idea has been confirmed by recent life-after-life studies.

Dr. Raymond A. Moody has collected accounts of near-death experiences of people who appear to have died and then were resuscitated. One patient who had a near-death experience as a child recalled that he saw life and its problems in a very different light following his near-death experience.

I never got wrapped up in family bickering like my brothers and sisters did. My mother said it was because I "had the bigger picture." I suppose that might have been true.

I just knew that nothing we were arguing about had any real importance. After meeting the Being of Light I knew that any arguing that went on was meaningless. So when anything like that started in the family, I would just curl up with a book and let other people work out their problems. Mine had already been worked out for me. I am the same way, even now—more than thirty years after it happened to me.[10]

You are literally a child of Heavenly Parents. Choices of thoughts, feelings, and actions from your real self will be a reflection of the glorious blaze of their divine presence. In this life you can approach their way of thinking, feeling, and acting. You, through your faith, can receive their power in your life. As you approach their purity, you will have clearer views, greater enjoyments, and more power to receive your promised blessings. The more experience you have in recognizing your divine nature, the easier it will be for you to remain in your real self, the less you will find yourself in your negative, and the more fruitful you will be in bringing to pass the things the Lord would have you do.

It is true that while in this mortal school certain amounts of adversity are necessary for your growth; but there are other forms of affliction that you create for yourself. In many cases, you have chosen your own sickness—it is the consequence of your negative mental diet.

THE THOUGHT-FEELING-ACTION PYRAMID

Your spirit and your mind have tremendous influence on your flesh. You literally have power to affect your own health. Human beings only, of all creatures of earth, can change their thought patterns. We are each the architect of our destinies. We become what we allow ourselves to think about—even when we don't think so. Our thoughts are important specifically because they have such a total impact on our feelings and actions. Alma warned that our words, works, and thoughts will condemn us (Alma 12:14). Jesus explained that "every idle word that men shall speak, they shall give an account thereof in the day of judgment" (Matt. 12:36).

John-Roger and Peter McWilliams[11] have suggested that in order to make progress in the physical world, three things are necessary—a thought, a feeling, and an action (or a directed activity). These three form a pyramid as shown in Figure 4.

If you have thoughts and feelings to match, but no action is taken, you are just spinning your wheels. If your thoughts and feelings are negative, this usually results in worry, depression, and problem dwelling. If your thoughts and feelings are positive but no action is taken, you are left with unproductive "positive thinking."[12] Physical action is necessary to give expression to your thoughts and feelings. This may be one of the reasons why the Lord has given us ordinances (actions) to provide outward form for our inward covenants (thoughts) and testimony (feelings).

If your thoughts and actions are not sustained by feelings, your actions will probably not continue for long. Our testimonies (thoughts and feelings) keep us faithful and active. Your feelings are your greatest motivators to action, taking ascendency over the mind in most cases. Your mind sparks your feelings, but your feelings move you to action. You take action because you anticipate a beginning or a continuation of good feelings. The purpose of our existence is connected with feelings: "Men are, that they might have joy" (2 Ne. 2:25). Christ endured the agonies of Gethsemane and the cross because of the love that he feels for all of us.

When you experience feelings and actions with no thoughts, no correct principles to guide you, you are headed for troubled waters. Feelings without thoughts, or without guiding principles, are like a ship without a rudder. The Prophet Joseph Smith warned the Relief

Figure 4. The progress pyramid.

Society sisters of zeal (that is, strong feelings and actions) without knowledge (or correct thoughts).[13]

If one of the sides of your pyramid is missing, the structure will collapse. You cannot experience productive, enduring, life-enhancing work without all three sides functioning in a progressive order: thoughts, feelings, actions. This being the case, you can see how important it is to control your thoughts. You must control your thoughts as you control your very life, because your thoughts determine your life, your world, your reality. Truly, "as [a man] thinketh in his heart, so is he" (Prov. 23:7).

Habits developed in your thought-feeling-action pyramid eventually affect your mental and physical health. Habitual positive thoughts produce health. Habitual negative thoughts produce illnesses and disease. The law of the harvest affirms that what you sow, you reap. I am not saying that negative thinking always causes disease, or any other life-threatening illness. Germs are the primary cause of illness. But repeated negative thinking promotes conditions in the body that make it possible for the germs, viruses, and other agents to take root. Your entire immune system is affected by the thoughts you persist in. Negative thinking can become an addiction. Clinical depression can be, in addition to genetic or disease-related biochemical imbalances, a consequence of habitual problem dwelling.

The idea that negative thinking is an addictive disease is sometimes a controversial subject. The medical doctors who have taken a close look see that the pattern of negative thinking, in its extreme, fits all the criteria of addiction in the medical sense. Thirty years ago, most of the medical establishment wouldn't admit that thoughts had any causal effect on organic illness. The generally accepted theory among the medical people now is that thoughts are a contributing factor of symptomatic illness, and that improving one's thoughts can help improve one's health.

As a psychotherapist, I see on a daily basis people who are in emotional and physical pain. The faces of these people change, but the problems they describe follow certain identifiable patterns. Usually, people who are in pain suffer because of (1) their own negative thinking, (2) difficult interpersonal relationships, or (3) unfavorable environmental or biochemical conditions. In most cases, the greatest contributor to this pain is their own negative thinking. This is not to minimize the influence that other people may have had in their life or the difficulty that environmental factors may have presented. What I do want to stress is that although people may not always be able to control the actions of others, or factors outside themselves, they can generally control what goes on inside themselves—the thought patterns that they choose. I have observed a common, recurring negative pattern: rather than accept the burden of responsibility themselves, people usually want to blame their emotions and problems on other people and on circumstances they believe are beyond their control.

Understanding that thoughts are contributing factors to your health is one of the grand keys to improving your physical and mental health. Many hospital beds are filled with patients who have been hospitalized as a consequence of addictive thoughts which have affected them physically—actually caused or contributed to their illness. Attempts to heal these types of illnesses without correcting the underlying thought patterns is like applying a Band-Aid to broken bones. The external treatment for internal causes is patchwork at best, and in many cases, constitutes a major effort in futility. Physical causes require physical therapy, but mental and spiritual causes require the therapy of faith. Paul warned us of seeking carnal solutions to spiritual problems: "For to be carnally minded is death; but to be spiritually minded is life and peace" (Rom. 8:6).

Spiritual-mindedness includes the ability to recognize your thought patterns and then make connections between true principles and specific situations within your own life. Let's consider this in more detail.

SEEING PATTERNS AND MAKING CONNECTIONS

Patterns are things that repeat themselves over and over. Your mind seeks to organize things into patterns. In your infancy, your mind began recognizing patterns in everything around you—in the faces of your family (eyes, ears, noses, and hair all generally located on heads with about the same arrangement), in the wallpaper, in clothing styles, and even in the seasons. This recognition of patterns is an automatic process. As you grew and matured, you began to form patterns of your own. You developed habits in virtually everything you did: in your walking, talking, writing, working, and also in your thinking— in your attitudes. You may not have stopped to realize that your attitudes and moods have been formed according to a pattern of your own design. Internal thought processes follow distinct patterns just as much as your handwriting and voice reflect a style all your own.

The scriptures describe two dichotomous types of thought patterns—one positive and the other negative. The thought-feeling-action pyramid, within a gospel context, can be expressed in a positive pattern as faith (thoughts), hope (feelings), and charity (actions). A negative pattern can be expressed as carnal (thoughts), sensual (feelings), and devilish (actions). (See Figure 5.) Whichever pattern you have developed over the years has had a great influence on your mental, spiritual, and physical health.

We find examples of these two distinct patterns in the scriptures. The Book of Mormon, especially, presents good and evil in discrete, mutually exclusive categories. This is done for instructive purposes. Like a textbook, the Book of Mormon provides abundant examples of how the Nephites and Lamanites from time to time followed either the positive faith patterns or the negative carnal patterns and received the inevitable blessings or consequences of their choices.

When people are faithful to the Lord and honor his covenants, they are blessed and protected. When they are not obedient, they are destroyed. The patterns are clear. These scriptural examples are given to us so we can liken ourselves to these people about whom we are reading. This enables us to choose gospel patterns and live more fully the abundant life and avoid the death and destruction of the wicked. (See 1 Ne. 19:23.)

Understanding that thought patterns are learned and that things learned can be adjusted, reformed, and reshaped to promote more health and happiness is a key to healing your troubled soul. To unlock faith's healing power, you must learn how gospel patterns operate in your life. Faith-power grows as you learn to see things from our Heavenly Father's point of view. As you immerse yourself in the scriptures and the teachings of the prophets, and as you observe your own actions and the behaviors of people around you, you will begin to see these patterns. You clearly see positive faith-hope-charity examples that bring life, health, and happiness, and the negative carnal-sensual-devilish examples that bring death, disease, and sorrow.

As you continue to look for patterns, examples, and models, you will find yourself extracting principles and making connections (applications) between newly recognized principles and your own situation. For example, when Jesus visited the Nephites, he healed all their sick.

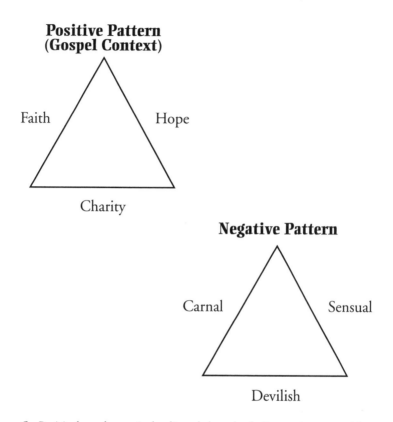

Figure 5. Positively and negatively aligned thought-feeling-action pyramids.

His disciples did the same during a long period after Jesus' final ascension. In the Doctrine and Covenants we read that when the Saints become united, including a temporal equality, then the abundant gifts of the Spirit will be made manifest. (See D&C 70:14.) I see a pattern here. I believe that when we Latter-day Saints are finally united as a people, when we live the gospel like the Nephites did, we will have similar gifts of the Spirit: visions, miracles, and the blessed healings of all diseases, spiritual and physical.

In your search to find healing patterns, the Holy Ghost will lead you along the way by providing sudden strokes of insights, ideas, and connections. As you seek, you will find. Truths will be revealed to you about how the principles you have learned apply to your own condition.

In the beginning, the process of seeing gospel patterns and making personal connections may be a little slow for you. But once you understand the procedure, you will sometimes find yourself having a hard time sleeping at night because your mind will be so active in making connections. Making connections is like dropping a ping-pong ball in a room full of loaded mouse-traps: one sets off another until all have been set off. Similarly, one truth leads to another and all truth fits together. You will find that this process is a wonderful and exciting learning experience. You will find that this is *real* learning. All else is simply data processing.

Memorizing scriptures or long lists of principles is not the most productive kind of learning. Simple memorization, as necessary as it is to learning, is not as much fun as making connections and seeing relationships. It is certainly not as productive in affecting our lives. Relational learning is seeing patterns, extracting principles, making connections, and thereby becoming empowered to make wise decisions in choosing our thoughts, feelings, and actions.[14] Relational learning is a process that works well in almost all fields of learning: table tennis, biology, music, economics, history, English, *and* mental health.

STRUCTURING YOUR OWN PYRAMID

Can you see how important your thoughts are to your health? Your faith-power is enhanced or limited by your thoughts. Your divine nature is hungry for more light and knowledge to act upon. Do not deny it proper nourishment. Your health is so tightly connected to how you think and feel about yourself.

The gospel of Jesus Christ teaches that you are a child of God. You are taught in the Church that this is a literal relationship. What other faiths take figuratively regarding this doctrine, Latter-day Saints take literally. You are a real child of God—you are his offspring. The seeds of deity are within you. You possess his divine nature. You have a glorious destiny that, for the present time, is incomprehensible and unimaginable. "As it is written, Eye hath not seen, nor ear heard, neither have entered into the heart of man, the things which God hath prepared for them that love him" (1 Cor. 2:9). You have forgotten who you are and what your divine heritage is, and until you are taught about your divine nature, you are susceptible to the influence of the adversary.

The antithesis of your divine nature is your carnal nature. The scriptures refer to this side of you as "the natural man." As you ponder your heavenly origins and the promised blessings of the gospel, your divine nature's thought patterns are set in motion. You are empowered with light, truth, peace, and joy that affects your mental and physical health. On the other hand, if you doubt your heavenly origins and continue to cling to the carnal comforters of the natural man, you will lose spiritual light and experience distress, which will negatively affect your health. You have the God-given agency to choose your own thought patterns. Whichever voice you choose to follow will have its consequences—health and happiness or disease and sadness. Why would people ever choose to be ill? That is the subject of the next chapter.

NOTES

1. Sigmund Freud as quoted by McWilliams, *Negative Thought,* 10.

2. An important work by Deepak Chophra, *Quantum Healing: Exploring the Frontiers of Mind/Body Medicine,* (New York: Bantam, 1990), contains the latest research and reasoning on healing. This book was a national best-seller and is an important work for anyone interested in maintaining and restoring health.

3. Mary Jaznowski, "Mind Power Opportunities" *Bottom Line* 12 (15 October 1991): 9.

4. *Teachings,* 189–90.

5. *Journal of Discourses,* 9:122; emphasis added.

6. As quoted in Garth L. Allred, *The Eternal Plan for the Children of God* (Hurricane, Utah: Homestead, 1986), 10–11.

7. Carolyn Pearce Ringger, *My Life Is a Joy to Me* (Mesa, Ariz.: Carolyn Pearce Ringger, 1985), 33.

8. Sterling G. and Richard G. Ellsworth, *Getting to Know the Real You.* (Salt Lake City: Deseret Book Co., 1981), 32.

9. Marion G. Romney, *Conference Report,* April 1973, 136.

10. Raymond A. Moody, Jr., *The Light Beyond* (New York: Bantam, 1989), 66.

11. McWilliams, *Negative Thought,* 193.

12. Please note that doing meditation, contemplation, visualization or pondering do not fall into the "unproductive" category, *if* they are intended to provide initial direction for feelings and actions.

13. *Teachings,* 201.

14. William Fox, Kurt Kanks, and Gerrald L. Pulsipher have developed an approach to learning that involves these principles. They formed the Relational Learning Group and are associated with the research and development division of the Franklin Quest Co., P.O. Box 2068, Salt Lake City, Utah 84110. I have found relational learning principles to be powerful instruments of learning and change.

7

The Origins of Illness—
Weeds of Error

Cursed is he that putteth his trust in the arm of flesh. Yea, cursed is he that putteth his trust in man or maketh flesh his arm.

—2 Nephi 4:34

There is a disease spreading in the world that affects each one of us—the disease of loneliness. This cosmic loneliness is the number one psychological disease afflicting mankind. University students are among the most lonely people in the world, followed by divorced people. The rich and famous are lonely, too. Country and western music depicts lonely people in serial love affairs. Alcoholism and drug abuse are sad symptoms of people who feel desperately alone. Lonely people make love and still feel very separated.

Some people are lonely because they have lost their loved ones in death or in sin. Even though their present sufferings are keen, faith in the Lord's promise can strengthen them. He will "wipe away all tears from their eyes; and there shall be no more death, neither sorrow, nor crying, neither shall there be any more pain: for the former things are passed away" (Rev. 21:4).

Our lonely feelings are actually caused by our separation from God—because of Adam's transgression and our own sins. We haven't always been lonely. In our premortal life, we basked in the warm glow of heaven's love and perfection; we were daily the delight of our Heavenly Parents (Prov. 8:22–25, 29–30). We were loved by God, and we ourselves had acquired great powers to organize and control physical and spiritual matter. (See D&C 131:7.) In a vision given to Abraham, he was shown certain noble and great spirits who were with the Savior in the creation of the world (Abr. 3:22, 24). You were no doubt among these noble and great ones.

Now you have come to this fallen earth, "trailing clouds of glory, from God who is our home."[1] Here in mortality, you have forgotten that you were among the "favorites of heaven."[2] The veil of forgetfulness is drawn across your mind. You do not remember your former dignity and power. There you were loved and belonged to the royal family of God. Here, when we are without revelation and knowledge from above, you and I wander in a lonely sphere where death, darkness, and disease reign. In this school of mortality we are tested. As the Lord said, "And we will prove them herewith, to see if they will do all things whatsoever the Lord their God shall command them" (Abr. 3:25).

We have an inner yearning to keep God's commandments because we are literal children of God.[3] We are his offspring. Mortality is a time for us to prepare to be like him. Adam fell that men might be. The Fall introduced both physical and spiritual death. As a consequence, we inherit death, disease, pain, and suffering; these we receive because we are children of Adam. Added to these are the separation and loneliness that we feel as effects of our sins. We all feel so, so, so alone in this world! We are commanded to heal our loneliness by drinking living waters and by eating the bread of life—by receiving the gospel of Jesus Christ. Instead, we sometimes try to drink from broken cups and eat of forbidden bread—the carnal comforters of the world around us. In your loneliness, what do you choose to comfort you? Is it faith in the Lord Jesus Christ, or is it a misplaced trust in the carnal comforters of the world?

CARNAL, SENSUAL, DEVILISH, AND DISEASE PATTERNS

Your thoughts have exceptional power to draw on the negative and positive energies around you. When you persist in drawing on the negatives, the result affects your moods and even your physical health by weakening the body's natural defenses. This is especially true when your negative thoughts are centered on yourself. We are at our most self-centered state when we are depressed. Nothing can sap our natural strength and health as much as prolonged depression because it is based on the lie of hopelessness. It focuses on our own powerlessness and denies the hope of Christ's deliverance and strength. But when we make the effort to connect ourselves to the Savior's power, to move ourselves away from our self-centeredness and begin to concentrate on the needs of others and how to serve them, we begin to heal. Christ-centered service is a balm to both the spirit and body.

Whereas the faith-hope-charity pattern will reveal all things, enlighten your mind, enlarge your soul, and show you things to come—things that will become delicious and healing to your mind and body, the carnal-sensual-devilish pattern of the natural man will lead you to darkness, disease, and even death. By persistently following this dark pattern, the light of Christ, and certainly the influence of the Holy Ghost, will eventually flicker and die out, "My spirit will not always strive with man," says the Lord (Gen. 6:3). Figure 6 shows how the carnal-sensual-devilish pyramid operates in the life of the natural man.

Carnal thoughts. In our fallen world we are all faced with adverse events such as rejection, disappointment, death, disease, betrayal, tribulation, false accusations, or "even the very jaws of hell." (See Figure 6.) Your false self imposes a negative subjective interpretation on the situation. You begin to think that the adverse event or situation *causes* you to feel the way you do. Satan whispers to you that something is wrong with you, that you are not okay or these things would not be happening to you. Since your negative self is not in tune with heavenly gifts, you seek earthly or carnal solutions. You choose carnal thoughts because of ignorance, sin, or because of the false traditions of your parents. (See D&C 93:39–40.)

When your faith in Christ is weak, you have no sure foundation that can truly bless your life or heal your pain. The natural man places his trust in Satan-inspired worldly comforters. You may be tempted to believe that peace and pleasure can be found in the physical world in things such as money, power, drugs, popularity, or passions. In an attempt to make your pain and loneliness go away, you may get caught up in extreme or unwise fad therapies and man-made false remedies. Of this trend toward carnal things the Lord has warned, "My people have committed two evils; they have forsaken me the fountain of living waters, and hewed them out cisterns, broken cisterns, that can hold no water" (Jer. 2:13).

Sensual Feelings. From your carnal thoughts come the sensual feelings of anxiety, doubt, depression, and a host of other feelings that lead to despair. Feelings become sensual because they are earthbound, hedonistic, self-centered, self-stroking, or self-punishing. Sensual feelings involve moods of loneliness, alienation, hopelessness, bitterness, resentment, and guilt. These emotions are sensual because, while in your false self, you are without hope, without hope in your own self-worth and in the Lord's power to save. Without faith in the Lord Jesus Christ or in your own inner ability to find a remedy, you get locked into mortality, the carnal world around you, knowing only what your five senses tell you. Your efforts become counterproductive to growth and well-being. In extreme cases, pain becomes so severe that even the five senses can betray you—some people experience hallucinations or delusions.

Devilish Actions. Our sensual feelings seek expression in devilish actions. We want to overreact (to fight) or to underreact (to take flight).[4] Satan seeks to entice us into extreme behaviors, to lure us into vertical kinds of thinking, whether we overreact or underreact. Satan does not care which way we act, because either way we are in his power. When we fall for carnal comforters, our vision is blocked and we feel trapped. Without hope in Christ and his power to bless us, we succumb to the devilish behaviors described by Nephi:

> And there shall also be many which shall say: Eat, drink, and be merry; nevertheless, fear God—he will justify in committing a little sin; yea, lie a little, take the advantage of one because of his words, dig a pit for thy neighbor; there is no harm in this; and do all these things, for tomorrow we die; and if it so be that we are guilty, God will beat us with a few stripes, and at last we shall be saved in the kingdom of God. (2 Ne. 28:8)

Rather than esteeming our brother as ourself, we succumb to the existential mentality of grabbing for the last piece of pie.

When sensual feelings occupy your heart, the heavens withdraw and your false self is left, or so it seems, with no solution except to either overreact (to blame, fight, yell, scream, shout, demand, and use unrighteous dominion) or underreact (to submit, withdraw, give in, give up, or become a wimp—a person with no courage or backbone).

Too many people think that all human relationships exist along the vertical plane: "If you're not a winner, you're a loser." They think

The Natural Man's Carnal Comforters

Event (Adversity)	Thought (Negative self-talk)	Feeling (Sensual feelings)	Action (Devilish Actions)		Disease and Death (Aggravated Physical Conditions)
			Overreact	Underreact	
Rain	I'm not OK	Anxiety	Blame	Please	Headaches
Slush	My thoughts are evil	Despair	Yell	Conformity	Ulcers
Pain	I must be bad	Frustration	Hostile	Submitting	Backaches
Death	I don't belong	Worry	Mean	Dependent	Constipation
Darkness	I don't count	Guilt	Vulgar	Alcoholic	Diarrhea
Disease	I'm an outsider	Nervousness	Rude	Insane	Insomnia
Discomfort	I'm inadequate	Shame	Abusive	Suicidal	Chronic fatigue
War	I'm a failure	Anger	Rebellious	Overeating	Obesity
Destruction	I'm dependent	Shyness	Competitive	Drugs	Stuttering
Betrayal	I'm weak	Helplessness	Shrewish	Withdrawal	Allergies
Tribulation	I'm not lovable	Panic	Agitating	Denial	Arthritis
False accusations	I'm not capable	Apprehension			Psychotic breaks
	I am nothing	Terror			

Figure 6. The natural man seeks carnal comforters which often lead to devilish actions and even disease and death.

if they are not in the top position (if they are not number one, the best, the prettiest, or most handsome) then they are a loser. They think in mutually exclusive opposite categories—black/white; rich/poor; winner/loser; good/bad; and so on. Overreacting and underreacting behaviors are devilish because they are Satan-inspired, selfish choices. They are ineffective in solving problems.

To help you understand the overreacting and underreacting competitive relationships, imagine or hold a pencil in the vertical position. Think of the top of the pencil as the place for overreactors, those who use unrighteous dominion (abusers, controllers, and blamers), and then think of the bottom of the pencil as the position of the underreactors (submitters, pleasers, and wimps). Figure 7 will help you visualize vertical relationships.

The opposite of a vertical relationship is a horizontal or level relationship. Level relationships (see Figure 8) represent a balance of strength and tenderness in contrast to overreacting and underreacting. Cooperation and mutual respect are important qualities. There is room for everyone. These level kinds of relationships are closely related to healing power and will be discussed in the next chapter.

Disease and Death. An important connection exists between habitual use of carnal comforters and illness. The more frequently you use carnal comforters, the greater is the likelihood of emotional distress (such as, shame, guilt, sorrow, worry) and physical suffering (headaches, backaches, ulcers, tics, skin disease, and even death.) Overreacting and underreacting behaviors, both carnal comforters, bring us into bondage, sin, and captivity. When you allow yourself to get caught in the grip of such repeated and unnecessary patterns, it puts enormous physiological stress on your body. These tendencies usually continue to escalate over time. Like revving up a car engine and not putting it in gear to move forward, overreacting and underreacting build up stresses in your body to the point that your electrochemical balance is affected and something has to give. What gives? Your health!

It has long been known that we get ulcers, not because of what we are eating, but because of what is eating us: unresolved conflicts, unrealistic expectations, refusing to repent of sins, and problem dwelling instead of problem solving. All of these represent the negative self's futile effort to find healing peace. Instead of peace, you get more pain.

Vertical Relationships

Overreactors

Underreactors

Figure 7. Vertical relationships. People at the top are overreactors; they seek dominion and control. Those on the bottom are underreactors; they submit, try to please, and avoid confrontations.

Horizontal Relationships

Strong   Tender

Figure 8. Horizontal or level relationships. People with level relationships have a balance of strength and tenderness; they seek mutual respect and cooperation.

The carnal-sensual-devilish pyramid, with its overreactions and underreactions, provides an illusion of relief or no one would ever choose it. People think if they drink more, sin more, or gamble more they will find a cure for their loneliness. The drunkard, while he is drunk, thinks he has no problems. In fits of anger, abusers think that they are gaining the victory, while at the same time the victims of such abuse submit to the evil in martyr-like ways. They think they are pleasing God by not resisting the abuse, or they falsely believe they are to blame for the problems themselves: "Where did I go wrong? What do I need to do better so these things won't happen again?"

Because Satan is miserable, he seeks the misery of all mankind (2 Ne. 2:18). He tries to spoil our happiness in many ways, but his efforts are directed primarily at getting us out of balance. He wants us to become intemperate and indulge in extreme behavior.

FIG LEAVES AND CARNAL COMFORTERS

After Adam and Eve ate the fruit of the Tree of Knowledge of Good and Evil, Satan had them sew fig leaves together to cover their nakedness. Here, the reference of "nakedness" is no doubt a metaphoric allusion to the couple's feelings of self-consciousness and unworthiness before the Lord. The figure can be extended to describe how we all feel after we sin. Using ineffective fig leaves—carnal comforters—we try to ease our loneliness and make the pain go away. They provide only an illusion of relief. These false comforters only escalate our stress; the harder we try to ease our pain by using them, the worse things get!

In contrast, our Heavenly Father provided Adam and Eve much better covers for their nakedness than fig leaves. They were given coats of skins—which symbolize light and truth. These garments, when honored, cover, heal, and protect. Through obedience and faith, they cover our nakedness (our vulnerability, our low self-esteem, our depression, and our feelings of unworthiness) before God.

After the Fall, Adam rejoiced by saying, "My eyes are opened, and in this life I shall have joy, and again in the flesh I shall see God" (Moses 5:10). Likewise, Eve said, "Were it not for our transgression we never should have had seed, and never should have known good and evil, and the joy of our redemption, and the eternal life which God giveth unto all the obedient" (Moses 5:11). They realized they could not be shielded from adversity and still grow. They realized that they could only progress and be happy by facing and overcoming opposition.

Unfortunately, many people, like the cartoon character Linus, try to avoid opposition by using carnal comforters for warmth and security—the carnal-sensual-devilish patterns they think will protect them. In their mortal pains, they react vertically, returning evil for evil instead of returning good for evil as commanded by the Lord.

It is virtually impossible to eliminate our own carnal comforters without the light of Christ and without knowledge of his gospel of peace and salvation. Our health and happiness are linked to our knowledge of and faith in the plan of salvation. Knowledge that brings peace begins with an understanding of our premortal existence.

As a child of God, having come from his glorious presence, you have descended into this world of grief, pain, sorrow and disappointment. At times you sense a divine discontent, a loss of your former heaven and security. You sense that your capacity for happiness is much greater than what you are experiencing here and now. You miss your former closeness with God and his righteousness. You feel that all is not right here. You are not complete. You sense your unworthiness. This is more than a mere feeling or a passing thought. It is your very ground of being, your deep-seated belief that "I'm just not good enough." You have lost the happy child within you and you feel insecure, undeserving, unloved, and incapable of coping.

These feelings of unworthiness undermine all your thoughts and seem to validate all your negative perceptions. When you get caught in these false perceptions, you feel as though you are in a dream world. Nothing seems real or solid or lasting. You cannot escape without help, because everything you see you interpret according to your past experiences and mindset.

This kind of negative thinking has an addictive quality. It may become a habit—a bad habit—which, over time, degenerates into an addiction. Negative thinking is a disease like alcoholism, compulsive overeating, or drug abuse. It is addictive to each of the pyramid sides: the mind, the emotions, and the body. Such an addiction blocks progress toward better health and imprisons you in a jail of your own making. You remain confined until you understand that you have chosen—by the thoughts you think—this hopeless way of looking at yourself and the world around you. You have made this choice either because you have not known of Christ's power to heal and save, or you have chosen to ignore it. By learning about the Savior and choosing to apply what you know, you become empowered to make choices that lead to true comforters born of the Spirit. Such comforters always bring greater freedom, health, and happiness.

True comfort comes in knowing the truth, by no longer denying the reality of things. Truth is knowledge of things unalterable, eternal, and unambiguous. Truth can be unrecognized or ignored, but it cannot be changed. Our first parents taught their children truths about their real selves and their relationship to God and the world around them. But "Satan came among them, saying: . . . Believe it not; and they believed it not, and they loved Satan more than God. And men began from that time forth to be carnal, sensual, and devilish" (Moses 5:13). They began to perceive reality in the cracked mirror of Satan's carnal comforters.

Many people believe that their false perception of things is actually reality. They believe the way they see the world is the way the world really is. Can you see how this way of thinking can cause destruction and disease? This earth is not our real home. It is not our real life. We don't really belong here. Your pains are not forever. Thinking otherwise is a product of your earthbound false self. When your false self is in control, you become locked into a worldly illusion rather than a correct vision of things as they really are and can be through the Lord Jesus Christ. When you are in your false self, you do not realize the negative impact you have had on yourself because of the ideas you have been entertaining over the years. You have chosen your poor opinion of yourself, and you are never at your best when you are operating out of this frame of mind. For this reason you will typically fall—your own fall from grace—by choosing the false comforters of overreacting and underreacting.

In this world we are subject to Satan's influence because we inherit the effects of the Fall. Furthermore, after reaching the age of accountability, we have all yielded to his temptations. In this fallen world, fraught with death, disease, pain, and sorrow, we learn to react in fallen ways. Within each of us there is a highly integrated and instantaneous response to danger known as the "fight-or-flight" response. For example, you are in the woods at night and hear a twig snap in the distant darkness. You see a huge shadow moving slowly toward you and in response you probably feel considerable anxiety or fear. You typically react to such a threat with a surge of adrenaline, and you either pick up a weapon and prepare to fight or take flight—to run in the opposite direction of the sound. These responses, first described by American physiologist W. B. Cannon, are automatic physiological responses to danger, either real or imagined. From a religious point of view, they are the responses of the natural man. If they are not controlled, they can destroy our relationships with one another and eventually express themselves in physical, emotional, and spiritual disease. Why? Because they are responses that operate without faith. In using this automatic response mechanism, we become *reactive* instead of *proactive.*

While reactive responses serve us well in primitive societies where "lions, tigers, and bears" are real threats, the fight-or-flight response works against us in our relationships with each other. If you fight or take flight every time you encounter a stressful situation, you are not taking positive, constructive action. Therefore, you won't be very effective in solving your problems or improving your health. Although at times the fight-or-flight response is a wise course to take (Alma 48:14–15), in most cases this response is a reactionary product of our fallen world—something that we must overcome. The Apostle Paul declared, "to be carnally minded is death; but to be spiritually minded is life and peace" (Rom. 8:6).

OVERREACTING

People who overreact cover their deep-seated feelings of unworthiness or loneliness by pretending to be very confident. They assume an air of self-confidence and an overbearing manner that is obnoxious and arrogant. They nurse their wrath to keep it warm so they can dump their anger on anyone who disagrees with them. They always want to engage in a fight. They refuse suggestions from those who want to help. Even constructive criticism is unacceptable because this, in their mind, would diminish them in some way.

From all outward appearances, it seems that these people need a heavy dose of recognition of their unworthiness; they seem to need someone to put them in their place. Actually, the opposite is true. Misbehaving children and misbehaving adults are actually very discouraged people. In their pain, they act out the role of superiority to compensate for their unworthy feelings. Does this sound familiar to you?

If you are one who overreacts, your false self will defend your illusions of superiority by thinking that you can intimidate people into conforming to your expectations. You will attack anyone who tries to get you on the level because you feel that any change from your mental vertical positioning would take away your assumed power and expose the error of your ways. This curious circle of striking out hardest at those who could benefit you the most is one of the most difficult problems with which you have to deal. Jesus Christ was rejected and killed by those whom he could have benefited the most. They were angry with him because he exposed their carnal thoughts, feelings, and actions.

A primary emotion generated by the fight response is anger. When you feel like fighting, you are usually overreacting. This response is motivated by your false self's need for power and control. Characteristically, other emotions associated with overreacting are hostility, resentment, guilt (anger at oneself), rage, seething, depression, and hurt. Characteristic actions include being mean, vulgar, rude, aggressive, and abusive.

One writer related a time when he overreacted:

> While on vacation, I received a traffic ticket from a particularly obnoxious police officer. A ticket *plus* insults! Too much. I stormed over to the local police station and reported the offending public servant to his superior. While listening to my story, the police captain was tapping into his computer. I thought he was recording some sort of formal report. Oh, boy. The nasty policeman was really in trouble now. What the captain was doing, however, was looking up my driving record. He discovered that I had an unpaid traffic ticket from a vacation I had taken seven years before. I was placed under arrest. The anger quickly turned to fear. My anger cost me $110 and several hours in the cooler. Now I know why they call it the cooler.[5]

When people overreact, as in the story above, they usually see relationships through a vertical win/lose belief window instead of a level win/win belief window. They tend to rank themselves and others according to the relative position they and others occupy on the vertical scale that we discussed earlier. Some people strive viciously for power that will elevate them to a higher position. Their actions may even be considered devilish in the sense that they are aggressive, demanding, abusive, compulsive, rude, crude, and controlling in their relationships. Overreacting people seek out others they can manipulate and control. For example, sadistic people (who like to hurt others) seek out masochistic people (who believe they deserve to be hurt). Codependent relationships like this are established when each partner depends on the other person to confirm their false beliefs about themselves. People who overreact need people who underreact to complete the interdependence of the relationship. These relationships are complementary because the balance of power, of decision making, is inequitable.

Overreacting is a form of unrighteous dominion—it is motivated by the thought that other people are our adversaries and block our way to a higher position on the vertical scale. Competition, jockeying for power and position, or one-upmanship is the name of the game. The spirit of overreacting is the spirit of Babylon. The Lord has warned us, "Go ye out from among the nations, even from Babylon, from the midst of wickedness, which is spiritual Babylon" (D&C 133:14). If we choose to remain in Babylon, we will suffer the plagues that will come upon her. (See D&C 64:24.) Because so much of our society operates on this level, we are so used to everything about Babylon that we just assume that this is the way things always have been, are now, and ever will be. In our distorted way of thinking, we may believe that overreacting is the natural way to go—that the world could not operate in any other way.

Someone once said that the last thing a shark would realize would be that it is swimming in water. In other words, water is so commonplace, so natural, that sharks take it for granted. They do not know of any other alternative; they don't know that birds fly and men walk on the earth. By comparison, some people don't know that there are alternatives to overreacting and underreacting because they are so immersed in competitive cultures.

We tend to take competition for granted. We learn competitive behaviors from our associations, the media, from the workaday world, and then we take these traits home to our marriages and families and wonder why there is so much emotional distance and pain. In our fallen world, where "if you are not a winner, you're a loser," it is hard for us to conceive of, let alone maintain, win/win relationships. Our illusionary successes with overreacting in spiritual Babylon—in acquiring wealth, power, and worldly honors—may be directly related to our failures in marriages and families where the spirit of sacrifice and selfless service is so critical.

As little children, we are exposed to competitive relationship patterns—the one-upmanship games we learn in the elementary years.

We learn overreactions such as "My dad is smarter than your dad" and "My dog can beat up your dog!"

In later years, the objects change: "My clothes are more expensive than yours;" "My car is better than yours;" "My dad is a doctor. What does your dad do for a living?"

In a university setting, students brag that their GPAs are higher than others, their wards are better than others, or their missions were highest in the number of convert baptisms. We pay lip service to the idea that "it is not where one serves, but how," but our competitive minds don't seem to believe it. Our negative self believes we must hold prominent positions in the Church or we are not acceptable to the Lord. We are too often more interested in being visible in the eyes of men than in keeping an eye single to the glory of God.

Listen in at any board meeting or dinner party, and you can hear the difference between people participating in an exchange of ideas (acting on a horizontal level) and people trying to score points (acting on a vertical level). Our problems with competitive communication crop up and rise to great heights in business and sports. Alfie Kohn, an expert on competition, states: "We have turned our just-for-fun sports into an overblown, institutionalized, codified worship of winning."[6]

This competition is motivated by pride. Pride, according to President Ezra Taft Benson, is the great stumbling block to Zion. He was speaking of vertical relationships when he said:

> The central feature of pride is enmity—enmity toward God and enmity toward our fellowmen. Enmity means "hatred toward, hostility to, or a state of opposition." It is the power by which Satan wishes to reign over us.
>
> We are tempted daily to elevate ourselves above others and diminish them. (See Hel. 6:17; D&C 58:41.)
>
> The proud make every man their adversary by pitting their intellects, opinion, works, wealth, talents, or any other worldly measure device against others. In the words of C.S. Lewis: "Pride gets no pleasure out of having something, only out of having more of it than the next man. . . . It is the comparison that makes you proud: the pleasure of being above the rest. Once the element of competition has gone, pride has gone."[7]

Prideful people use force, intimidation, and manipulation to maintain their control. Denial, minimization, and especially blame are also used. These latter forms of control are almost always found in abusive relationships. An abusive husband, for example, will first deny that he beats his wife; then, when confronted with her bruises, he minimizes the abuse by saying, "Well, she bruises easily" or "It was her fault because she provoked me."

These kinds of vertical behaviors infect almost all of us to one degree or another. Joseph Smith warned, "We have learned by sad experience that it is the nature and disposition of almost all men, as soon as they get a little authority, as they suppose, they will immediately begin to exercise unrighteous dominion [and in other ways to overreact]" (D&C 121:39). Unrighteous dominion has many faces and can range from physical abuse to harboring resentments.

RESENTMENT IS VERTICAL

Resentment is a very common type of vertical behavior. It is a warped tool used by emotionally handicapped people to get their way. With resentment they try to coerce others to conform to their wants and wishes.

We feel resentment when others do not live up to the images and expectations we have for them. We start to believe that what applies to objects also applies to people. We are disappointed in people the way we are disappointed in a car that does not run as we expect it to. But when we resent others, we are only protecting our images because it is easier (so we may think) to change others than it is to change our views of them. However, since the images and expectations are ours, the resentment is also ours. We own it all!

We have inherited our basic views of the world from our parents and teachers. We have a lot invested in our world view and in our expectations. We have spent many years refining these beliefs. Now that all of our views are solidified we think, "Why should I change my shoulds, musts, and oughts about others just because they are not smart enough to conform?" This is the way we negatively talk to ourselves.

When you harbor resentment, you are hard to live with because you are always uptight. The slightest inconvenience sets you off with outbursts of anger directed toward those around you. Resentment is riddled with judgment and criticism. It is vertical because when you feel resentment you look down on others. Instead of motivating others with love, gentleness, meekness, and love unfeigned, you fall for the Satan-inspired trap of contention and unrighteous dominion. (See 3 Ne. 11:29–30; D&C 121:41–42.) When you are filled with resentment, you dwell in your problems instead of looking objectively for ways of solving problems.

Some people believe that resentment is only natural. It is true that the natural man holds resentment—but "the natural man is an enemy to God" (Mosiah 3:19). The natural man will justify his contentious anger by calling it righteous indignation, and will cite as an example the time Jesus cleansed the temple in Jerusalem of the money changers. However, there are strong differences between the two. Contentious anger is marked by forcing our will on others, choosing to be out of control, overreacting to the situation, and hanging on to the anger with a sense of false righteousness.

Righteous indignation, on the other hand, is marked by maintaining free will, choosing to be strong but in control, maintaining an energy equal to the situation, and choosing to be charitable. Jesus was not contentiously angry—he was righteously indignant. His actions were motivated by love, not resentment.

In the Bible we read that we are not to be angry without cause. (See Matt. 5:22.) This point is clarified by the Joseph Smith Translation, which corrected this statement by omitting the qualifier "without cause." In other words, we are not to get angry with one another at all. This was affirmed by the Savior when he taught the Nephites that "he that hath the spirit of contention is not of me, but is of the devil, who is the father of contention, and he stirreth up the hearts of men to contend with anger, one with another. Behold this is not my doctrine . . . but this is my doctrine, that such things should be done away" (3 Ne. 11:29–30).

Resentment is one of the most dangerous emotions you can harbor. It does far more damage to you than it does to the other person— or object. (The traffic doesn't care how angry you get. It just keeps backing up!) Resentment is damaging to your cardiovascular system. It is one of the most unpleasant emotions, too. "Hating people is like burning your own house down to get rid of a rat."[8] You have to work a lot harder to hate than to love.

In addition, if we do not forsake the spirit of contention, it can poison our relationships, inhibit growth, and stifle our expansion. Resentment creates feelings of unworthiness in ourselves and hatred toward others. It puts enormous stress on the mind, the emotions, and the body. Unresolved anger and contentious relationships can kill. I have seen this happen several times over the years.

The solution to resentment? Change the mental image or the physical action. In this case, change the image. When you realize that your resentment is based not on others' actions, but on your reactions to their actions, you are on the road to freedom. You really only get angry with others when you imagine they have something you need or want. By contrast, when your being is centered in Christ, recognizing that all good things come from him, then you are free to conclude that nobody has anything that is worth getting angry about.

When you are angry with yourself, you have the option to change either your image or your action. You do not, however, have the right to change anyone else. You have the right to inform other people regarding your thoughts and feelings about their behavior, and you have the right to tell them what action you will take if they continue theirs, but you have no right to directly change another's behavior. In close relationships (like husband and wife), people sometimes feel they have special rights to change the other person. They feel justified in using harsh language or coercive actions to make the other person submit to their images. Not so! That belief is the cause of more disastrous relationships than probably any other cause.

We can't change other people's behaviors, but we can change the way we view them. When people treat you unfairly, you have a responsibility to talk to them in firm but loving ways and let them know how you feel. If they continue, rather than letting resentment build up, change your image. Without being condescending, say to yourself something like, "They probably are doing the best they can according to what they understand. I will continue to pray for them so that we both can see things more from God's point of view."

If abuse and hostility continue, you must take action yourself. You may have to create physical distance between you and the other person. This is what Nephi had to do in the Promised Land when he and his family packed up their goods and left Laman and Lemuel and their families behind. The same principle was at work when King Mosiah left the land of Nephi-Lehi and went to Zarahemla, when the Israelites left Egypt, and when the Latter-day Saints left Nauvoo and went to the Great Salt Lake Valley. Sometimes, to avoid further entanglements with vertical people, you just have to pack your stuff and leave—but remember to leave your resentment behind, too.

John-Roger and Peter McWilliams suggest that to eliminate resentment we can add to our self-talk, or images, the expression ". . . and sometimes they're not." For example, to the expectation that "Friends are always honest," we need to add, "and sometimes they're not." Likewise, "Doctors are always meticulous, and sometimes they're not." "Waiters are always friendly, and sometimes they're not." "Traffic should always run more smoothly, but sometimes it doesn't."

Why do you think Jesus commanded you to "love your enemies, bless them that curse you, do good to them that hate you, and pray for them which despitefully use you, and persecute you" (Matt. 5:44)? Could it be that the Savior gave this commandment, not necessarily to benefit all those evil people who do such bad things to you, but to benefit you personally? Much more helpful to your mental and physical health than anger is for you to extend love, blessings, goodness, and prayers to your enemies.

UNDERREACTING

The primary emotion generated by the flight response is fear—fear of confrontation or of not being adequately prepared for a stressful situation. Related feelings are anxiety, timidity, shyness, inhibition, reticence, apprehension, and even terror. Sometimes people who feel that they just can't cope any longer choose to run away when they should, in fact, stand their ground and face their adversaries. Characteristically their underreactions involve withdrawing, submitting, getting ill, giving in and giving up, or escaping though the use of drugs, alcohol, food, sex, insanity—or the great escape (or so some think), suicide.[9]

People who underreact are at the bottom of vertical relationships. Often they are people who try to please everyone else but themselves. They defer, submit, give in, and give up when they need to take an active stand for truth and justice. Herbert Byard Swope said, "I cannot give you the formula for success, but I can give you the formula for failure—which is: try to please everybody."[10] People who underreact sometimes falsely cast themselves as peacemakers. Underreacting is a false comforter because it shows weakness and is often accompanied with thoughts of being more righteous than people who overreact.

"Pride is a sin that can readily be seen in others but is rarely admitted in ourselves," said President Benson. "Most of us consider pride to be a sin of those on the top, such as the rich and the learned, looking down at the rest of us. (See 2 Ne. 9:42.) There is, however, a far more common ailment among us—and that is pride from the bottom looking up. It is manifest in so many ways, such as faultfinding, gossiping, backbiting, murmuring, living beyond our means, envying, coveting, withholding gratitude and praise that might lift another, and being unforgiving and jealous."[11]

Sometimes pride is manifest in underreacting by people who think they are so unworthy that not even Christ can save them. In their agony of disbelief, they withdraw more and more from others through the use of drugs, alcohol, sex, and sin. To them, their unworthiness is not an illusion—it is reality! They cling to their negative thought-feeling-action pyramid. Their negative thoughts about themselves evoke desperate feelings of loneliness and detachment, and no matter what suggestions you give to such people, they are inclined to play the "Yeah, but . . ." game. "Yeah, but that won't work because . . . ," and they list all the reasons why they believe that nothing—literally nothing—can rescue them from their problems.

When you underreact, you visualize negative results in everything you try—so you do nothing. You are afraid to commit yourself to any constructive action because of your fear of failure. You do not want to disappoint your family and friends by making commitments that have been broken so often in the past. You may know the doctrines of the gospel quite well, and you attend your meetings; but you think that you must overcome your habits through your own power because you are unworthy of any divine assistance—you feel you are not loved by the Lord.

Sometimes people who underreact are motivated by a desperate desire to be loved. To them, being loved is more important than being respected, and they act as enablers for people who overreact. They will stay in a relationship much longer than is wise or expedient. With real intent, they sing to themselves the lyrics of the popular songs, "As Long as He Needs Me" or "Stand by Your Man." They believe they should stay in unhealthy relationships at all costs, even if it means submitting themselves to extreme physical, emotional, or sexual abuse. Underreactors placate overreactors and make excuses for the other person's vertical behavior. They take responsibility and absorb the consequences for the choices made by overreactors.

An example of how underreactors make excuses comes from the life of a woman named Jane. Jane's father was a very successful salesman. He was rarely home during the week and was often tied up in meetings on the weekend. When he was home, he was demanding and aggressive. At times he was even physically abusive to Jane and her mother. He clearly favored his eldest son, who was a star athlete at the local high school. Jane's mother, a very quiet, socially inactive, inhibited, and submissive woman, would not stand up to her husband in his unrighteous demands. Instead, she would do all she could to avoid a confrontation.

Later, Jane married a man who was very similar to her father. He was six years her senior, sexually demanding, and physically and verbally abusive. A coach in the community baseball leagues, he was extremely competitive and would remind his team, "Winning's for winners, losing's for losers!"

In her tenth year of marriage, Jane came in for marriage counseling. Her medical doctor had referred her to me because of chronic guilt feelings (for not doing enough to make her marriage work) and headaches and backaches that had no medical basis. In addition to the aches and pains, Jane complained that she felt like she was losing her mind as well as her own identity as an individual. She was trying so hard to please her parents, who lived across the street, her husband, and her two very demanding sons.

In therapy, Jane learned quickly that she almost always underreacted in an attempt to win the love of the men in her life. Her father, brother, husband, and sons all overreacted to insure that they got their way and controlled their relationships. Jane and her mother had both adopted underreactions to placate their men. Jane's coping crisis involved coming to grips with her constant pattern of trying to please others, and not validating herself as a person with rights and needs equally as valid as those of the men around her.

It was not until her husband joined the therapy sessions that real progress was made. Resistant at first, he finally came to see that if he were more cooperative, less demanding, and less competitive, Jane could be more responsive and loving to him. In the therapy sessions, Jane cautiously and gradually began asserting herself. She even found herself overreacting, but in time reached a balance of strength and tenderness. Her backaches and headaches began to diminish after the third week and were completely gone at the end of the fifth week. She no longer harbored feelings of guilt for not doing enough to make the marriage work.

Jane's initial concerns may be much like yours. How do you know when it is proper to endure the vertical behavior of others and when it is proper to confront them? We have been commanded to resist not evil. (See 3 Ne. 12:38–39.) But the scriptures contain examples of times when war was necessary. When to turn the other cheek and when to go to war is not an easy question to answer, but we find our individual answers as we obtain the mind of the Lord through reading the scriptures, listening to the words of living prophets, and gaining direction from the Holy Ghost. Without proper guidance, we tend to be extreme in our behaviors. The Doctrine and Covenants provides a powerful lesson on when we are justified in defending ourselves. In speaking to the Saints, the Lord said:

> If any nation, tongue, or people should proclaim war against them, they should first lift a standard of peace unto that people, nation, or tongue; and if that people did not accept the offering of peace, neither the second or the third time, they should bring these testimonies before the Lord, then I, the Lord, would give unto them a commandment, and justify them in going out to battle against that nation, tongue, or people. (D&C 98:34–36)

At times the Lord will command us to courageously stand our ground and not be moved out of our place. We need not feel guilt-ridden when we have done all we can to establish peace and then must actively defend what is right by firm action.

GUILT CAN BE VERTICAL

People like Jane feel guilty when they cannot conform to all the expectations of other people. Having guilt is a form of underreacting. Putting guilt on others is a form of overreacting. Only one kind of guilt is productive—when the Spirit of the Lord lets you know that you are doing wrong and motivates you to repent. These spiritual nudges are necessary for guidance and spiritual progress. When you feel this kind of guilt, you need to cease and desist your thoughts, feelings, and behaviors that are evoking these promptings from the Spirit. If you ignore them, you cannot progress and the Spirit will eventually leave you.

The Spirit of the Lord will not always strive with us when we persist in doing evil. (See Gen. 6:3.) When the Spirit completely withdraws we no longer feel guilt; it is like having our conscience "seared with a hot iron" (1 Tim. 4:2). This analogy refers to physicians in biblical times who would apply a hot iron to a blood vessel to stop bleeding. So it is with our conscience when we persist in evil. We no longer feel guilty, and we lose our sense of evil. As Alexander Pope declared, "Vice is a monster of such frightful mein, as to be hated needs but to be seen, yet seen too oft, familiar with her face, we first endure, then pity, then embrace."[12]

It is not always easy to differentiate between positive, Holy Ghost–imposed guilt and negative, self-imposed guilt. This second kind of guilt is really anger directed toward yourself: you are fighting with yourself about something you should or should not have done. This guilt has a tendency to build over time and in some cases can actually kill. Of course, other factors are also involved; but guilt is paramount. The most tragic thing about this kind of guilt is that it is completely, totally, and thoroughly unnecessary. It is a waste of time because you spend your energies dwelling on the problems instead of solving them.

Here is how these guilt feelings get started. Let's say that you have a pretty good sense of self-worth, but you are overweight and so you decide to diet. Chocolate ice cream is not on your diet, but in a moment of weakness you eat a carton of chocolate ice cream. You then feel guilty. You spend the entire day feeling guilty. (Similar guilt feelings will spring up when people give in to their addictions to drugs, alcohol, tobacco, sex, anger, and other obsessive thoughts and compulsive behaviors.)

Each time you set goals and fail, you feel guilty. The more serious the offense, the greater the guilt. Eating chocolate ice cream creates one level of guilt; whereas, incest or spouse abuse creates a much higher level.

As you gradually learn the process of choosing correct thoughts, feelings, and behaviors through faith in the Lord and in your own divine nature, you will feel happier because you have a greater sense of control. The more you can do this, and complete the steps of repentance as required, the more you become free in the present because you are a new creature in Christ. You *used* to have a problem, but *now* you are set free.

Guilt-ridden people have a hard time putting their sins in the past, but the difficulty of the task does not negate the necessity of it.

Guilt-ridden people dwell on their problems instead of solving them. These people moan, groan, blame, and complain about many things to anyone who will listen to them, but they never come up with any solutions to the problems they dwell upon. They belong to the

"Ain't It Awful" club. You know people like this; maybe you have even been a member of the club.

Complaining is often an attempt to get attention. Complaining and blaming are ways of underreacting. John-Roger and Peter McWilliams have suggested two ways of overcoming this bad habit.

1. *Only complain to someone who can do something about the problem.* If your water bill seems too high, there's no point in telling anyone but the water company. If your reception on cable TV is not working, telling a friend will do no good unless your friend happens to work for the TV company. Long discussions about hunger and pollution and politics and corruption serve little purpose so long as no action is taken.

2. *Compliment at least as often as you complain.* Listeners will have a tendency to tune you out or turn you off if you complain all the time. Try to keep a balance in your conversations between your negative and positive observations. In fact, if you will find something positive to say before you complain, you will find the other person more willing to listen to your complaints and you will be training yourself to find the positive in things.[13]

Complaining people are mentally locked into a false dilemma—a belief state in which you think you have only two choices and both of them are bad. For example, when a judge confronts an abusive husband about beating his wife, the man may respond by saying, "What do you want me to do? Be a henpecked wimp? She needs to be disciplined." The abuser believes that if he doesn't abuse his wife, he will be a weakling. He has created a false dilemma. On the other hand, when an abused wife is encouraged to take firm action regarding her hostile husband, she may say, "What do you want me to do? Be, a witchy, rude, and non-supportive wife?" She believes that no matter how abusive he is, in order to be a good wife she should stand by her man and take the insults—another false dilemma.

Without help, people who believe in false dilemmas remain forever convergent in their thinking. They have tunnel vision: they can see only vertical choices for their behavior. Their false self holds the narrow view that overreacting and underreacting are their only real options. The false self will not seek new knowledge or other alternatives to replace the vertical self-defeating thoughts. The false self is without hope and remains so until the real self is empowered with additional knowledge and control. Critically depressed persons, like Donna who who cut off all her hair, are caught in false dilemmas when they conclude that they must be miserable forever, or they must commit suicide. They cannot think divergently or see that level alternatives exist.

You cannot allow yourself the luxury of false dilemmas. They fly in the face of light and truth and can ruin your health and lead to physical symptoms that result from emotional stress.

PSYCHOGENIC PAIN DISORDERS

False dilemmas put enormous physiological stress on our physical bodies. Pain and sickness that result from such mental stresses are called psychogenic pain disorders—*psycho,* mind; *genic,* origin. Medical doctors have difficulty treating psychogenic disorders since they do not seem to have any physiological basis.

Traditional medicine has recognized the influence of thoughts on physical health and has, in the past, used the term *psychosomatic* to refer to illnesses without a clearly identifiable physical basis. However, psychosomatic disorders have tended to be considered imagined, not real. More recently, the physical pain is recognized as being real and the expression "psychogenic pain disorder"[14] is used more commonly. This expression recognizes a fundamental interdependence between mind and body in all states of illness and health. The sickness is real, but its origin is in negative thinking, feeling, and acting. "Researchers and clinicians today are increasingly aware that virtually all disorders are psychosomatic in the sense that they involve the continual interplay of mind and body in their origin, development, and cure."[15] Rene Dubos has stated that, "Whatever its precipitating cause and its manifestations, almost every disease involves both the body and the mind, and these two aspects are so interrelated that they cannot be separated one from the other."[16]

You do not need to fall for false dilemmas nor succumb to their inevitable psychogenic illnesses. Other alternatives are available, such as those described in this book, which can empower you to avoid overreacting and underreacting and get on the level with yourself and others. It is vital that you learn what these alternatives are. An important key to remember here, in connection with the healing power of faith, is that the mind is not only an instrument of potential illness, it also plays a significant part in getting well. But the choice of how you use your mind—for health or disease—is yours. Do not fall for the Satan-inspired belief that by using carnal comforters like false dilemmas you can find peace, control, or happiness.

President Spencer W. Kimball said that the reason people sin is to satisfy some deep unmet need.[17] This observation helps us understand the paradox in sinning. People sin thinking it will bring them happiness—satisfy their need—but in the end their unhappiness and pain, the consequence of sin, is greater than the temporary pleasure.

Another observation I have made about why people sin is that sometimes people do unworthy things to prove to themselves that they are indeed "right" about their unworthiness. That way, in their mind, there is no need to repent, to choose a pathway of happiness. They are so unworthy, so much a loser, that there is no chance for their recovery. I remember a patient in a hospital in which I once worked who had tattooed on his knuckles of both hands "B-O-R-N L-O-S-E-R".

There is a certain payoff for sin—a short-lived benefit. When people dwell in and advertise their pain, they get a lot of attention. This attention seems to fill their unmet need for love. For them, a temporary carnal comforter will be sufficient. They conclude, "Complaining to others about my problems gets me love." They may get extra amounts of cuddling, or pampering—the payoff for illness or suffering.

To further understand the payoff of complaining, we must understand the underlying principle that "the one who is sickest, gets his way." One person might say, "I have a headache." The other says, "I have a *migraine* headache." So the former has to take care of the latter.

These attention-getting mechanisms are not necessarily conscious creations. Somewhere along the line, people have learned to fake illness in order to stay home from school or to get extra attention. These things become programmed into their brains, and they are used over and over again, bringing with them hosts of related illnesses—mental, physical, and relational.

With understanding and with faith in the truth, however, you can break out of these attention-getting processes. Negative patterns are learned behaviors; anything *learned* can be *unlearned*, and more positive ways of coping from your real self can be put into practice.

Your real self recognizes that every problem can be viewed from an eternal context. When your real self is in control, you will have the faith to endure and to manage your problems in a spirit of peace. You might want to take an honest look at what kind of payoff you are getting from your negative thoughts, feelings, or physical illnesses. Could it be that you are choosing to be sick? Don't be afraid of the truth. Recognize how your false self will betray your ultimate happiness. Sections 121–23 of the Doctrine and Covenants may help to put your own problems into proper perspective. These revelations came to the Prophet Joseph Smith during times of extreme trial for him and the Saints. These revelations may help you understand why you have had horrible things happen to you. Be assured that there was purpose in why you were not reclaimed according to your personal time schedule. Only by trusting Christ in his almighty power to heal and by obeying his commandments can we truly find the bread of life and living waters through which we will never hunger nor thirst again.

SELFISHNESS VERSUS SACRIFICE

In the New Testament the Apostle Paul said, "For as in Adam all die, even so in Christ shall all be made alive" (1 Cor. 15:22). Ever since the Fall, everything dies. I believe that the Fall introduced what is known in scientific circles as *entropy*. The Second Law of Thermodynamics states that all things left unattended move toward entropy—a state of undifferentiation, uniformity, simplicity, decay, or degeneration. Everything moves toward death. For example, if I were to leave my watch on the beach, it would not, by itself, charge or replace its own battery, rather it would lose energy, rust and decay, and begin to break down into its elemental components. All things physical follow this trend toward entropy. Mountains wear down, cars rust, toys break. Everything we see, including our bodies, grows old and dies. This process is all around us, and Satan, eager to seduce us, suggests to our minds and hearts that the only way to deal with entropy is to "eat, drink, and be merry, for tomorrow we die" (2 Ne. 28:7). (See also Luke 12:19–20.)

The natural man recognizes that he will die, but he does not trust that in Christ all things will be made alive again. Natural men and women grab for things of this world while they have opportunity. Grabbing and taking, instead of giving and sharing, places a strain on our relationships; strained relationships create stress, and unresolved stress can eventually affect one's health.

Without the plan of salvation, without hope, we succumb to the siren call of materialism. Satan whispers to us that by acquiring, hoarding, competing, and using unrighteous dominion we can grab what we will need to make us happy. To be the richest man in the graveyard is the object of this hedonistic game. The adversary whispers, "There is no other way." He fosters false principles: selfishness instead of sacrifice, hate instead of love, exploitation instead of cooperation. He wants us to speak instead of listening; take instead of give, to destroy instead of create. The natural man, faced with the threat of entropy, adopts the last-piece-of-pie mentality: "Since there is only one piece of pie left, I will grab it before anyone else does."

This type of thinking is very common in our modern world. "Find happiness by grabbing all the stuff you can while you can!" In our despair, we spend our time working in the service of a self-image that includes sufficient money, stocks, bonds and the acquisition of gold and silver to provide power and position.

We seek to escape from the challenges or boredom of daily living through drugs, alcoholism, or blaming others for our faults and failures. The natural man overreacts, grabbing all he can before others take it from him. He hoards, withholds, steals, controls, climbs, and exploits. He lives by the motto, "Do unto others before they do it unto you!" Faced with the threat of loss, he becomes ever more dominant, aggressive, competitive, and selfish.

The Lord asks, "Wherefore do ye spend money for that which is not bread? and your labor for that which satisfieth not?" (Isa. 55:2). He commands, "Seek not for riches but for wisdom" (D&C 6:7) and again, "Lay not up for yourselves treasures upon earth, where moth and rust doth corrupt, and where thieves break through and steal" (Matt. 6:19).

Submissive people react to the process of entropy but choose to underreact instead of overreacting. They are afraid of offending others and thereby losing love. People who underreact will not stand for principles even if it means losing respect. President Spencer W. Kimball has warned:

> Few men have ever knowingly and deliberately chosen to reject God and his blessings. Rather, we learn from the scriptures that because the exercise of faith has always appeared to be more difficult than relying on things more immediately at hand, carnal man has tended to transfer his trust from God to material things. Therefore, in all ages when men have fallen under the power of Satan and lost the faith, they have put in its place

a hope in the "arm of flesh" and in "gods of silver, and gold, of brass, iron, wood, and stone, which see not, nor hear, nor know" (Dan. 5:23)—that is, in idols. This I find to be a dominant theme in the Old Testament. Whatever a man sets his heart and his trust in most is his god; and if his god doesn't happen to be the true and living God of Israel, that man is laboring in idolatry.[18]

The antithesis to all this hedonistic grabbing and stockpiling is the gospel principle of sharing, giving, extending ourselves to others. Giving in the face of shortage is not natural, which is why the natural man is an enemy to God. Herein lies the major test of mortality. It is in giving that we are blessed to receive. "Blessed are the merciful: for they shall obtain mercy" (Matt. 5:7). The gospel teaches us that sacrifice brings forth blessings. Coming unto Christ involves giving if we want to receive, listening if we want to be heard. We must learn to cooperate instead of forever competing against one another as the natural man does.

This gospel works against everything the natural man works for. The gospel of Jesus Christ, including his atonement and the eventual renewal of all things, is the counter power to the process of entropy. Men and women of faith willingly share their resources, their time, their talents, and their material goods rather than frantically trying to safeguard and protect them from others. Sacrifice, sharing, and service are ways we can demonstrate our faith in the Lord's promises that by giving we will receive. If we desire the grace and peace of the Lord, we must be willing to offer grace and peace to others (D&C 93:20). If we will trust the Lord and willingly give to others, we will be opening the door to allow him to help and heal us.

As in Adam all die (entropy), even so in Christ shall all be made alive (atonement). Jesus will make all things right again. Through the Lord's unfathomable suffering there will come about the great atonement. We need to look to our Savior for the way out of our disease and stress-causing vertical relationships. Only through faith in the Lord Jesus Christ and in our own divine natures can we overcome the tendencies of the natural man. "But without faith it is impossible to please him" (Heb. 11:6), but with faith *all* things are possible (Matt. 19:26).

NOTES

1. William Wordsworth, cited in *Richard Evans' Quote Book* (Salt Lake City: Publishers Press, 1971) 99.

2. *Lectures on Faith* 6:4.

3. For a discussion of Adam and Eve being children of God, see chapter 3 of Allred, *The Eternal Plan.*

4. This thought-feeling-actions-health pattern is presented here simplistically for didactical purposes. In reality, these variables are continuous and branching, but they are neither mutually exclusive nor linear.

5. McWilliams, *Negative Thought,* 37.

6. Alfie Kohn, *No Contest: The Case against Competition* (Boston: Houghton Mifflin, 1986), 80.

7. Ezra Taft Benson, "Beware of Pride" *Ensign,* May 1989, 4.

8. Harry Emerson Fosdick as quoted in McWilliams, *Negative Thought,* 450.

9. Rather than being an escape from all your problems, suicide only aggravates your problems as you enter the world of spirits with the same emotional problems plus suicide on your hands. (See Alma 34:34–35.)

10. As quoted in McWilliams, *Negative Thought,* 206.

11. Benson, "Beware of Pride," 5.

12. As cited in *Richard Evans' Quote Book,* 199.

13. McWilliams, *Negative Thought,* 206.

14. See *Diagnostic and Statistical Manual of Mental Disorders,* Third Edition (Washington, D.C.: American Psychological Association, 1980).

15. Capra, "Can Science Explain Psychic Phenomena," 327–28.

16. Rene Dubos, *Man, Medicine and Environment* (New York: Praeger, 1968), 64.

17. Spencer W. Kimball, *The Teachings of Spencer W. Kimball* (Salt Lake City: Bookcraft, 1982), 481.

18. Spencer W. Kimball, "The False Gods We Worship," *Ensign,* June 1976, 4.

III

The Therapy of Faith

Faith in the Lord Jesus Christ leads to faith in your own divine nature. Your faith grows as your mind and heart awaken and respond to the promptings of the Spirit. You set the stage through your own mental exertion directed toward truth. You ask and you receive; you knock and it is opened unto you. You grow in grace, light, power, and peace. You face adversity more calmly because your real self is in control and you know that the Lord loves you and is aware of your suffering. You know that he will strengthen and help you, and that you are not alone.

As your faith-power grows, so will your ability to receive all things. This was the nature of the faith-power possessed by the Former-day Saints as described in the Lectures on Faith:

> *The Former-day Saints viewed the plan of salvation [as] . . . a system of faith—it begins with faith, and continues by faith; and every blessing which is obtained in relation to it is the effect of faith, whether it pertains to this life or that which is to come. To this all the revelations of God bear witness. . . . And through the whole history of the scheme of life and salvation, it is a matter of faith: every man received according to his faith—according as his faith was, so were his blessings and privileges; and nothing was withheld from him when his faith was sufficient to receive it. He could stop the mouths of lions, quench the violence of fire, escape the edge of the sword, wax valiant in fight, and put to flight the armies of the aliens;*

women could, by their faith, receive their dead children to life again; in a word, there was nothing impossible with them who had faith. *All things were in subjection to the Former-day Saints, according as their faith was. By their faith they could obtain heavenly visions, the ministering of angels, have knowledge of the spirits of just men made perfect, of the general assembly and church of the firstborn, whose names are written in heaven, of God the judge of all, of Jesus the Mediator of the new covenant. (Lectures on Faith 7:17; emphasis added)*

Although your faith-power may not be at the same high level these Former-day Saints attained, don't be discouraged. Their examples provide hope, vision, and direction for us. They describe what we too may eventually receive when we learn the healing power of faith.

8

The Healing Power of Faith— Seeds of Truth

Yea, I know that God will give liberally to him that asketh.
Yea, my God will give me, if I ask not amiss.
—2 NEPHI 4:35

In the previous chapters of this book, we discussed the importance of developing faith in Christ and in your own divine nature. We also looked at the origins and manifestations of illness when you allow your carnal nature, your false self, to take over. We will now look at the healing power of faith.

Healing faith requires putting your real self in charge of your thoughts, feelings, and actions. This means that instead of choosing things carnal, sensual, and devilish you choose faith (thoughts), hope (feelings), and charity (actions).

The Doctrine and Covenants explains that "faith, hope, charity and love, with an eye single to the glory of God, qualify him for the work" (D&C 4:5). Your *work* is developing your faith in the Lord Jesus Christ and in your own divine nature. This faith will infuse your being with feelings of hope—hope for the present and the future. This hope empowers you with feelings of love so you can be truly charitable in reaching out and blessing the lives of others.

Faith, hope, and charity eliminate the stresses and strains experienced by the natural man. Your being is infused with love for your real self, for truth, and for the good in others. Christlike love is a healing power because it enables you to draw on the powers of heaven. Charity never faileth. It becomes a constant source of strength and power when you learn how to tap into it. You become more robust, more self-disciplined in exercising, in balancing your diet, and in forming good nutritional and other health-promoting habits. Good health habits in all aspects of your life lead to greater peace and happiness. The whole purpose of the Savior's ministry was to teach us eternal truths that would entitle us to receive healing power into our lives and which will enable us to return to our Heavenly Father's presence.

THE BEATITUDES—STAIRWAY TO HEALING

Some of the most basic and beautiful teachings of the Savior are found in the Sermon on the Mount. These rules for Christlike living are recorded in Matthew, chapters five through seven, and in 3 Nephi, chapters twelve through fourteen. The Beatitudes form an integral part of this important discourse and were presented in taxonomic form; they are meant to be completed sequentially. The Book of Mormon record contains the most complete account of this sermon. Figure 9 shows the Beatitudes diagrammed in taxonomic form.

Here is how the upward progression works. From 3 Nephi 12:3 we read, "Blessed are the poor in spirit who come unto me, for theirs is the kingdom of heaven." In and of itself, there is nothing good about being poor in spirit. The Lord wants us to be rich in spirit, a quality which comes by repenting and coming unto him. It is repenting and coming unto the Lord that qualifies us for the kingdom of heaven.

Next, Jesus said, "Blessed are all they that mourn, for they shall be comforted" (3 Ne. 12:4). Here the Lord is not only instructing us to mourn for our lost loved ones, but also to mourn for our sins. A godly sorrow for past mistakes will qualify us for the comforting and healing influence of the Lord.

"Blessed are the meek, for they shall inherit the earth" (3 Ne. 12:5). When we are meek, we are open to truth—we are childlike, humble, and teachable. This humility prepares our minds and hearts for revelation from the Holy Ghost. "Blessed are all they who do hunger and thirst after righteousness, for they shall be filled with the Holy Ghost" (3 Ne. 12:6). A slight desire for truth is not sufficient to achieve great

Resentment from Others

Blessed are the persecuted, for theirs
is the kingdom of heaven.

True Peacemaker

Blessed are the peacemakers, for they shall be
called the children of God.

Sanctification

Blessed are the pure in heart,
for they shall see God.

Charity—The Pure Love of Christ

Blessed are the merciful, for they shall obtain mercy.

Actively Seek after Truth

Blessed are those who seek righteousness,
for they shall be filled with the Holy Ghost.

Childlike Humility

Blessed are the meek, for they shall inherit the earth

Godly Sorrow for Sin

Blessed are they that mourn, for they shall be comforted.

Repentance

Blessed are the poor in spirit who come unto me.

Figure 9. The Beatitudes in taxonomic form.

faith-power; you must hunger and thirst after it. If you knock, it will be opened to you; if you don't knock, it won't be opened. If you ask, you will receive; if you don't, you won't receive. Once you receive, then you must be willing to share what you have received if you expect to grow in faith-power.

"Blessed are the merciful, for they shall obtain mercy" (3 Ne. 12:7). A hand that is opened to give is also opened to receive. If you give love, you get love. If you impart knowledge, you receive knowledge. As you give, you get.

"Blessed are all the pure in heart, for they shall see God" (3 Ne. 12:8). "Charity is the pure love of Christ" (Moro. 7:47) and qualifies us to enter the presence of God and receive of his abundant healing power. The Holy Ghost purifies and sanctifies us, but we have to be humble and childlike to receive of his influence. Charity is not just purity in appearance, but the purity of heart that qualifies us to enter the presence of God. A person who has this sacred privilege is in a position to know the mind of God and the requirements for peace on earth.

"Blessed are all the peacemakers, for they shall be called the children of God" (3 Ne. 12:9). The prophets and righteous men and women throughout time who have known the mind of God have declared repentance as the prerequisite to peace on earth. Lovingly helping others to repentance is being a peacemaker.

"Blessed are all they who are persecuted for my name's sake, for theirs is the kingdom of heaven. And blessed are ye when men shall revile you and persecute, and shall say all manner of evil against you falsely, for my sake; For ye shall have great joy and be exceedingly glad, for great shall be your reward in heaven; for so persecuted they the prophets who were before you" (3 Ne. 12:10–12). Declarations of repentance offend the carnal mind, and those who declare such truths are persecuted by evil men and women of the world.

Thus, as people move upward in the Beatitudes, their faith-power increases and eventually they acquire Christlike charity: they become sanctified before the Lord, and they become true peacemakers. Because the natural world works in opposition to the things of God, they are persecuted for righteousness' sake.

Central to the Sermon on the Mount is the idea that we receive mercy for mercy. We are healed as we seek to heal others. Ultimately, the work of the atonement, and therefore the gospel, is the work of healing, making us complete, helping us to overcome the sins of the

world, and making us whole in Christ in every respect. Our Lord and
Savior, Jesus Christ, has promised that if we walk "in obedience to the
commandments, [we] shall receive health in [our] navel and marrow
to [our] bones" (D&C 89:18). Jesus "shall change our vile body, that
it may be fashioned like unto his glorious body, according to the
working whereby he is able even to subdue all things" (Philip. 3:21).
Jesus has atoned for your sins and can empower your soul with his
healing grace and peace.

THERAPY OF FAITH PRINCIPLES

As the Sermon on the Mount began with repenting and coming
unto Christ, so also does healing faith begin with coming unto the
Lord. To paraphrase the first Beatitude we might say, "Blessed are the
poor in spirit and health who come unto me."

Coming unto Christ requires a change of thinking, a new way of
looking at things. Your faith-power begins with your thoughts.
Remember, when you work by faith, you work by mental exertion.
You mentally exert yourself to focus on three things: (1) the love the
Savior has for you personally, (2) the power he possesses as God's Son
to take away your pain, and (3) the capacity your real self has to qualify for these desired blessings.

We have been commanded to cleanse the inner vessel (Alma
60:23–24). We need to elevate our diet of thoughts and behaviors to
those which better match our real selves. We do this by using our
agency to erase negative thought patterns and replace them with positive ones. Basically, healing faith involves spending more time focusing on and nurturing the positive (accentuate the positive), spending
less time dwelling on problems (eliminate the negative), and squeez-
ing the most enjoyment out of each moment of life (affirm the present as a part of eternity) regardless of circumstances that appear to be
beyond your control. That is it! It is simple. And yet, the process is not
to be grasped all at one time. This book is a text, a road map for your
journey. Though the path may be long for some and short for others,
you can learn to enjoy the faith, hope, and charity pathway to better
health and happiness.

FAITH, HOPE, CHARITY, AND HEALTH PATTERNS

Your real self structures your thought-feeling-action patterns along healing lines—faith, hope, and charity. This pattern facilitates higher self-esteem, greater feelings of well-being, and more positive interpersonal relationships—all of which facilitate better physical health.

Faith: Thoughts. In this fallen world you are faced with adverse events such as rejection, disappointment, death, disease, betrayal, tribulation, and false accusations. At times it seems that "the very jaws of hell . . . gape open the mouth wide after thee" (D&C 122:7). (See Figure 10.) When these problems arise, you allow your real self to take control. Through mental exertion, your real self places positive interpretations upon the events through "self talk." You choose to have faith thoughts which evoke within you positive feelings. You talk to yourself in positive, objective ways. Instead of saying, "This should not be happening," you say, "This situation is really difficult, but there is something Heavenly Father wants me to learn through it."

When problems arise, you remember that the negative events themselves do not cause your feelings. Your thoughts cause your feelings and you can control your thoughts. Even though the problem may sting and burn, the real you is still okay. Remember that you will be healed through the power of Jesus Christ who is the embodiment, the personification of all truth. He is the great physician. He is Son of the Almighty God. He is "Alpha and Omega, the beginning and the ending" (Rev. 1:8). Through him all things are possible.

When Satan whispers to us that something is wrong with us—that we are not okay or these things would not be happening to us—we know that he is lying. We must remind ourselves that there is a purpose in adversity, and that in spite of our stresses and strains we are loved by a wise and kind Heavenly Father. We also remind ourselves that God does not want us to suffer any more than is necessary for our growth.

Even Jesus had to learn by the things he suffered (Heb. 5:8). "In that he himself hath suffered being tempted, he is able to succor them that are tempted" (Heb. 2:18). The knowledge that Christ has power to heal us is vital to our faith-power. Knowledge makes it possible for you to ask in faith for your righteous desires, knowing that you will receive. (See Moro. 7:26.) Because you exercise faith in Christ, you hope for things which are not seen which are true. (See Heb. 11:1.)

The Therapy of Faith

Event (Adversity)	Thought (Faith-talk)	Feeling (Feelings of Hope)	Action (Charitable Actions, Balanced) Strong	Action (Charitable Actions, Balanced) Tender	Health and Happiness (Physical and Spiritual Health)
Rain	I am a child of God	Peace			"And all saints who remember to keep and do these sayings, walking in obedience to the commandments, shall receive health in their navel and marrow to their bones; and shall find wisdom and great treasures of knowledge, even hidden treasures; and shall run and not be weary; and shall walk and not faint. And I, the Lord, give unto them a promise, that the destroying angel shall pass by them, as the children of Israel, and not slay them" (D&C 89:18–21).
Slush	I am OK	Happiness	Just	Merciful	
Pain	I am loved	Joy	Powerful	Friendly	
Death	I belong	Optimism	Capable	Dignified	
Darkness	I count	Contentment	Competent	Modest	
Disease	I am adequate	Harmony	Dependable	Flexible	
Discomfort	I am doing it	Confidence	Disciplined	Compassion	
War	I am strong	Cooperative	Intelligent	Caring	
Destruction	I am capable	Relaxed	Firm	Loving	
Betrayal	I am coping	Grateful	Logical	Sensitive	
Tribulation	I am balanced	Courageous	Rational	Warm	
False accusations	I am interdependent	Assertive	Industrious	Spontaneous	
		Cheerful	Prudent	Intuitive	
		Compassionate	Assertive	Benevolent	

Figure 10. As we apply the therapy of faith, the events in our lives no longer control us, and as a result, we perform charitable actions and have health and happiness.

Hope: Feelings. Faith brings hope. Additional fruits of faith are harmony, cheerfulness, happiness, comfort, and peace. Hope is both a physical and spiritual feeling of anticipation. It is a feeling that good will come of the trust you place in the Savior and in his ways of doing things. When your hope is strong, you feel good about yourself and relate with others in a Christlike manner.

There are actually two kinds of hope: positive, healing hope and negative hope. The negative kind has to do with cliff-hanging or tolerating a situation and waiting for it to change. No doubt this was the kind of hope Benjamin Franklin was referring to when he said "He that lives upon hope will die fasting."[1] The other kind of hope—healing hope—has to do with climbing (or progressing) and is the kind of hope involved in healing faith. Healing hope is something you feel; it is the feeling of peace. Hope is the inescapable consequence of faith. "Wherefore, whoso believeth in God might with surety hope for a better world, yea, even a place at the right hand of God, *which hope cometh of faith,* maketh an anchor to the souls of men, which would make them sure and steadfast, always abounding in good works, being led to glorify God" (Ether 12:4; emphasis added).

Charity: Actions. Hope in Christ and in your own divine nature—that you are lovable and capable—sets the stage for charitable actions. We act according to how we feel. When you feel good about yourself, you have something to offer others. You become a giver instead of a taker. When you have feelings of hope and peace, you feel like being charitable. With hope you are able to interact with others in a Christlike manner. Moroni explained that "charity is the pure love of Christ" (Moro. 7:47).

When you are truly charitable, you are able to maintain a Christlike balance of strength and tenderness in all your relationships; you are not likely to overreact or underreact. Some people have a mistaken notion that expressions of charity are limited to just tenderness and compassion. This is not the complete picture. Charity also requires that you be strong in defending truth and virtue. Christ fearlessly called the scribes and Pharisees to repentance and cleansed the temple of the money changers. You too can stand up for what is right, good, and true. You can set limits for the behavior of your children and others. You can say, "This far and no further!"

Being both strong and tender are important traits of a Christlike person. They are manifestations of your divine nature—the real you.

It is helpful at this point for you to contrast balanced, level behavior involving strength and tenderness with the imbalanced, vertical actions involving overreacting and underreacting that were discussed in the previous chapter. The more time you spend pondering and contrasting these two ways of acting, the more you will make connections and gain insights into how these behaviors are manifest in your own relationships with others. You may recognize, for example, that overreacting is a false form of being strong, and underreacting is a false form of being tender. Fearing they may be seen as weak, some vertical people overreact; they become mean, vicious, crude, and abusive. Fearing they may not be tender and loving enough, other vertical people choose to underreact; they become pleasers, weak, inhibited, withdrawn, and shy. As you continue to observe your own and others' behavior, you will make more and more connections between the principles we have been discussing and their application in real life.

The important point is to be aware of your own tendencies to overreact or underreact and to learn to focus on your divine nature in order to stay in balance. You can be firm and loving at the same time. Your real self wants to maintain the Christlike balance of warmth and strength, mercy and justice, faith and works, love and logic, spontaneity and dignity, flexibility and firmness. The Holy Ghost will lead you progressively toward the light of these principles, toward what you need to know in order to grasp your desired blessing. As you seek, you will find. As you knock, it will be opened to you. Learning to love the good in yourself and in others is a beginning principle. Without this kind of charity, we have not power to either heal or be healed.

In stressing the importance of charity, Paul said:

> Though I speak with the tongues of men and of angels, and have not charity, I am become as sounding brass, or a tinkling cymbal. And though I have the gift of prophecy, and understand all mysteries, and all knowledge; and though I have all faith, so that I could remove mountains, and have not charity, I am nothing. . . . And now abideth faith, hope, and charity, these three; but the greatest of these is charity (1 Cor. 13:1–2, 13.)

An important dimension of charity was stressed by Elder Dallin H. Oaks, who defined charity as a condition of the heart as well as actions of compassion. He referred to King Benjamin, who explained that even when we do not have sufficient resources to give to the poor, our attitude should be "if I had, I would give."[2]

Health and Happiness. Faith, hope, and charity all work togeth-er toward your health and happiness. This is the basic gospel pattern involved in unlocking the healing power of faith. When you are able to exercise charity in your relationships with others, you receive grace for grace, you increase in light and truth, your control over your car-nal self is increased, and you are able to commune more and more with the infinite powers of heaven.

As your faith increases, your righteous power increases. You become qualified to receive blessings promised in the Word of Wisdom.

> And all saints who remember to keep and do these sayings, walking in obedience to the commandments, shall receive health in their navel and marrow to their bones; And shall find wisdom and great treasures of knowledge, even hidden treasures; And shall run and not be weary, and shall walk and not faint. And I, the Lord, give unto them a promise, that the destroying angel shall pass by them, as the children of Israel, and not slay them. (D&C 89:18–21)

A man once asked President Harold B. Lee the question, "How is it that some people keep all the commandments and still are not healed?" President Lee replied, "We need to put more periods after the Lord's promises and fewer question marks!" President Lee was empha-sizing that the Lord will honor, when the time is right, all his promis-es. "When we obtain any blessing from God, it is by obedience to that law upon which it is predicated" (D&C 130:21). The time involved in receiving the blessing is up to the Lord. He may not always grant us our blessing when we want, but he will never be late. His time schedule will always work for our best good.

The fruits of faith will always be peace to our soul and the power of deliverance (1 Ne. 1:20). The Savior exemplified this principle through-out his mortal ministry. He himself had to pass through the most terrible trials: "O my Father, if it be possible, let this cup pass from me" (Matt. 26:39). But he was finally delivered according to the mercy and power of his Father. Just as Jesus was healed of his broken and torn flesh, we too can be healed according to the tender mercies of our Heavenly Father.

FAITH PRECEDES THE MIRACLE

The Savior performed many miracles during his mortal ministry that delivered afflicted souls from various kinds of suffering and dis-ease. Miracles exist in the restored Church today as well. But, as

Moroni explained, "It is by faith that miracles are wrought; . . . where-fore, if these things have ceased, then has faith ceased also" (Moro. 7:37–38). But we must always remember to seek the Lord's will in our asking, to be certain that what we ask will be for the good of all con-cerned. Moroni explained that "Whatsoever thing ye shall ask the Father in my name, which is good, in faith believing that ye shall receive, behold, it shall be done unto you" (Moro. 7:26).

A powerful example of asking for a righteous blessing is found in early Church history. At Haun's Mill, a small settlement of Mormons on Shoal Creek, Missouri, an angry mob who believed the Mormons to be their enemies rode into the settlement and began shooting the residents. Many of the Saints fled to the blacksmith's shop for safety. The mob stuck their rifles through the spaces in the logs and shot those who were frantically trying to hide within. After taking the horses and belongings of their victims, the mob rode off, howling like renegade Indians. Willard Gilbert Smith recalls the following:

> As soon as I was sure [the mob] had gone, I started for the shop [from the woods nearby]. I was the first person to enter this holocaust (wholesale destruction by fire and sword), stepping over the dead body of my father in doing so. I looked around and found my brother, Sardis, dead, . . . and my little brother, Alma, almost lifeless, lying among a pile of dead where he had been thrown by the mob, who evidently thought him dead. I picked Alma up from the dirt and was carrying him from the shop when I met my mother, who screamed and said, "Oh! They have killed my little Alma!" I said, "Alma is alive but they have killed father and Sardis." I begged mother not to go in but to help with Alma. Our tent had been dev-astated by the mob, even the straw tick [was] cut open and straw scattered about, taking the tick with them. Mother leveled the straw, laid some clothes over it and on this awful bed we placed Alma, and cut his pants off. We could then see the extent of his injury. The entire ball and socket joint of the left hip was entirely shot away, leaving the bones three or four inch-es apart. It was a sickening sight, one I shall never forget. Mother was full of divine, trusting faith, a most marvelous, wonderful woman. As soon as Alma could talk, mother asked him if he knew who made him. He said "Yes, mother, God did." She then told him that the wicked mob had shot his hip away and asked, "Do you think God can make a new one?" Alma replied, "Yes, I know He can." Mother then said, "All right, let's pray to the Lord and ask Him to do so." So we all gathered around him on his bed of straw and mother prayed, dedicating him to the Lord, asking God to spare his life if He could make him strong and well but to take him to Himself if this were impossible. In her terrible excitement and sorrow, her only help seemed her Heavenly Father. So she prayed for guidance, pleading for help

in this dire extremity. By inspiration her prayers were answered and she knew what to do. She placed little Alma in a comfortable position on his stomach, telling him, "The Lord has made it known to me that He will make you well, but you must lie on your stomach for a few weeks."

Mother was inspired to take the white ashes from the campfire, place them in water to make a weak lye, with which she washed the wound; all the crushed bone, mangled flesh and blood were thus washed away, leaving the wound clean and almost white like chicken breast. Then she was prompted how to make a poultice for the wound. Mother asked me if I knew where I could get some Slippery Elm tree roots. I said I knew where there was such a tree. . . .

The prayers of implicit, trusting faith were answered. A new hip gradually replaced the one that was shot away. Alma was fully restored to health, walked without a limp, and was a dancing master in his young days. He devoted years of his life to missionary work, a man of faith, full of integrity, beloved by all who knew him.[3]

In our own day, the Lord has instructed us:

Whosoever among you are sick, and have not faith to be healed, but believe, shall be nourished with all tenderness, with herbs and mild food, and that not by the hand of the enemy. And the elders of the church, two or more, shall be called, and shall pray for and lay their hands upon them in my name; and if they die they shall die unto me, and if they live they shall live unto me. . . . It shall come to pass that he that hath faith in me to be healed, and is not appointed unto death, shall be healed. (D&C 42:43–44,48)

Another example of trusting faith is described in this simple and beautiful experience of a young mother and her four-year-old daughter. The little girl climbed up on a chair to help her mother fix pancakes. In her excitement to help her mother, she slipped and fell, hurting her leg. The mother offered to rub the leg and kiss it better. The child refused and said, "Heavenly Father will make it better." Whereupon she limped to the living room, kneeled down, and pleaded for Heavenly Father to make her leg stop hurting. In a few moments, the child, full of love, came running to her mother and said, "Look Mom, my leg has stopped hurting." In spite of her stress, the daughter was able to focus her young mind and heart on the healing power of Christ, and her pain was taken away.

Such innocent and believing virtue is the key to all learning and healing. Could it be that the Lord had this kind of childlike humility in mind when he said, "Suffer little children, and forbid them not, to come unto me: for of such is the kingdom of heaven" (Matt. 19:14)?

When we are humble, the Lord's Spirit can work more powerfully with us. When we are earnest in our seeking, the Holy Ghost can reveal solutions to our problems—both emotional and physical. Sometimes the solution will be patience in the season of trial, but often the solution will involve ways and means of finding release from pain. Humility to be healed is a characteristic of the real self, but we must grow in humility day by day.

WEAK THINGS TO BE MADE STRONG

When we offer the Lord a broken heart and contrite spirit, his "grace is sufficient . . . [to] make weak things become strong" (Ether 12:27). When you humble yourself and decide to focus on Christlike thoughts, your real self will place adversarial conditions within a spiritual, eternal context, for "unto the pure all things are pure: but unto them that are defiled and unbelieving is nothing pure; but even their mind and conscience is defiled" (Titus 1:15).

When you are sufficiently humble, you will see yourself and your stressful condition from a constructive point of view. As Viktor Frankl said, "The last of the human freedoms [is] to choose one's attitude in any given set of stressful circumstances, to choose one's own way." Though he was a prisoner in a concentration camp, Dr. Frankl recognized that he could have peace in spite of his circumstances:

> And there were [in the concentration camps] always choices to make. Every day, every hour, offered the opportunity to make a decision, a decision which determined whether you would or would not submit to those powers which threatened to rob you of your very self, your inner freedom; which determined whether or not you would become the plaything of circumstance, renouncing freedom and dignity to become molded into the form of the typical inmate.
>
> Seen from this point of view, the mental reactions of the inmates of a concentration camp must seem more to us than the mere expression of certain physical and sociological conditions. Even though conditions such as lack of sleep, insufficient food and various mental stresses may suggest that the inmates were bound to react in certain ways, in the final analysis it becomes clear that the sort of person the prisoner became was the result of an inner decision, and not the result of camp influences alone. Fundamentally, therefore, any man can, even under such circumstances, decide what shall become of him—mentally and spiritually. He may retain his human dignity even in a concentration camp.[4]

You can make these kinds of choices in spite of adversity. When you see growth potential in adversity, your thoughts, feelings, and actions will be more consistent with the mind and will of the Lord. You can even rejoice in adversity, because there is so much that you are able to learn. When you are able to view things this way, you can feel happy, cheerful, and optimistic. The extent to which these eternal feelings fill your heart, your relationships with others, as we have pointed out, will be marked by a Christlike charity.

The Lord gives us weakness and sometimes illness and pain, so that we may be humble; and the Lord promises that his "grace is sufficient for all men that humble themselves before me; for if they humble themselves before me, and have faith in me, then I will make weak things become strong unto them. Behold, I will show unto the Gentiles their weakness, and I will show unto them that faith, hope and charity bringeth them unto me—the fountain of all righteousness" (Ether 12:27–28).

You may ask the question, "So how do I come unto the Lord? How do I focus my thoughts, feelings, and actions on Christ so as to draw on the powers of heaven and enjoy health and happiness?" The answer is "with all thy heart, and with all thy soul, and with all thy mind, and with all thy strength" (Mark 12:30). We must commit our whole lives to the Lord. We must strive honestly to follow the promptings of the Spirit. The Spirit will not shout at us, but will come as a still small voice, and the impressions upon our minds and our hearts will be unmistakable. We must commit to the Lord that we will be guided by his Spirit and by correct principles—that we want to be grounded in truth, according to the covenant we made at baptism.

We receive truth "even by study and also by faith" (D&C 88:118). Study of the gospel brings the Spirit as well as insight into making changes. We receive this kind of light, line upon line and precept upon precept. (See Isa. 28:10.) Elder Boyd K. Packer explained,

> True doctrine, understood, changes attitudes and behavior. The study of the doctrines of the gospel will improve behavior quicker than a study of behavior will improve behavior. Preoccupation with unworthy behavior can lead to unworthy behavior. That is why we stress so forcefully the study of the doctrines of the gospel.[5]

The healing of our physical and spiritual selves will not require as many of the tubes, instruments, and machines of a finely equipped hospital as it will require a refinement in the way we think our thoughts. Many hospital beds are filled with people whose aches and pains are compounded through the contamination of unhealthy thoughts and beliefs. The Lord has exhorted us to

> Let virtue garnish thy thoughts unceasingly; then shall thy confidence wax strong in the presence of God; and the doctrine of the priesthood shall distil upon thy soul as the dews from heaven. The Holy Ghost shall be thy constant companion, and thy scepter an unchanging scepter of righteousness and truth; and thy dominion shall be an everlasting dominion, and without compulsory means it shall flow unto thee forever and ever. (D&C 121:45–46)

Although your recovery from pain to peace is a relatively simple course, you must be willing to forsake your figurative fig leaves, your earthly addictions, even when you think giving these up will seem to leave you comfortless. To give up your self-defeating habits may be frightening, but the Lord has said that he will not leave you comfortless. If you repent of your sins, forsake them, and exercise faith in him, he has promised that he will send you peace. (See John 14: 18, 27.)

Unless you have committed murder, there is nothing you have done that cannot be corrected by the healing power of Christ's Atonement. The steps for salvation are clearly defined in the scriptures.

Christ wants you to nail your sins to the cross. Your sins have already been paid for. Precious blood has already been spilt to pay the price. You need only to reach out to the Savior with humility—a broken heart and a contrite spirit—and trust in his divine power to heal. By accepting his ordinances and honoring your covenants, you will be delivered. You will receive your desired blessings. You can become sanctified and made whole before him, for "as many as received him, to them gave he power to become the sons of God, even to them that believe on his name" (John 1:12). Giving heed to the light of Christ and the promptings of the Holy Ghost are the only means by which we can break out of the illusions—the fig leaves and false comforters—which originate with the false self. By coming to Christ, we achieve a balance of both strength and compassion, justice and mercy, power and sensitivity.

TRUE CHARITY—BALANCING STRENGTH AND COMPASSION

The Book of Mormon defines charity as "the pure love of Christ" (Moro. 7:47). We must not confuse charity with excessive sympathy and giving to others when it would harm them. President Ezra Taft Benson has often said, "You cannot help people permanently by doing for them what they can and should do for themselves."6 The Book of Mormon clearly states that mercy cannot rob justice. (See Alma 42:25.) In other words, faith, hope, and charity do not lead us to be so loving, so merciful, that we ignore important consequences; if rules are broken, penalties must be imposed.

The four sons of Mosiah, because they had developed faith, hope, and charity, were empowered to bless the lives of others. Ammon and his three brothers left Zarahemla to preach the gospel of Jesus Christ among the Lamanites in the land of Nephi-Lehi. In recounting their story, Mormon first identified Ammon, the eldest, as "chief among them," then Mormon explained that Ammon, "did *administer* unto them" (Alma 17:18; emphasis added). Mormon did not want his readers to think that a vertical relationship existed among the brothers. Instead, he emphasized the level, cooperative relationship that existed among these brothers. Their efforts and their strengths were directed toward serving one another and bringing salvation to the Lamanites, not toward competition for position or recognition. This message of selfless service toward one another was the same message Jesus sought to teach his disciples when he washed their feet. (See John 13:5.)

Had the four sons of Mosiah been competitive and position-conscious as missionaries, the spirit of the Lord would have been grieved and their remarkable successes would not have been realized. The spirit of cooperation and charity was an outgrowth of their hope in the Lord Jesus Christ which came from "much prayer, and fasting; therefore they had the spirit of prophecy, and the spirit of revelation, and when they taught, they taught with power and authority of God" (Alma 17:3).

When you have true charity, as these men did, you will not only be loving, kind, friendly, soft, gentle, approachable, merciful, and full of love, but you will also be strong, firm, just, consistent, and courageous. True charity reflects a proper balance of both strength and tenderness. For example, what effect would it have on your children if you were kind and giving but did not exercise strength to set limits to their behavior? What effect would it have on them if you were stern in your justice and discipline but showed neither warmth nor tenderness? One of the Christian myths about Jesus is that he was simply loving and compassionate, that he never really raised his voice or his arm in defense of truth and justice. While it is true that Jesus was full of love and compassion, he was also firm, just, and strong. His feelings of mercy did not rob his sense of justice.

A correct view of the Savior, a balanced view, has the Son of God Almighty, rising in the magnificence of his royal dignity, in perfect power, and challenging the Pharisees and the Sadducees in their deceit. He had power to calm the waters, to heal the sick, and to raise the dead.

Some of us show more love than strength in our relationships, while others of us demonstrate more strength than tenderness. None of us has arrived at a perfect balance yet. The Prophet Joseph Smith said:

> God has created man with a mind capable of instruction, and a faculty which may be enlarged in proportion to the heed and diligence given to the light communicated from heaven to the intellect; and that the nearer man approaches perfection, the clearer are his views, and the greater his enjoyments, till he has overcome the evils of his life and lost every desire for sin; . . . But we consider that this is a station to which no man ever arrived in a moment: he must have been instructed in the government and laws of that kingdom by proper degrees, until his mind is capable in some measure of comprehending the propriety, justice, equality, and consistency of the same.[7]

The nearer we approach true charity, the clearer will be our views, and the greater our enjoyments. We will also be on the pathway to better health and happiness. The healing power of faith starts with faith thoughts. You strengthen your real self by carefully selecting what you allow to enter and remain in your mind.

STRENGTHENING YOUR REAL SELF

Church membership offers us a chance to serve and develop cooperative feelings that are a true manifestation of charity. The scriptures enlighten us with the idea that truth clings to truth. "For intelligence cleaveth unto intelligence; wisdom receiveth wisdom; truth embraceth truth; virtue loveth virtue; light cleaveth unto light; mercy hath compassion on mercy and claimeth her own; justice continueth its course and claimeth its own" (D&C 88:40).

I like to think of true principles as little magnets that are constantly in motion seeking out other truth magnets. When they find each other, they click together in bonds of friendly association. So it is with us when we are in our real self. The more I get to know my own real self, the more I love me. The more I get to know the real self of my wife and children, the more I love them. The more I get to know any person's real self, the more I love them. When I am positive, I bond with other people's positive—it is impossible not to.

When I counsel people with severe problems, I consciously focus my attention on something good about them. I can always see something good. I focus on that good in my mind, and do you know what? It grows.

Whatever you focus on will grow in your mind. This is one of the reasons certain Freudian approaches to healing were fraught with problems. A patient who focuses full attention on all the problems experienced in early childhood years and stays there usually walks out more depressed than when he walked into the analyst's office.

It is important to take a look at the past for diagnosis and assessment, but it is more important to get into the present as soon as possible and begin dealing with what is going on in our heads, hearts, and relationships *now*. The question, "Why do I think and do things like that?" is not as important as, "What can I do with the Lord's help about the problem now?" The answer lies in empowering your real self with light and knowledge by triggering your thoughts with faith-talk and faith-pictures, which will be discussed later. Positive thinking is necessary, but is not sufficient to full healing. Only by faith in the Lord Jesus Christ and in your own divine nature can all things be accomplished.

LIMITATIONS OF POSITIVE THINKING

As I have pointed out, thoughts are powerful agents of change, more powerful than most people give them credit. They are not, however, all-powerful. Positive thinking without matching actions has a down side.

With thoughts alone, without doing anything physical, you cannot open a carton of milk, or turn the corner of this page. Thoughts are powerful, but "as the body without the spirit is dead, so faith [thoughts] without works [actions] is dead also" (James 2:26).

Literally millions have been helped by reading the great self-help books on thinking positively when they wanted to solve problems in their lives. Most people could benefit from Dr. Peale's great book, *The*

Power of Positive Thinking. However, as important as many of these ideas are, they are not sufficient. Why not? Because thoughts must be connected with actions.

Positive thinking alone is not sufficient to bring about great healing changes, especially if the structure of thought itself is negative. For example, the decision "I am not going to ever again think a negative thought," which some people consider to be positive thinking, is in reality a negative thought. For this reason, school children should not be required to write on the board one hundred times, "I will *not* be late for school." If a positive thought is structured in the negative, the mind is preoccupied with the negative. It would be more instructive for them to write: "I am always on time for school."

If you tell yourself that from today onward you will never again think negatively, and then don't give yourself a specific word-for-word vocabulary of the right things to say to yourself (self-talk), you will soon slip back into the comfortable old habit of negative thinking.

Research shows that your mind cannot focus on two things at the same time. This is a blessing, in a way, because as your real self chooses to focus on virtuous thoughts, you automatically erase the negative. This is how you detach yourself from your false self and empower your real self. Erasing and replacing is something you need to do constantly as you strive for better health and a more abundant life.

You need not let other people influence your thoughts either. Just because others are being negative does not mean that you have to be. You are like one instrument in an orchestra. Just because the person next to you gets off key, must you? If someone close to us has a bad day or gets angry, we often jump to the conclusion that we caused it or that we can't help being angry when they are angry. Erase the thought that you caused the anger and replace it with a desire to help!

Now let's get down to the basic actions you can take to increase the faith-power of your real self and help you to break the grip of your false self.

AFFIRMATIONS—FAITH-TALK

The first step in unlocking the healing power of faith is learning to control your thoughts. This is best done by looking at how you talk to yourself. You talk to yourself in your head constantly, and your thoughts generally have either a positive or negative content. Most people are incredibly negative in their self-talk by repeating such thoughts as, "I'm too fat," "I'm so ugly," "I'm so stupid," "I'm such a klutz."

Your addictions begin with the diet of your self-talk. When you learn to detect the negative self-talk, if you erase it and replace it with positive self-talk, you will change the way you feel about yourself. Shad Helmstetter offers the following story to stress the importance of substituting positive self-talk to replace the old, worn out, negative self-talk that is so characteristic of the false self.

> Imagine for a moment your "mental apartment"—the place you live with your thoughts. That mental apartment is furnished with everything you think about yourself and the world around you; it is furnished with your thoughts. Much of the mental furniture in this mental apartment is "hand-me-down" furniture. It is the old negative ways of thinking which were handed down to us from our parents, our friends, our teachers, and everyone else who has been helping us program our subconscious minds: they gave us the furniture which we have kept and which we use in our mental apartment.
>
> Imagine that most of that "furniture" (your negative thinking), because it was hand-me-down furniture, is weary with age. The old tattered sofa is sagging and worn. The chairs are broken and shaky, ready to fall apart if sat in too heavily. The pictures, hanging crookedly on the walls, are yellowed and faint. The kitchen table leans at an angle, the dishes chipped and cracked, no cup has a handle, long since broken away. . . .
>
> Now let us say that I agree to come over to your home, this mental apartment, and help you get rid of all the old furniture. I tell you that I am going to help you get rid of your old negative thinking once and for all. . . .
>
> By six o'clock that evening we have finished, and I leave. After I leave you stand in the middle of your mental apartment. It is empty and spotless. There is not a negative thought, not a sofa, a picture, a book or chair in sight. You look around you and think, "This is great! I've gotten rid of all my old negative thinking. Now I can be a positive thinker!"
>
> You stand around, walk through your mental apartment, and then stand around some more. A little later that evening, after spending an hour or two with nothing but yourself and an empty apartment, what do you suppose you will do? You will go out into the garage, where the old furniture is stored, and get a chair! A little later, you will make another trip to the garage and bring in a table, and maybe a dish or two.
>
> We are most comfortable with the thoughts we have lived with the most. It makes no difference if those thoughts aren't the best for us—they are what we know, they are what we are most secure in keeping at our side. By nine o'clock you may even have retrieved the trusty old TV. One by one, you will begin to bring your old trusted and time-worn negative thoughts back into your mental apartment! Why? Because when I helped

you remove the old furniture I didn't give you any new furniture to replace it with—I didn't give you any positive new thoughts to replace the negative old thoughts.[8]

If you only decide to stop thinking negatively, and do not have an immediate, new, positive vocabulary to replace the old, then you will always return to the comfortable, old, negative self-talk of the past. Healing faith requires that you replace negative thoughts with positive ones. The more your thoughts focus on Jesus Christ and on your divine nature, your real self, the more healing power you will be able to tap into from heaven.

There are several ways you can go about erasing and replacing thoughts. Memorizing scriptures and the words to hymns are effective ways. Another powerful way is to use affirmations—statements designed "to make firm" positive things about yourself.

Affirmations, another word for self-talk, are worded in the present tense and usually begin with the words "I am . . ." Examples: "I am happy, cheerful, and optimistic." "I am calm, relaxed, and tranquil." "I am able to handle difficult situations as they arise." "I am getting better—every day and in every way." Healing faith requires that you replace your old self-talk with affirmations that reflect your faith in the Lord Jesus Christ and in your own divine nature.

From here on in this book, we will call gospel-centered affirmations *faith-talk*. Faith-talk or self-talk may be one form of the mental exertion that the Prophet Joseph Smith described as the process of working by faith. Faith-talk is a very powerful tool because it is a first person (I), present tense (am) statement that reflects the power of Christ and the divine nature of your real self (a child of God). When you learn to use faith-talk correctly, you are empowered by the Holy Ghost and you will be able to make wonderful, healing changes in your life.

The power of the "I am" form of faith-talk is profound! As a Latter-day Saint psychologist, I find important doctrinal significance in this approach to health. Jehovah (or Yahveh) in the Hebrew is translated as "I am" in English. Jesus Christ is the Jehovah of the Old Testament. It was he who told Moses that his name was "I am" or Jehovah. He is alpha and omega, the beginning and the end. Jesus is the embodiment of all truth. He declares, "I am the way, the truth and the life" (John 14:6). Faith-talk is like bearing your testimony to yourself of the truth—of things as they were, as they are, and as they will be. (See D&C 93:24.) Faith-talk affirms the reality and power of your real self—the premortal you who was valiant in that war when the adversary aligned himself against the Savior.

By practicing faith-talk, you make firm your commitment to things good, true, and beautiful. You are committing to let your real self have dominion in your life by coming unto Christ, becoming like he is. As you learn the power of faith-talk, you can begin to appreciate what Emerson meant when he said, "The currents of the Universal Being circulate through me; I am part and parcel of God."[9] By practicing faith-talk, you remind yourself who you really are and what you must do to find peace and healing power. You establish a firm foundation in Christ.

An example of faith-talk formed from Paul's admonition may take the form of, "I *am* honest, true, chaste, benevolent." Other examples drawn from the scriptures might be, "I *am* always willing to walk by faith." Some people are troubled by using self-talk that, according to their present perceptions, is not true. This problem is resolved when you remember that faith-talk is a *goal* you are working toward. As a goal, it can be stated as an absolute, because that is the target you are righteously aiming for.

Once, when I asked a patient how she was feeling, she replied, "I am happy, cheerful, and optimistic." I asked her if that was faith-talk or something she had arrived at. She said, "That is faith-talk because after the faith-talk comes the state of being." She had learned an important lesson regarding how faith-talk works. What you say is what you get—faith precedes the miracle.

Let me give you another example of how faith-talk works. If I walk into a classroom and affirm in my mind that these students are my best friends, I am likely to have a good experience with them. Because of loving thoughts, I interact with my students in a loving manner; the students respond in a loving way; and my affirmation is realized. The loving affirmation becomes a self-fulfilling prophecy.

On the other hand, suppose I walk into a classroom doing negative self-talk and say to myself, "What a bunch of knot-heads these kids are! They don't want to learn anything." If I take this approach, I will certainly experience resentment from the students. Whatever we affirm, we eventually get. This pattern is repeated in every aspect of our lives.

Saying the words alone is not sufficient to bring about change. To make your faith-talk work for you, you must legitimately embrace the feelings you are affirming. If you do not embrace these feelings, then your self-talk can work against you and become a form of self-deception. President David O. McKay warned:

> Thoughts are the seeds of acts and precede them. Mere compliance with the word of the Lord, without a corresponding inward desire, will avail but little. Indeed, such outward actions and pretending phrases may disclose hypocrisy, a sin that Jesus most vehemently condemned.[10]

On the other hand, when you do accept the feelings that go with the faith-talk it results in great blessings of health and happiness.

Faith-talk works best when your mind and body are relaxed. Early morning is a good time to rehearse. Don't try to work on too many affirmations at a time. Be sure to keep them in the present tense and positive. See Appendixes A and B for examples of affirmations that you can use to get started; but the best ones will be those you create to suit your particular needs.

When your real self takes charge with faith-talk, you see through the eyes of truth. You become more accepting of others, and you desire not to condemn but to reach out and help and bless their lives. Your real self controls your level of tolerance so that you do not swing from one extreme to another—from anger to submission. As you pay attention to your real self and the messages you receive from the Spirit of the Lord, you learn to trust your real self and the Lord in a cooperative partnership. You build momentum as you change. As you allow your real self to take control, you will find that moving forward becomes a natural healing process.

FOCUSING WITH FAITH-TALK

Faith-talk is a powerful tool you can use to overcome negative beliefs and help you reach your goals of peace and health. At this point it is important to point out the need for a reality check with trusted others as you form your faith-talk statements. A trusted friend, bishop, or counselor may be of great help. Otherwise, you might end up affirming old worn-out destructive thoughts. How can you bring about specific results by pinpointing your faith-talk?

In order to make lasting changes in your life, you must begin by changing the way you perceive the world—the way you talk to yourself about things. Much has been written about the process of making changes in our lives. Some have argued that it is easier to *act* your way into a new way of thinking than it is to *think* your way into a new way of acting. Christ has said, "If any man will do his will, he shall know of the doctrine" (John 7:17). However, the power or motivation to act must come from the thoughts and desires of the inner man. Through righteous, humble petitioning, the Holy Ghost can influence our inner selves. This influence will take many forms, including helping you to form and use your own faith-talk to make changes in your life.

You will want to form new faith-talk statements each day to use along with the ones you obtain from this chapter. One effective way to practice faith-talk is to personalize the scriptures. For example: "[I] cheerfully do all things that lie in [my] power; and then . . . [I] stand still, with the utmost assurance, to see the salvation of God, and for his arm to be revealed" (D&C 123:17). You will notice marked results as you apply the same pattern to other health-related scriptures.

Faith-talk statements are targets or goals that you stake everything on. You banish every contrary thought. You waste no energy on doubts, fears, or reconsideration. Faith-talk statements need to be written down; you need to write down your wants. One lady told me that when she hears conference talks she writes down exhortations from the Church leaders in faith-talk form. She showed me the following list that helps her deal with adversity.

Notice that affirmations can also take the form of commitment:

I give thanks for everything! All that the Father hath shall be given me.
I feel that life at its worst is a fascinating experience.
I have faith that all things that happen to me are for my good.
Here are several other examples of faith-talk one might form using gospel exhortations we hear frequently:
I ponder the scriptures daily, particularly the Book of Mormon.
I liken the scriptures unto myself.
I remember that Christ's atonement is the power behind my ultimate forgiveness. I look to Christ and his atonement in everything [I read].

As a bishop, I was happy to notice that the Young Women's values are stated in faith-talk form. Young women throughout the Church are encouraged to repeat these values at their meetings and remember them throughout the week.

Faith. I am a daughter of a Heavenly Father who loves me, and I will have faith in his eternal plan, which centers in Jesus Christ, my Savior. (See D&C 14:7.)

Divine Nature. I have inherited divine qualities which I will strive to develop. (See 2 Pet. 1:4–7.)

Individual Worth. I am of infinite worth with my own divine mission which I will strive to fulfill. (See D&C 18:10.)

Knowledge. I will continually seek opportunities for learning and growth.

Choice and Accountability. I will remain free by choosing good over evil and will accept responsibility for my choices. (See Josh. 24:15.)

Good Works. I will nurture others and build the kingdom through righteous service. (See 3 Ne. 12:16.)

Integrity. I will have the moral courage to make my actions consistent with my knowledge of right and wrong. (See Job 27:5.)

Use these examples of faith-talk to begin your own collection. The idea is to use them and then adapt them to your own specific needs. Faith-talk coupled with faith-pictures empowers your real self to draw upon the heavenly powers of the Spirit to make positive changes in your life.

I have President Kimball's famous statement, "Do it now!" on the wall of my office, but I have changed the sign into a faith-talk statement that reads, "*I am* doing it now!" One student asked if I were *always* doing it now, and I replied, "No, but that is my faith-talk. That is what I am committed to, and that is what I am working toward. That is how I reach my goal."

A faith-talk statement that I use a lot is, "*I am always on time for my meetings!*" I try to see myself doing whatever is necessary so that I am always on time. In connection with this self-talk statement, a friend of mine said, "I thought you said in class it is not wise to use absolutes like 'always.'" I explained that in formal papers and in speech it is not a good idea to use absolutes like "always," "never," and "only." However, when you are doing faith-talk you use absolutes to more effectively program your brain. An absolute statement has a greater impact and allows for no exceptions which your negative self can use to justify not reaching the goal expressed in your faith-talk statement. For example, the expression "I am *usually* on time for my meetings" does not carry the same impact as "I am *always* on time for my meetings!" The affirmation creates a picture of the goal you are working toward.

Sometimes I hear people say, "Well, this seems like a lot of hype to me! You want me to say that I am happy, cheerful, and optimistic when, in fact, I am really depressed." When I hear this argument, I suggest to them that their last statement was a negative affirmation and is really a form of negative hype. You *feel* according to how you *think*. You choose your own self-talk. "Which would you rather be," I then ask, "happy or depressed?" You choose your own self-talk, so you choose indirectly how you feel about things, then you act according to your feelings.

VISUALIZATIONS—FAITH-PICTURES

In 1926, Gertrude Ederle, of the United States, was the first woman to swim the English Channel. The circumstances surrounding her success are very interesting. She had been promised that if she were successful in swimming the channel, she would be awarded $25,000 in cash and a new, red automobile. When she was three-fourths of the way across the channel, she became very exhausted. She was ready to give up and have the boat that ran alongside her pick her up. Just as she was about to admit defeat, she visualized in her mind a red car on the shore and someone standing beside it with the keys to the car extended to her. This image gave her fresh determination to finish the swim, and she became the first woman to ever swim the channel.

The power of our minds to first create mental images and then have them affect our physical world is nothing short of miraculous. Children have a marvelous imaginative capacity. They can play in a sand pile for hours, pretending they are building roads, houses, and cities. When you were a child, did you ever use your imagination to create animal pictures out of clouds? Carl Jung said, "Without this playing with fantasy no creative work has ever yet come to birth. The debt we owe to the play of imagination is incalculable."[11] Though this is true, there is one caution. While visualizations can be used for positive, creative, and constructive purposes, such as empowering your real self, they can also be used in negative, destructive, and devastating ways. We must be careful how we choose to use our imagination because, like a computer, the data we program into our minds will be what comes out in our actions.

We have referred to affirmations centered on Christ and your own divine nature as faith-talk. Now we will refer to visualizations centered on these same truths as faith-pictures. Both faith-talk and faith-pictures program your biological, mechanical brain. Here is how the process works: (1) From all the stimuli around you, your spirit as a free agent chooses what to attend to, what to think about; (2) When you choose to focus on positive images through faith-talk and faith-pictures, these words and images become programmed, through repetition, into your brain; (3) Conscious and unconscious information from your brain causes your body to act; (4) Repeated acts become habits, and habits determine the very nature of who you are, of what you have and will become.

When you choose faith-talk and faith-pictures, you empower your real self with light and truth. Your sustained thought patterns eventually impact both your spiritual and physical health. This brain programming is sometimes called cognitive structuring or neurological imprinting.

Many of our thought patterns, or neurological imprinting, take place at the unconscious level. We do not realize it is happening. We often think thoughts without being consciously aware that we are thinking, but our brain gets programmed just the same. It is something we are always doing, whether we recognize it or not. From the prophet's sermons to TV advertising, other people suggest images for our minds to dwell upon. But in the end our thoughts are our choice, and they impact our very being. Perhaps this is why Jesus said, "Whosoever looketh on a woman to lust after her hath committed adultery with her already in his heart" (Matt. 5:28). And whether you focus on light or darkness, your choices will impact your health—for good or evil, health or sickness.

IMPRINTING YOUR MIND WITH FAITH-PICTURES

Elder Richard G. Scott has spoken about the importance of visualization in increasing our faith:

> To better understand prayer I have listened to the counsel of others, pondered the scriptures, and studied the lives of prophets and others. Yet what seems most helpful is seeing in my mind a child approaching trustingly a loving, kind, wise, understanding Father, who wants us to succeed.[12]

Elder Scott has recognized the benefit of visualization while in the act of prayer. This is a form of faith-picturing.

I believe that all the prophets and good and faithful people the world over use faith-talk and faith-picturing, although they may not have identified what they do with these expressions. From the life of President Ezra Taft Benson, for instance, we find a beautiful account of how his faith brought about miraculous results. On one occasion he flew to Paris at the beginning of a journey that would take him, during his first 50 days in Europe, to 102 cities in 13 countries, some of them in the occupied areas of Germany. We read of the difficulties he overcame in traveling from one place to another during this time.

> Complicating what would have been a staggering schedule even under favorable conditions were the facts that highways throughout Europe that had been bombed and strafed with gunfire were nearly impassable, bridges had been demolished, telephone and telegraph facilities were restricted, food was scarce, and all priority space on trains and planes was reserved for military personnel. The challenge of traveling throughout Europe appeared to be a strategical nightmare.
>
> In trying to get from Paris to The Hague in the Netherlands, Elder Babbel was informed by telegram that President Benson would arrive at a certain station. Elder Babbel hurried to the station, but the station master insisted the train in question was a local shuttle service, and any passenger arriving from France would come into another station a mile away, where a train from Paris was due. Babbel hurried there, but Elder Benson was not aboard the train. Back and forth he went between the stations, looking for Elder Benson.
>
> Finally he called the Hotel des Indes and learned that Elder Benson had arrived. "How did you get here?" Babbel asked, amazed. "On the train about which I wired you," Ezra replied. "But the stationmaster insisted no passengers from Paris could possibly be aboard that train." "Yes, I know," Elder Benson answered, "they told me that in Paris."
>
> In Paris, Ezra had learned that he and Chaplain Badger would be delayed a full day getting to the Netherlands. Just then he noticed a train preparing to leave for Antwerp, Belgium. The stationmaster warned him against taking the train, as all connections between Antwerp and the Netherlands were cut off. But Ezra felt otherwise, and he and Chaplain Badger boarded the dilapidated train with cardboard windows and wooden slats for seats.
>
> In Antwerp an angry stationmaster insisted the two Americans must backtrack. Again Ezra spotted a train preparing to leave. This one was to stop at the Dutch border, where the Maas River Bridge had been demolished. Again Ezra felt prompted to take it, and over the stationmaster's protest he and Chaplain Badger boarded. As warned, at the Maas River all

passengers were forced to pile out, but before long an American Army vehicle approached, and the driver was persuaded to take them to a small village just inside the Dutch border. There they found the local shuttle train leaving for The Hague.

Fred Babbel was amazed at the event, though he would learn to take such developments in stride. During the coming months he would see Elder Benson's faith and determination at work countless times.[13]

Similar examples could be cited from the lives of men and women who have learned, like President Benson, that by viewing their tasks with an eye of faith instead of seeing things through the natural eye, they can overcome what seem to be insurmountable obstacles and receive their righteous desires.

This process of faith-picturing (creating mental images of desired outcomes) is an eternal gospel principle. It was involved in the creation of the world. From the scriptures and from the teachings of the prophets, we learn that before the physical creation, the gods discussed their plans for the worlds and all things that in them are. Plans and preparations were made in the minds of the gods before the actual creation took place. (See Abr. 4.)

God's ability to visualize the creation of the world and all life upon it is beyond our comprehension. You also have a mind capable of tremendous creative imagination. You are a free agent. You can create, organize, and bring about new and interesting conditions in your life by the things you picture. If you want to make changes in your life, you must visualize the goal you want to accomplish, whether it be improved health, gaining wealth, acquiring knowledge, remodeling your kitchen, or rendering service to others. Then visualize the steps you must take to accomplish your goal. This process of visualizing the steps to take is sometimes called doing a task analysis. This means you identify each step you must take to reach your goal and visualize yourself taking the step. Do all this in your mind. Repeat the images over and over, working out every detail. When it comes time to actually perform the labor, you are prepared. You have already done it in your mind with faith-picturing many, many times. The actual task will then be much easier.

To illustrate how faith-pictures can help you reach your targets, the following accounts may be helpful. Recently my family and I were invited to present the sacrament service in the Tongan Ward in Honolulu, Hawaii. We live in Hauula, about forty miles up the coast on the North Shore of Oahu. It takes at least one hour and fifteen minutes to drive from where we live to where the Tongan Saints have their meetings. Because of certain delays in my own ward, we were not able to leave until 2:00 P.M. The Tongan Ward meeting started at 3:00 P.M. My children wanted to call and excuse our family from the meeting. I wanted to help them realize that the Lord can bless us if we have faith in him and ask for things that are good. I suggested to them that they practice faith-talk, "Our family is always on time for our meetings," and then picture our family walking into the meeting at exactly 3:00 P.M. Every time one of the children would say, "Dad, we are going to be late!" I would remind them to use faith-talk and picturing. The traffic was particularly bad that day with a lot of Sunday drivers enjoying the beautiful Hawaii coastline. We tried to hurry without being rushed—God does not expect us to rush. And you know what? We walked into our meeting at exactly 3:00 P.M. All during the meeting, I could hear one of my teenage daughters saying, "I can't believe we got here on time! I can't believe we got here on time."

As a young missionary, I was to give an Easter Sunday talk in a branch in East Liverpool, Ohio. It was to be my first presentation in a sacrament service as a missionary, and I was very nervous. A wise companion took me to the chapel on the preceding Saturday afternoon when no one was around. He had me stand at the pulpit and present the talk to an imaginary audience. He even had me imagine I was making eye contact with some of the most supportive and friendly members of the ward. When the time came for me to make my presentation I found myself quite relaxed and comfortable, because I had already given the talk in my mind.

Now, as a professor at BYU-Hawaii Campus, I find myself doing as my companion had instructed by presenting my daily lessons in my mind before I ever walk into the classroom. This way I can make adjustments and corrections in my mind before I actually give the lesson.

Astronauts, champion athletes, great stage performers, skilled surgeons, and truly professional executives and salesmen practice flawless techniques in their minds over and over again. So do influential teachers, prophets, and Church leaders. They know that thoughts beget habits, and they discipline their thoughts to create the habit of uncommon performance—one of the marks of the true spirit self.

As you exercise yourself and your faith by using faith-talk and faith-picturing, you will be able to let your spirit soar above the trials and tribulations of this fallen world. With an eye of faith, you will be able to see yourself as you really are. This process was described by Elder Parley P. Pratt when he said, "Let the candidate for celestial glory forget, for a moment, the groveling sphere of his present existence, and make the effort to contemplate himself in the light of eternity, in the higher spheres of his progressive existence, beyond the grave." He continued by saying you should contemplate the eternal nature of your real self as being

> a pure spirit, free from sin and guile, enlightened in the school of heaven, by observation and experience, and association with the highest order of intelligence, for thousands of years; and clothed with immortal flesh, in all the vigor, freshness and beauty of eternal youth; free alike from pain, disease, death, and the corroding effects of time; looking back through the vista of far distant years, and contemplating our former sojourn amid the sorrows and pains of mortal life, our passion through the dark valley of death, and his sojourn in the spirit world, as we now contemplate a transient dream, or a night of sleep, from which we have awakened, renewed and refreshed, to enter again upon the realities of life.
>
> Let us contemplate, for a moment, such a being, clothed in the finest robes of linen, pure and white, adorned with precious stones and gold; a countenance radiant with the effulgence of light; intelligence and love; a bosom glowing with all the confidence of conscious innocence, dwelling in palaces of precious stone and gold; bathing in the crystal waters of life.[14]

This is a description of the real me and the real you, isn't it? One of the most beautiful things about these truths is that it helps us recognize error. By truly knowing your real self, you can know who and what you are not. You can learn to see yourself in this eternal light by casting out your negative images and by learning and affirming truths about yourself through faith-talk and faith-pictures. You can learn to overcome adversity and heal your pain. Sometimes you will learn quickly, and sometimes you will learn more slowly.

LEARNING THROUGH TRAUMA OR REPETITION

You will never know everything there is to know in this life. But you can learn what you need to know to stop unnecessary pain. Learning new ways of thinking, feeling, and acting come to us through trauma (shock) experiences or through repetition (daily practice).

If you witness an automobile accident, the shock of it will impact your mind immediately, and you will drive much more carefully for some time. Learning to play the piano, however, cannot come through one dramatic experience, but requires patient practice. Likewise, if you want to acquire the habit of remaining calm when someone provokes you, you will have to learn through practice also. You will have to practice patience for a period of time until you form the habit of forbearance. A tense, determined will to practice is not the key, but continual commitment to calmness in the face of adversity coupled with faith-talk and faith-picturing: "I am always calm in the face of adversity; when others get angry, I become cool and rational." When you take these steps, calming powers will flow unto you like the dews from heaven, and you will be healed. (See D&C 121:45–46.)

The Lord wants us to repent and exercise faith in him because he loves us. If we do not repent of our own free will, he will allow things to happen in our lives that we will not like, but these unwanted events are designed to motivate us to repent. As an example of this principle, we read, "Wherefore, this people shall keep my commandments, saith the Lord of Hosts, or cursed be the land for their sakes" (Jacob 2:29). In other words, God will curse the land in order to bring us to repentance.[15] We can choose to repent daily, or we can expect hardships in our lives because our Heavenly Father loves us.

This is not to say that all suffering is a consequence of sin. Sometimes it is. If we do not live up to the covenants we make with the Lord, we are vulnerable to Satan's influence. It takes sincere and hard repentance to once again become eligible for the blessings of the Lord. For example, Alma the younger was redeemed through his traumatic experience with the angel and the cleansing process that followed. He was never the same after that experience. He declared: "After wading through much tribulations, repenting nigh unto death, the Lord in mercy hath seen fit to snatch me out of an everlasting burning, and I am born of God. . . . My soul was racked with eternal torment; but I am snatched, and my soul is pained no more" (Mosiah 27:28–29). There are other recorded experiences in which changes were wrought upon people in dramatic, traumatic ways, such as the conversion of King Lamoni and his father, and Paul on the road to Damascus. However, for most of us, changes will come through patient repetition of virtuous thoughts, feelings, and behaviors. You can't see grass grow, but it surely does. Likewise, your new habits will be acquired slowly but surely.

The average habit may take from five to twenty-one days to break. You break bad habits by substituting good ones. The more attention given bad habits, the harder they are to break. You eliminate bad thoughts by substituting good thoughts. You must with vigilance focus on the desired behavior, not the bad. The process is not one of white-knuckled willpower, but free-flowing creative imagination. You consciously replace the old habit with one you would prefer simply through affirming the new. For example, when you catch yourself in a nervous habit (nail-biting, head-scratching), substitute taking a deep breath and smiling instead. It is important to keep at it for at least three weeks. As with physical habits, it takes time and practice to establish better spiritual habits. The things of God are learned through patient repetition or study.

The Prophet Joseph described the progressive nature of our development when he said,

> The nearer man approaches perfection, the clearer are his views, and the greater his enjoyments, till he has overcome the evils of his life and lost every desire for sin; and like the ancients, arrives at that point of faith where he is wrapped in the power and glory of his Maker and is caught up to dwell with Him. But we consider that this is a station to which no man ever arrived in a moment: he must have been instructed in the government and laws of that kingdom by proper degrees, until his mind is capable in some measure of comprehending the propriety, justice, equality, and consistency of the same."[16]

This process begins as you learn to mentally exert yourself in more positive, growth-promoting, and healthful ways through faith-talk and faith-picturing.

THOUGHT DETECTION—THINKING ABOUT YOUR THOUGHTS

You need to consider the content of the thoughts that stream through your head. In a way, you must learn to be a mind detective by discovering those specific thoughts that evoke negative (or positive) feelings and actions. The more you are able to do this, the more you will be able to erase thoughts that are self-defeating and replace them with thoughts that are healing.

To break the chain of repeated negative ideas, you must start by thinking about your thoughts. Once you identify your unwanted and destructive thought patterns, you can erase them and replace them with more constructive thoughts. You *erase* and *replace!* The process begins by thinking about what you think about. The next step is selecting appropriate and more positive thoughts.

THOUGHT SELECTION—CHOOSING YOUR THOUGHTS

In order to replace unwanted thoughts, you need alternative thoughts. Your ability to do this will increase as you gain knowledge. This book is designed to give you more knowledge, not only of how the erase-and-replace process works, but also of principles of light and truth that you can use as replacement thoughts. Additionally, as you listen to trustworthy mentors, prophets, teachers, physicians, and psychotherapists, they will suggest other ideas you can substitute for the unhealthy thoughts you may have previously held.

Your God-given ability to change your thoughts is the basis of your free agency. You have the freedom to choose your thoughts, just as you do to change channels on a television. When you persist in thinking a certain way, habits are formed that are hard to break. That does not mean as you get older that you cannot change, but it does mean the process is harder and demands more energy and attention. You break destructive habits by identifying them and replacing them with more constructive ones.

The following profile is a quick way of assessing your present thought patterns and will also give you specific faith-talk and faith-pictures that will give you more control of your thoughts, feelings, actions, and health.

YOUR PERSONAL THOUGHT PROFILE

Although the the Personal Thought Profile found in Appendix C has not been validated, it can provide a quick, general inventory of your thought patterns to give you a personal thought profile. It is not intended to provide a complete assessment of your mental processes. Important decisions should not be made on the basis of this brief test without confirmation from other sources. The profile is meant only to give you a rough idea of your strengths and indicate the areas in which you might need to make changes in the thoughts you select.

You will benefit most if you complete the profile before reading the remainder of this chapter.

IDENTIFYING FAITH-TALK FOR PERSONAL IMPROVEMENT

Once you have graded yourself in each of the nine Thought Profile areas, you are ready to identify your own targeted areas for improvement. Now, how do you go about making changes? Do you say, "That's just the way that I am;" "I can't improve or change;" "I've tried before;" "I can't do anything about it;" "I've always been this way"? These are all negative affirmations. What you say or think about yourself is what you are. If you tell yourself that you can't, you are right. But if you believe you can, you are right.

To counteract these ideas from your false self and to empower your real self, do the following:

1. In the statements listed below, circle the corresponding letter from each category in which you received a C grade or less in your Personal Thought Profile.

    A.   I am composed: calm, relaxed, and tranquil.
    B.   I am lighthearted: happy, cheerful, and optimistic.
    C.   I am energetic: enthusiastic and socially involved.
    D.   I am expressive: talkative, spontaneous, affectionate, and demonstrative.
    E.   I am sympathetic: kind, understanding, gentle, and compassionate.
    F.   I am objective: rational, reasonable, and logical—as detached as needed.
    G.   I am assertive: confident, firm, strong, and self-assured.
    H.   I am patient: accepting, loving, and caring.
    I.   I am self-disciplined: controlled, methodical, and persistent.

2. These become your faith-talk statements. Repeat them to yourself many times every day.

3. Form a faith-picture for each statement. Visualize yourself being and doing these things. Get as many of your senses involved as you can with each statement. As you do your faith-picturing, what specifically do you see, hear, feel, etc.?

Working through your personal profile has helped you get started in creating your own faith-talk statements. These sentences are broad and very general. Now you will benefit from personalizing and localizing your own faith-talk, which means that you need to modify, adapt, and shape your self-talk and pictures in more specific ways. Since each of us is unique and each of our situations is different, we must tap into our *own* healing powers and processes. Time, experience, and the Holy Spirit will show you the way. Working towards targets or goals is fun. It generates interest and enthusiasm and makes life an exciting adventure.

A very dear friend of mine, one who has formed a deep trust in the Lord through struggles with her own health and relationships, shared with me her faith-talk formed from talks given by Elder Neal A. Maxwell[17] and Boyd K. Packer.[18] These affirmations prepared her to have a peak experience in her spiritual growth. Whereas she once struggled with annoyances in the behavior of people close to her, she now expresses joy that those annoyances "just don't matter any more." These are her affirmations:

> I am in total self-control, freed from judging others because I am patient and make allowances for others to exercise their agency.
> I have complete trust in the Lord. My irritations, fears, and worries cease. The electro-chemical change triggers my brain and causes joy unspeakable. This process activates an internal chemical balance and brings physical, emotional, mental, and spiritual health.
> My resistance to the operation of the laws regulating the Holy Ghost in my life is removed, and his Spirit fills my being. The Holy Ghost is free to magnify, purify, and sanctify. The fetters and shackles of the "natural man" fall away and I am free. It is the most wonderful feeling and is very thrilling.
> I am filled with thanksgiving to the Lord for his patience with me. I'm grateful for the prayers of others, the influence of my deceased progenitors, and the support of my family.
> I use my free agency to follow the counsel of the prophets and my freedom is increased. I obey the divine laws that I know exist. I earn and protect my freedom by obedience to the laws of the gospel. Freedom is not a self-preserving gift. My individual preferences and differences are irretrievably enmeshed with others, so I am patient and long suffering. I submit to the "process of time." I know that patience is linked with faith in the Lord. I know that impatience says I know what is best better than the Lord.
> I must not just endure, but endure well and gracefully those things the Lord seeth fit to inflict upon me. I submit cheerfully and with patience to the will of the Lord. There is simply no other way for real growth to occur.

You can use faith-talk and faith-pictures to help you overcome any challenge, problem, or weakness you may face. For example, a member of my ward came by my home wanting to have his baby blessed. He and his wife were active members, but they had not yet been sealed in the temple. As I commented on the fact that the child was not born in the covenant, I asked him when he was going to the temple to have his family sealed. He qualified for a recommend except for the payment of tithing. He said, "We always put our tithing money aside, thinking we will pay it later. Things come up where we have to use the money; then we think we will pay double next time, but we never do."

I introduced this good brother to faith-talk and faith-pictures. I told him, "You must never again say what you just said. Instead, you should say this: 'We always pay our tithing first!' Then create a mental picture of cashing your check, requesting correct change to pay your tithing. See yourself making out the slip and putting the money in the tithing envelope and licking and sealing the envelope. Next, picture yourself dropping the check off to the bishop."

He said, "I should be able to do that."

I smiled and said, "Don't say 'should.'" Say, 'I always pay my tithing first!'"

When you do your part and commit and visualize in this manner, the powers of heaven are released in your behalf, miraculous doors are opened, and you are able to accomplish the things the Lord has commanded you. I reminded this brother that "the Lord giveth no commandments unto the children of men, save he shall prepare a way for them that they may accomplish the thing which he commandeth them" (1 Ne. 3:7).

This dear brother went away with a happy heart. In his mind he is a full tithe payer; he has seen it in his mind. Even the visualization made him happy. He will be even happier when he and his wife actually are full tithe payers and are prepared to kneel at the altar of the temple and be sealed for time and eternity.

You can create your own faith-talk in the same way. The pattern to follow is to first ask yourself the following questions:

"What is it I am feeling?" "What is it that I want?" and "What is it that I am afraid of?"

In most cases, people who are hurting will answer from the negative, false self. "I am feeling angry, hurt, annoyed, and depressed!"

Now challenge the answer to the first question with faith-talk: "I am really, by nature, a very happy person." Next, use faith-pictures, visualizing a time when you were happy, cheerful, and optimistic. If you can't think of a time or situation when you were happy, borrow a mental picture or visualize someone you like and can identify with and superimpose that picture on yourself. Tell yourself, "That is what the real me is like." Repeat your statement and the picture many times a day.

Your false self may answer, "I want to get even, hurt back, or run away." Counter this with the following faith-talk: "I follow the counsel of the Savior and I pray for those who have harmed me. The Lord and I together are a majority. Together we are invincible. I seek to bless the lives of others in all circumstances and in all ways."

Another negative answer may be, "I am afraid that this hurting will never stop." Challenge this with, "I trust the Lord in all that I do. I am full of courage and can meet any situation. I accept all things the Lord, in his perfect wisdom, chooses not to change and that I can't change now. I know that all my losses will be made up to me in the resurrection, provided I continue to be faithful. Joseph Smith said, 'By the vision of the Almighty I have seen it.'[19] I have this promise of the Lord."

As you get into the habit of turning negatives around by faith-talk and faith-pictures, you will find that things change. One friend of mine said that "even colors change." She meant that her view of the world changed so much that even the colors of such things as flowers, trees, and the sky took on a new hue and intensity. Another insightful person worked through his patriarchal blessing and put many of the promises and counsels of the patriarch in affirmation form: "I was one of the valiant ones in the premortal life, and I am valiant here in mortality, too. I love doing missionary and genealogical work."

By making a conscious effort to detect and erase your negative self-talk and replace it with faith-talk and faith-pictures, you are making a decision to exercise your faith so that the Lord can heal you. The Lord has said, "Behold, I will tell you in your mind and in your heart, by the Holy Ghost, which shall come upon you and which shall dwell in your heart. Now, behold, this is the spirit of revelation" (D&C 8:2–3). The spirit of revelation—of light and understanding—will come to you in the solitude of your thoughts as you go to the Lord in your own sacred grove.

If you wanted to become an artist, you would need an art room to do your work. The same is true if you wanted to become a carpenter, pianist, or cook; you would need a special place to do your work. If you want to become proficient in using the healing power of faith, you will benefit from your own sacred grove. Your own sacred grove can be an actual place, or it can be a place you build in your imagination. It is a place for you to go to pray, ponder, visualize, contemplate, meditate, make decisions, solve problems, get direction from the Spirit of the Lord, and sanctify and heal yourself. It is your own sacred grove because the expression conveys feelings of sacred retreat, revelation, preciousness, safety, and refuge.

In your own sacred grove, do your faith-talk and faith-pictures. If one of your faith-talk statements is, "I am lighthearted: happy, cheerful, and optimistic," try to picture times when you have been happy. Make the picture as clear as you can. Try to visualize in your mind places, people, and circumstances in your mind when you were happy. Try to visualize color, smells, textures, etc. The more detailed the picture, the more indelible will be the neurological imprinting. Of course this is true of your false self too. You must utterly avoid creating mental pictures of things carnal, sensual, or devilish.

The imprinting of these new mental habits becomes progressively more indelible as you practice them in your thoughts, mental pictures, speech, and actions, and through your influence on others. Thinking healing thoughts through faith-talk is helpful; creating mental pictures through faith-picturing is better; speaking about our goals (bearing testimony) is still better; but acting upon them and encouraging others to participate is best yet.

We have this promise from the Lord: "Teach ye diligently and my grace shall attend you, that you may be instructed more perfectly . . . in all things that pertain unto the kingdom of God, that are expedient for you to understand" (D&C 88:78). In other words, you receive knowledge for knowledge, grace for grace. You receive the blessings of the Atonement in your life as you extend to others the blessings of the gospel. You receive knowledge as you seek to impart knowledge to others. You are healed as you seek to heal others. You are saved as you seek to save. This important gospel principle, as you give you get, is at the heart of King Benjamin's statement, "When ye are in the service of your fellow beings ye are only in the service of your God" (Mosiah 2:17). The Lord will provide you with all the resources that you need to help you as you keep his commandments and seek to bless the lives of others. One of your greatest resources to make changes will be your ability to visualize your physical, emotional, and spiritual well-being.

PICTURING YOUR HEALTH

In cooperation with professional medical help, you can do much with faith-talk affirmations and faith-picture visualizations that can help you. Dr. Carl Simonton developed a technique that has become very popular and can help you heal from the inside out. For years he has been using nontraditional methods for treating cancer patients who were diagnosed as "terminal." His approach was to ask patients who were entering his clinic for an initial consultation, "When did you decide to die?" By asking this question, he was challenging the patient's *thoughts* about death.

Dr. Simonton's basic approach is very consistent with the therapy of faith. His idea is to imagine whatever is not healthy about you as the "bad guys" and your own healthy body parts as the "good guys." Then imagine them slugging it out. The good guys always win. For example, if you have cancer cells in your body, you can see those as villains in black hats and your white blood cells as heroes in white hats. They meet and engage in a powerful battle. The battle is real. Your mental exertions give added power to the good guys. You picture them gaining more and more power. Every minute and every hour they increase in power. Although they may lose one or two battles, they always win in the end.

You can picture viruses of various kinds mutating into non-life-threatening ones. You can visualize fear as an iceberg melting in warm summer sun. If your heart is not functioning right, visualize it going through repair with little reconstructive workers who are master craftsmen.

When you develop true faith, you will be more calm, relaxed, and tranquil. It is also true that when you learn to relax, your faith-talk and faith-pictures will have greater strength in forming new habits of thinking, feeling, and acting. Take the time to learn to relax. For some reason, the neurological imprinting process is improved when our bodies are in a state of relaxation. Good times for practicing your faith-talk and faith-pictures are early in the morning and at night just before you go to sleep, while your body is relaxed.

Many times, early in the morning, while your body is at rest, or just after you have awakened and are going about routine activities, you will have ideas come to you that will help you with your pain, in your lessons, relationships, and problem solving for the day. Keep a pad of paper near so you can write phrases and draw pictures, sketches of the things that come into your mind.

Sometimes relaxation is hard for people. Nevertheless, learning to relax is a powerful tool in making healing changes. See Appendix D for a relaxation exercise that you can read to yourself on a tape recorder. Then listen to your own voice as it becomes a cue for relaxation. Play the tape over as often as you need to in order to relax. You may also want to personalize the tape by including your own faith-talk and faith-pictures that are particularly helpful to you.

The options open to your mind are endless. Never lose your imagination. Be creative. Have fun. When you learn to enjoy the process of healing, you will find that your health is more enjoyable, too. Remember, worrying is a form of atheism. Exerting yourself with faith-talk and faith-pictures is the way to health and healing. Remember that your basic aim is to change your thought, feeling, and action patterns in order to heal your soul by receiving the blessings of heaven.

WHEN DARKNESS SURROUNDS YOU

After you have had strong spiritual highs—experiences in which you have felt the Spirit of the Lord and feelings of love, beauty, happiness, joy, and knowledge—you can expect a negative spirit to try to bring you down.

After walking on water, Peter almost drowned. This process of being spiritually high and then spiritually low happens to us frequently. Some of our experiences are very intense. Some are less so.

From the life of Moses, we learn an important key that can help us control spiritual darkness when it surrounds us. The episode describing Moses' vision of God and then his encounter with Satan provides us with a pattern for protection—a key of knowledge that enables us to *command* Satan to leave us alone. The Devil has only limited control over us. Those of us who have bodies have power over those who do not. (See *Teachings*, 181, 190, 305–6.) Through knowledge of this key and through faith, we can command Satan, and the darkness and misery he brings with him will be lifted.

The powerful key God gives us to command Satan is vividly demonstrated in scripture. In vision, Moses saw God and had the heavens open unto him:

[He] beheld the world upon which he was created; and Moses beheld the world and the ends thereof, and all the children of men which are, and which were created; of the same he greatly marveled and wondered.

Satan came tempting him, saying: Moses, son of man, worship me.

And it came to pass that Moses began to fear exceedingly; and as he began to fear, he saw [felt] the bitterness of hell.

And Moses received strength, and called upon God, saying: in the name of the only begotten, depart hence, Satan.

And it came to pass that Satan cried with a loud voice, with weeping, and wailing, and gnashing of teeth; and he departed hence, even from the presence of Moses, that he beheld him not.

And now of this thing Moses bore record; but because of wickedness it is not had among the children of men. (Moses 1:8, 12, 20–23)

Here we have the key that can dispel the powers of darkness and depression in our lives. *We can command in the name of Jesus that Satan leave us, and Satan must go!* As he leaves, our bodies, spirits, and emotions feel lighter. We experience a lifting sensation much like clouds lifting after a heavy storm, and we feel a sense of liberation and gratitude for our deliverance. We breathe easier.

Sometimes you may feel overwhelmed by the bitterness of hell. Darkness, loneliness, hopelessness, pain, and abandonment all seem to blend into a black hole, and there seems to be no way out. The "very jaws of hell [seem to] gape open their mouth wide after thee," and you forget for a time that you are still loved of the Lord and that all these things shall give you experience and be for your good—and that the Son of Man hath descended below them all. (See D&C 122:7–8.)

I have found the key offered in this scripture to be true and powerful. Because we love the Lord and *desire* to keep his commandments—it is not required that we have been perfect—we are authorized to use his name and power to dispel darkness. The Lord judges us according to our works, according to the desire of our hearts. (See D&C 137:9.) If we have a broken heart and a contrite spirit, we can exercise this key and have marvelous deliverance.

I have found the following faith-talk statements to be very powerful in dispelling the powers of darkness. You may just say them in your mind, and they are effective. You may say them aloud, when alone, with powerful results. As you say them, form faith-pictures of what you are saying. Faith-talk and faith-picturing are particularly powerful to use as you take the sacrament or when you are in the temple—in addition to your private times alone.

In the name of Jesus Christ, I command you, Satan, and all your hosts to leave this room, this house, and this property and never return.

I choose to worship Jesus Christ, the Son of the living God. Him alone will I love and serve.

I love Jesus Christ. He alone is God's almighty Son. My commitment is to him and him alone. He is my Savior, My Redeemer, my Great Deliverer.

I consecrate my time, my talents, and everything I have to the Lord Jesus Christ. I would give my life for him if I were asked. With every breath I take, I live for him and him alone.

In the name of the Only Begotten Son, even Jesus Christ—whom I love and serve—I command you, Satan, to leave my presence and take your evil influence with you.

These and other faith-talk statements that will come to you will give you great power over Satan. You will feel him leave, and you will be at peace. You will feel the love of God return to your mind and heart. We have the power to bind Satan. With these keys of knowledge and faith, we have power over him and can dispel the darkness around us. Through the use of these keys, Satan will be bound by the righteousness of the people. As Nephi described our day, he explained:

> And because of the righteousness of his people, Satan has no power; wherefore, he cannot be loosed for the space of many years; for he hath no power over the hearts of the people, for they dwell in righteousness, and the Holy One of Israel reigneth. (1 Ne. 22:26)

After Moses cast Satan out, the account continues:

> And it came to pass that when Satan had departed from the presence of Moses, that Moses lifted up his eyes unto heaven, being filled with the Holy Ghost, which beareth record of the Father and the Son; and calling upon the name of God, he beheld his glory again, for it was upon him; and he heard a voice saying, . . . lo, I am with thee, even unto the end of thy days. (Moses 1:24–26)

As it was with Moses, so shall it be with you, as you exercise your keys of knowledge and power—faith-talk and faith-pictures—to bind Satan now.

NOTES

1. McWilliams, *Negative Thought,* 242.
2. Dallin H. Oaks, regional fireside given at the Cannon Activities Center in Laie, Hawaii, 13 January 1992.
3. N. B. Lundwall, *Faith Like the Ancients* (Salt Lake City: N. B. Lundwall, 1950), 63.
4. Viktor Frankl, *Man's Search For Meaning* (New York: Pocket Books, 1963), 104–5.
5. Boyd K. Packer, "Little Children," *Ensign* (November 1986), 17.
6. Dew, *Ezra Taft Benson,* 107.
7. *Teachings,* 51.
8. Helmsettler, *What to Say,* 86–87.
9. McWilliams, *Negative Thought,* 578.
10. David O. McKay, *Gospel Ideals* (Salt Lake City: Deseret Book, 1976), 382.
11. McWilliams, *Negative Thought,* 498.
12. Richard G. Scott, *Conference Reports,* October 1989, 38.
13. Dew, *Ezra Taft Benson,* 202–3.
14. Pratt, *Key to Theology,* 160–61.
15. See also Hel. 10:6.
16. *Teachings,* p. 51.
17. Neal A. Maxwell, "Patience," *Ensign,* November 1979, 28–31.
18. Boyd K. Packer, "Free Agency and Obedience" in *Teachings of the Living Prophets,* Student Manual for Religion 333 (Salt Lake City: The Church of Jesus Christ of Latter-day Saints, 1982), 44–45.
19. *Teachings,* 296.

9

Focusing Your Faith on Correct Principles

I am the way, the truth, and the life.
—John 14:6

In earlier chapters we discussed how your feelings come from your thoughts: when you control your thoughts, you control your feelings and your actions. This chapter presents a potpourri of principles upon which you can focus your thoughts, feelings, and actions. These selected principles have helped many people find the healing grace and peace they have so earnestly sought.

You may not benefit equally from each principle. Rather, scan each principle and then focus on those that will be most helpful to you personally. Once you select individual principles, it is important to affirm their truthfulness in your own mind and heart by using them as affirmations and visualizations—faith-talk and faith-pictures. I have provided basic faith-talk statements for each heading.

As you study these principles, write down these faith-talk statements, along with those of your own creation, and repeat them over and over. As you do your faith-picturing, it is important to vividly visualize yourself involved with the principle. Where are you? What are you doing? What do you see? Hear? Smell? Remember that your mind programs your brain, and your brain controls your robot-like body. You make changes by the thoughts (or principles) you think about.

REVELATION PRECEDES FAITH

I know that I must have knowledge of Christ before I can have faith in him.

Before you can exert faith in the Lord Jesus Christ, you must have correct information about him. Information precedes faith. The more knowledge you have about the Savior and your own inner power to make changes, the more faith you will develop and the more control you will have over your life. An example of how knowledge must precede faith is found in the following story.

A young woman named Rhonda, a returned missionary, had been active in the Church all her adult life. She was recently disfellowshipped for fornication and was referred to me for counseling and therapy because, as her bishop said, "She wants to repent but feels no guilt or shame for her immorality, but she has continuous headaches."

Rhonda was a willing participant in the therapy sessions. When I introduced her to the thought-feeling-action pyramid, she readily recognized the interconnectedness of the three areas. Therapy for her was a process of helping her evaluate her thought processes—her beliefs, values, and knowledge of gospel principles—and see connections between her thoughts, feelings, and immoral behavior. Continued sessions revealed certain vacancies in her understanding of gospel principles, particularly regarding her temple covenants. Because of her lack of knowledge, Rhonda was vulnerable, and she simply followed her feelings, which eventually led to her immorality. Helping her gain a more accurate knowledge of the gospel principles and her temple covenants helped her become more integrated or connected in her thoughts, feelings, and actions. Rhonda's headaches eventually left her. As her faith and self-esteem increased, she gained a stronger hope in Christ. Rhonda made progress as she was able to receive and integrate light and truth. This is a form of receiving and utilizing revelation.

President J. Reuben Clark said that revelation is the *sine qua non* of the gospel—without which there is nothing. Joseph Smith said, "We never can comprehend the things of God and of heaven, but by revelation."[1] He also explained that "no man can receive the Holy Ghost without receiving revelations. The Holy Ghost is a revelator."[2] Revelation is food for the soul. Physical food causes us to grow in our youth and maintains our health in our adulthood.

Can you imagine going two or three days without eating and not getting hungry? After just a few hours, your body sends signals prompting you to eat. As time goes by, your body's call for food becomes louder and louder. Just as our physical bodies need to be fed physical food, our spirits need spiritual nourishment. We not only need to regularly feed both our physical and spiritual selves, but we also need to be selective in the quality of the food we choose. A common statement holds, "We are what we eat." In a similar way, "We are what we think about." Exerting ourselves with faith-talk and faith-pictures—expressing both faith in the Lord Jesus Christ and in our real self—provides spiritual nourishment and blesses us in both body and spirit. In our own thinking, we want to become one with God so we can receive of his healing power.

To be truly blessed of the Lord, you need to pray that your thoughts will be his thoughts, that your feelings will be his feelings, and that you may act as he would act if he were in your situation. "Salvation cannot come without revelation," declared the Prophet Joseph Smith.[3] This is because we need revelation (knowledge) to know how to detach ourselves from the strong negative influences around us that can affect our brains and bodies in destructive ways.

You need revelation to learn how to empower your real self. Just as microwave ovens, televisions, and CD players need electricity to function, so we need the Spirit of the Lord to enliven and empower us. Without his Spirit we are less than empty shells; we are vulnerable to Satan and his angels. Without the spirit of revelation, without the Atonement, we would be without hope in this life and become devils ourselves in the spirit world; the influence of Satan is that strong. (See 2 Ne. 9:9.) However, with revelation from God we can overcome the power of Satan.

It is the privilege of every member of the Church to receive knowledge through revelation. President Joseph F. Smith has explained:

> The spirit of inspiration, the gift of revelation, does not belong to one man solely; it is not a gift that pertains to the Presidency of the Church and the Twelve Apostles alone. It is not confined to the presiding authorities of the Church, it belongs to every individual member of the Church; and it is the right and privilege of every man, every woman, and every child who has reached the years of accountability, to enjoy the spirit of revelation, and to be possessed of the spirit of inspiration in the discharge of their duties as members of the Church. It is the privilege of every individual member

of the Church to have revelation for his own guidance, for the direction of his life and conduct.[4]

It is vital that we learn how to receive and recognize revelation. The Prophet Joseph Smith taught us how to recognize revelation:

> A person may profit by noticing the first intimation of the spirit of revelation; for instance, when you feel pure intelligence flowing into you, it may give you sudden strokes of ideas, so that by noticing it, you may find it fulfilled the same day or soon; (i.e.) those things that were presented unto your minds by the Spirit of God, will come to pass; and thus by learning the Spirit of God and understanding it, you may grow into the principle of revelation, until you become perfect in Christ Jesus."[5]

Knowledge born of the Spirit, sudden strokes of ideas, enables you to know the mind and will of the Savior. It allows you to get a glimpse of your life through his eyes. From this vantage point, you see what needs to be done and do it far better than you could on your own. Elder Richard G. Scott explained:

> Our Heavenly Father did not put us on earth to fail but to succeed gloriously. It may seem paradoxical, but that is why recognizing answers to prayer can sometimes be very difficult. Some face life with only their own experience and capacity to help them. Others seek, through prayer, divine inspiration to know what to do. When it is required, they qualify for power beyond their own capacity to do it.
>
> Communication with our Father in Heaven is not a trivial matter. It is a sacred privilege. It is based on unchanging principles. When we receive help from our Father in Heaven, it is in response to faith, obedience, and the proper use of agency.
>
> It is a mistake to assume that every prayer we offer will be answered immediately. Some prayers require considerable effort on our part. True, sometimes impressions come when we have not specifically sought them. They generally concern something we need to know and are not otherwise able to find out.[6]

Elder Boyd K. Packer described how the Spirit communicates with us:

> The Spirit does not get our attention by shouting or shaking us with a heavy hand. Rather it whispers. It caresses so gently that if we are preoccupied we may not feel it all. . . . Occasionally it will press just firmly enough for us to pay heed. But most of the time, if we do not heed the gentle feeling, the Spirit will withdraw and wait until we come seeking and listening.[7]

Of all the knowledge that the Holy Spirit may reveal to you, the knowledge that you are literally a child of God is probably the most powerful in bringing about healing change through faith-talk and faith-pictures. Trusting the Lord brings feelings of love and acceptance from the Spirit. You are loved. You do matter to our Father. Isaiah reminds us, "Can a woman forget her sucking child, that she should not have compassion on the son of her womb? yea, they may forget, yet I will not forget thee. Behold, I have graven thee upon the palms of my hands; thy walls are continually before me" (Isa. 49:15–16). The Lord will not desert you. He will remember you as you seek a correct knowledge of him and how he will bless you.

Because you are loved by your Heavenly Father, you can receive knowledge that may lead you to those who have the gift of healing; or you may be directed to competent medical practitioners. Sometimes your pain may have a physical basis. If such is the case, you may need medical attention. However, reliable data states that only about five percent of depression illnesses are primarily physiologically based, except among the aged. Physiologically based depression is referred to as "endogenous," meaning simply "from within." In these cases of depression the individual experiences an imbalance of chemicals in the brain that affect the entire physical system in such a way as to produce a major depression with all its concomitant symptoms. The important point to remember concerning endogenous depressions is that they have absolutely nothing to do with whether you are a good Mormon living the commandments. A person with this type of depression has an illness just as we have any other physical illnesses. Again, only about five percent of depressive illnesses are physiologically based.

Faith in Christ gives us authority over our false self. When we have faith in him, he empowers us to have dominion over our false self. This authority comes by knowledge—both that which we receive here as new knowledge and that which our real self remembers from our pre-existent past. When we have faith in Christ, he parts the veil for a moment and gives us the power and authority to access and use knowledge that we gained in our premortal sphere. We remember truths we once knew but forgot when we passed through the veil into mortality. The more we grow in faith, the more the Savior empowers us with this and other knowledge until we receive a fullness and become one with him and in him.

OBEDIENCE AND FREEDOM

Because I know and am obedient to the principles and ordinances of the gospel, I enjoy peace in this life.

Obedience does indeed determine the degree to which you will be able to cope with the challenges and stresses of your life. Elder Bruce R. McConkie, a man of great faith, said, "Faith is a gift of God bestowed as a reward for personal righteousness. It is always given when righteousness is present, and the greater the measure of obedience to God's laws the greater will be the endowment of faith."[8] In other words, the level of obedience to the laws and ordinances of the gospel determines the strength of our faith in the Lord Jesus Christ.

Elder Boyd K. Packer has explained that blessings of which we can hardly dream come into our lives when we willingly seek and obey the will of God.

> Some say that obedience nullifies agency. I would like to point out that obedience is a righteous principle. . . .
>
> Obedience to God can be the very highest expression of independence. Just think of giving to him the one thing, the one gift, that he would never take. Think of giving him that one thing that he would never wrest from you. You know these lines of the poet:
>
> > *Know this, that every soul is free*
> > *To choose his life and what he'll be,*
> > *For this eternal truth is given*
> > *That God will force no man to heav'n.*
> >
> > *He'll call, persuade, direct aright,*
> > *And bless with wisdom, love, and light,*
> > *In nameless ways be good and kind,*
> > *But never force the human mind.*[9]
>
> Obedience—that which God would never take by force—he will gladly accept when freely given. And he will then return to you freedom that you can hardly dream of—the freedom to feel and to know, the freedom to do, and the freedom to be, at least a thousandfold more than we offer him. Strangely enough, the key to freedom is obedience.[10]

"If ye are prepared ye shall not fear" (D&C 38:30). If we are obedient, we will prepare ourselves for what will come. Whether we are speaking of destructions in the last days by way of war, calamity, or fire, or the emotional trauma associated with circumstances of our environment, we have the promise that if we are prepared, we have no need to fear. How do you know if you are prepared? Who has the answer? Could it be that if you are afraid of the past, the present, or the future, you are not sufficiently prepared? How do you prepare then? By gaining further light and knowledge, and by living what has been given. Preparation is living what we presently know to be true.

If you do not live up to your covenants, Satan has great power over you. The following story illustrates this principle. A few years ago, a young elder went to his bishop because his mother-in-law continued to call him on the telephone and wanted him to come to her home and give her a blessing to cast out evil spirits. He was reluctant to do this because it happened so frequently, and because the mother-in-law had a man living with her outside the bonds of marriage. She knew she was not keeping her temple covenants, but she still wanted the priesthood blessings to save her from Satan. The bishop suggested to the elder that he encourage his mother-in-law to honor her covenants and to tell her that if she does not, she will continue to be in Satan's power no matter how many priesthood blessings she receives. Truly, if we are prepared by living the gospel covenants, we need not fear the power of Satan in our lives or the physical calamities that may come upon the wicked.

As you keep your covenants, you are showing your Heavenly Father that you love him and that he can trust you to keep your commitments with him. When we are obedient, the Lord reveals great and glorious truths that both strengthen and deliver us from fear and the calamities of the last days.

GAINING THE TRUST OF THE LORD

I am successful because the Lord trusts me!

The most important success in this life is gaining the trust of the Lord. Sometimes people get depressed because they cannot win the love and respect of people they consider important. Your most important success will be quietly gaining the trust of your Heavenly Father. The Prophet Joseph Smith explained the great blessing that can come to you when you do gain the trust of God. He explained that "when the Lord has thoroughly proved [you] and finds that [you are] determined to serve Him at all hazards, then [you] will find [your] calling and [your] election made sure, then it will be [your] privilege to receive the other Comforter, which the Lord hath promised the Saints."[11]

Although these blessings are the crowning blessings that come after a life of service and devotion, it is important that we ponder them, for "when there is no vision, the people perish" (Prov. 29:18). These lofty blessings come independently of your vocation, money, or worldly status. They are not independent, however, of *how* you perform your labors.

As you gain experience in that private and personal world with God, you will become less dependent upon the approval of others for your sense of personal worth. You will then come to understand what Hugh Nibley meant when he said,

> I have always been furiously active in the church, but I have . . . never held an office or rank in anything; I have undertaken many assignments given me by the leaders of the Church, and much of the work has been anonymous. No rank, no recognition, no anything. While I have been commended for some things, they were never the things which I considered most important—that was entirely a little understanding between me and my Heavenly Father, which I have thoroughly enjoyed, though no one else knows anything about it.[12]

Quietly gaining the trust of the Lord can give you a new perspective on your life. Among the comforting truths that he may reveal to you, may be his purposes behind the adversities you face as you seek to obey the commandments.

CHOOSING TO ACT

I choose to unlock the healing power of faith every day of my life.

You have read much that can help you unlock the healing power of faith, but until you choose to act, this information cannot bring you what you want and need. W. H. Murray has stressed the importance of deciding to decide in a beautiful narrative written in connection with the Scottish Himalayan Expedition.

> Until one is committed, there is hesitancy, the chance to draw back, always ineffectiveness. Concerning all acts of initiative (and creation) there is one elementary truth, the ignorance of which kills countless ideas and splendid plans: That the moment one definitely commits oneself, then Providence

moves too. All sorts of things occur to help one that would never otherwise have occurred. A whole stream of events issues from the decision, raising in one's favor all manner of unforeseen incidents and meetings and material assistance, which no man could have dreamed would have come his way. I have learned a deep respect for one of Goethe's couplets: "Whatever you can do, or dream you can, begin it. Boldness has genius, power and magic in it.[13]

Deciding to decide about worthy actions opens the doors of the heavens; and blessings are then, and only then, poured out in ways that to us were incomprehensible and unimaginable. It is the willingness to do, however, that creates the ability to do! There are some times, however, when "the spirit indeed is willing, but the flesh is weak" (Matt. 26:41). In such times, choosing to have a sense of humor and learning to laugh are important ingredients in strengthening your real self. The choice is yours.

ACCOUNTABILITY

I am accountable and responsible for my thoughts, feelings, and actions.

You are accountable for what goes on inside of you. No blame allowed! If you are angry with someone for something, they did not cause your anger. The anger is inside of you. For example, if you squeeze an orange, orange juice comes out. Do you know why? Because that is what is inside. If you squeeze a person and anger comes out, do you know why? Because that is what is inside. The external pressure with which a person is provoked did not create the anger. Anger came out because the person had learned the anger mechanism, a false comforter, to deal with pressure. Anything that has been learned, however, can be unlearned, remolded, or reshaped for the present. The first step in relearning is to stop blaming others for what is really inside of you. You are accountable for your own thoughts, feelings, and actions. If you are going to blame others for your failures, it's a good idea to credit others for your successes.

George Bernard Shaw said that "people are always blaming their circumstances for what they are. I don't believe in circumstances. The people who get on in this world are the people who get up and look for the circumstances they want, and, if they can't find them, make them."[14] In other words, they take responsibility for their own growth and do something about it instead of just waiting for something or someone else to make them grow. They take charge of their own lives and make things happen. Children and immature adults blame other people and circumstances for the bad things that happen to them. Their language reflects their blame. For example, when children drop a cup and it breaks, they will sometimes say, "*It* dropped out of my hand," or when they cut themselves with a knife, "The *knife* slipped and cut me."

Innocent expressions? Yes, I suppose, for children. But when we become adults, we need to take the responsibility: "I dropped the cup," "I cut myself." We need to own what happened instead of attributing our mistakes and problems to others or to inanimate objects. You are more accountable for creating, allowing, or promoting what happens to you than you may ordinarily think.

In 1890, William James roused himself from a prolonged depression with the realization that he had the freedom to choose between one thought and another. When this freedom is recognized and you come to know that you are independent of any and all external circumstances, then the evil of bondage, criticism, anxiety, and death itself, fades rapidly. This freedom is within you and is a part of you as a being of light and truth. This is the gift of free agency. The ability to make choices is a gift from God but also is a part of your divine nature. Responsibility for choices wasn't just "tacked on" to free agency as an annoyance but is a fundamental part of agency. It allows you to grow and progress.

This principle of accountability is best illustrated during the life of Christ. The Savior could easily have blamed others for the pain and suffering he endured at Calvary. Instead, while tormented and taunted on the cross, Jesus prayed to the Father for those who nailed him there, "Father, forgive them; for they know not what they do" (Luke 23:34).

We also find this principle exemplified in the life of Joseph Smith. He chose to feel peace instead of anger toward those who he knew would kill him. When the Prophet "went to Carthage to deliver himself up to the pretended requirement of the law, two or three days previous to his assassination, he said: 'I am going like a lamb to the slaughter; but I am calm as a summer's morning; I have a conscience void of offense towards God, and towards all men'" (D&C 135:4).

As the Mormon pioneers crossed the plains, they sang songs of optimism in spite of hardship. Perhaps the best known is

"Come, Come, Ye Saints." It reflects their choice to trust the Lord no matter what.

> And should we die, before our journey's through,
> Happy day! All is well!
> We then are free from toil and sorrow, too;
> With the just we shall dwell!
> But if our lives are spared again
> To see the Saints their rest obtain,
> Oh, How we'll make this chorus swell—
> All is well! All is well!15

Though their challenges were great, these faithful Saints trusted the Lord, submitted to his will, and accepted the responsibility for their own actions.

GUARD YOUR THOUGHTS

Things are not the way I think they are, but however I think, they are.

You create the world you live in by the thoughts you think. You subjectively interpret the world you see. You choose to see the bucket half full or half empty. If you choose the former, you are happier than if you choose the latter. This principle is all pervasive. You even create your own self-image by the way you choose to think about yourself. Your feelings about your spouse are connected with how and what you think about your spouse. This is also true about how you view your children and other significant people in your life—and even how you view your relationship with the Lord. All these are a consequence of your choice of thoughts. As you choose to think, you choose to feel and act. You do not create *objective* reality by your choice of thoughts, but you do create your own *subjective* interpretation of the world—the world from your point of view.

Since we as human beings are such social creatures, we are greatly affected by the thoughts, feelings, and actions of those around us. The closer the associations, the more profound the impact we have on each other. Parents have great influence on their children, as do peers upon their associates.

The gospel provides directions and patterns for influencing each other. When we learn of the gospel, we want to share it with others.

When we receive the blessings of healing and deliverance, we want to share these thoughts with others so they can grow too. As we have been fed, we want to feed others.

However, thoughts that are not fed will not grow. We may feel at times that God has deserted us, that he has cast us aside, and that is why we may cling so desperately at times to carnal things. But if we stop thinking such thoughts, what we refuse to feed will die. By not supporting negatives, we let them quietly go down to their grave where they belong. Even as weeds die without water, soil, and sun to sustain them, so will negative thoughts die if we do not feed them. We can spurn our false self's appetite for anger, discontent, impatience, fear, and lack of faith. We can let go of contention, resentment, and guilt. We can release the grip of negative thinking, and we will find light and truth—even joy. We can concentrate on the good within us. There is so much more to love about us than there is to hate.

The Lord loves us and he wants to help us. He is calling us to return to him, to come unto him for support and strength. "Yea, for thus saith the Lord: Have I put thee away, or have I cast thee off forever? For thus saith the Lord: Where is the bill of your mother's divorcement? To whom have I put thee away, or to which of my creditors have I sold you? . . . O house of Israel, is my hand shortened at all that it cannot redeem, or have I no power to deliver?" (2 Ne. 7:1–2). The Lord has not forsaken us, but we must guard our thoughts as we guard our very lives. We truly do become what we think about.

DIVINE DISCONTENT

I look forward to a better world, but I accomplish what needs to be done now.

Unless your unhappiness immobilizes you and keeps you from doing what the Lord wants you to do, your longings may merely reflect a "divine discontent." Your Heavenly Father does not expect you to find a fullness of happiness in this transitory life. You are not expected to settle in and accommodate the fallen conditions of this world. Sometimes your yearnings reflect a healthy discontent, a godly desire for a bright future and a glorious heavenly home amid loving family and friends. It is good and proper to consider these nostalgic feelings and yearnings as gifts of the Spirit. Even the ancient prophets and Saints confessed that they were "strangers and pilgrims" in this mortal and fallen world. (See Heb. 11:13; D&C 45:13.) Their faith and hope were centered on higher levels: "They desire a better country, that is, an heavenly: wherefore God is not ashamed to be called their God: for he hath prepared for them a city" (Heb. 11:16). This life is to be seen as a temporary schooling. But you will not be here forever. The pathway to peace in this life and the way back to your heavenly home have been prepared by your Lord and Savior, Jesus Christ.

When the Apostle Thomas asked Jesus how he could know the way to the peace promised by the Savior, Jesus patiently reminded him that "I am the way, the truth, and the life: no man cometh unto the Father, but by me" (John 14:6). Jesus will lead us to a better world— one free from sin, disease, death, and contention. But we have work to do now before we can go home.

WITH HIS STRIPES YOU ARE HEALED

Jesus is keenly aware of my suffering and will heal me and make all things right.

None of us can find true peace in this life, nor eternal life in the world to come, without a knowledge of both Jesus and the principles of truth he and his apostles taught. In our own dispensation, the dispensation of the fulness of times, we are instructed that the word of God, a knowledge of the true Savior, will come through the Prophet Joseph Smith. (See D&C 5:10.)

From the Prophet Joseph, we learn that we do not have to be perfect to be loved and blessed of the Lord. The gifts of the Spirit, including the gift of healing, are given to all those who love him and keep all his commandments, *and to those who seek so to do* (D&C 46:9).

"Surely he hath borne our griefs, and carried our sorrows . . . and with his stripes we are healed" (Isa. 53:4–5). There is no suffering that you can experience that Christ does not comprehend, nothing in which he cannot succor you. In connection with the depth and the reason for Christ's own suffering, we read that

> He will take upon him death, that he may loose the bands of death which bind his people; and he will take upon him their infirmities, that his bowels may be filled with mercy, according to the flesh, that he may know

according to the flesh how to succor his people according to their infirmities. (Alma 7:12)

Truly, Christ descended below all things that he might comprehend all things and succor us in our sorrow. (See D&C 88:6.) Elder Neal A. Maxwell offers this insight into Christ's empathy for us:

> I testify that He is utterly incomparable in what He is, what He knows, what He has accomplished, and what He has experienced. Yet movingly, He calls us His friends.
>
> Indeed, we cannot teach Him anything, but we can listen to Him, we can love Him, we can honor Him, we can worship Him! We can keep His commandments, and we who are so forgetful and even rebellious are never forgotten by Him! We are His "work" and His "glory" and He is never distracted.[16]

Because the Savior knows and understands your pain, he can succor you in your afflictions and help you as you travel the pathway that leads you home. The gospel is the pathway of happiness. The Savior himself declared, "I am come that they might have life, and that they might have it more abundantly" (John 10:10). From the Book of Mormon we read, "Adam fell that men might be; and men are, that they might have joy" (2 Ne. 2:25). The Prophet Joseph Smith explained that "Happiness is the object and design of our existence; and will be the end thereof, if we pursue the path that leads to it; and this path is virtue, uprightness, faithfulness, holiness, and keeping all the commandments of God."[17] Alma explained to his son Helaman, that "whosoever shall put their trust in God shall be supported in their trials, and their troubles, and their afflictions, and shall be lifted up at the last day" (Alma 36:3). Even as the Liahona directed the Nephites to their promised land, so "shall the words of Christ, if [you] follow their course, carry [you] beyond this vale of sorrow into a far better land of promise" (Alma 37:45). These statements all point to one thing: you can find peace. By keeping the commandments, you qualify to receive your Heavenly Father's mercy.

We prosper as we love the Lord and keep his commandments. The Lord is there for you when you need him. You may not always see him and may not prosper in the way you think you should, but you will prosper in the most important ways—the Lord will perform little miracles in your life that make a big difference. When you trust in the Lord, he will be with you and bring you peace.

SEEKING PRIESTHOOD BLESSINGS

I have the faith to ask for and receive priesthood blessings.

You can receive healing powers and gain an understanding of the Lord's will for you from many sources—the scriptures, answers to prayers, and especially priesthood blessings. These holy blessings can help you draw upon the healing powers of heaven. The scriptures teach and testify of the gift to heal and be healed.

> And whosoever among you are sick, and have not faith to be healed, but believe, shall be nourished with all tenderness, with herbs and mild food, and that not by the hand of an enemy. And the elders of the church, two or more, shall be called, and shall pray for and lay their hands upon them in my name; and if they die they shall die unto me, and if they live they shall live unto me. . . . And again, it shall come to pass that he that hath faith in me to be healed, and is not appointed unto death, shall be healed (D&C 42:43–44, 48).

Priesthood blessings are powerful sources available to the faithful Saint who is seeking peace, direction, and understanding. Remember that such blessings are not a substitute for repentance and the learning of principles involved in mental and physical health. When is it appropriate to seek a priesthood blessing? The answer to that question is whenever you desire one.

ATTENDING THE TEMPLE

The temple—the house of the Lord—is a place where I find answers to my prayers.

I have a young friend, a former student, who experienced chronic depression and suicidal feelings resulting from a very unstable home life. She responded cautiously to my outreach and gradually stabilized her life and accepted a mission call. After receiving the temple endowment, she wrote to me of the impact her temple experience had on her:

> [The] night was so beautiful! I feel so strangely comforted now; whenever I look in the mirror I see me but it's not me—do you understand? I think differently now, I feel differently, I see things differently, hear, taste, touch, speak, etc. . . .
> Talk about being weird—I have this urge to go up to everyone I meet and give them hugs. This is something I have never seen in me before . . . Is it normal? . . .

I will say this much, the way I'm feeling is the way I have always wanted to feel—I have felt it in dreams and in unseen visions. When I say
unseen visions I mean that I have had times where I'll be pondering over
things and I will get this beautiful feeling come over me and, at the same
time, I know that if I turn and look behind me I'll see something that isn't
on this earth—like Zion. I've had that happen and it was so neat! I never
turned around to confirm it but I know it was there. . . . I could see it in
my mind and it was Heaven!

This sister was able to get faith-pictures as a result of her temple
experience. The Lord established his house so that you and I could be
endowed with such power from on high and be prepared for additional things which are to come.

YOUR RESPONSIBILITY FOR OTHERS

*I am at peace because I teach others all I can and then allow
them to exercise free agency and choose for themselves.*

Do you have wayward children? Do you have parents who are not
keeping the commandments? Do you worry about what you could do
to help them? If you do, remember that our Heavenly Father and the
prophet Lehi both had children who were wayward. Each mourned
his loss, but they did not get depressed to the point that they were
immobilized by their grief.

God does not hold you responsible for the foolish choices made by
others because you do not have full control over their lives. When I first
encountered this principle, I felt the professor who introduced it to me
was "copping out." He said in class one day, "I'll accept complete
responsibility for my wayward child when I have complete control over
his life." I had been taught all my life that I was to be a good parent and
that a good parent is responsible for the actions of his children, that a
bishop is responsible for the welfare of his ward, and that missionaries
are responsible for the conversion of every soul in their assigned area.
This emphasis on responsibility is not totally accurate. For instance, I
sometimes hear scriptures quoted to stress our responsibility toward
others. In the dialogue between God and Cain, Cain asked smugly, "Am
I my brother's keeper?" The answer to that question is probably no, or
Cain would not have asked it. We are not our brother's *keeper*, but we
are our brother's *brother*. We may not have the power to cage and keep
our brother and thus be totally responsible for his thoughts, feelings,

and actions, but we do have the responsibility to teach him and testify to him. However, we are never required to force our will on another human being. Force not only alienates them from us, but violates the basic law of the gospel—free agency.

Jacob explained our responsibility: "Now, my beloved brethren, I, Jacob, according to the responsibility which I am under to God, to magnify mine office with soberness, and that I might rid my garments of your sins, I come up into the temple this day that I might declare unto you the word of God" (Jacob 2:2). Jacob's responsibility was to declare the word; it was not to *make* his hearers repent.

I have heard some parents declare, "But if I don't *force* my children to be good, how I can I *make* them behave?" The answer is that we are to follow the example of the Savior as we work with others. He never used handcuffs, as it were, to force men to follow him. He used spiritual magnets to attract others. He attracted them, and us, through promises and covenants. All covenants are entered into voluntarily or not at all. Even if the choice were covenant or die, there is still a choice. Because covenants and promises preserve agency and bring power and happiness, they are a means of drawing us to Christ. He said, "My sheep will hear my voice" (John 10:27). He called, and they came. He never used dogs to round up his sheep, as a sheepherder does. He was the "Good Shepherd." Too often, in our attempt to rid ourselves of guilt when others do not heed our counsel, we are tempted to call out the dogs and make them obey. This is the wrong spirit and can provoke others to reject not only us, but our values as well. It is well to remember the statement by Joseph Smith, "I teach them correct principles and they govern themselves."[18]

Sometimes we are remiss in teaching correct principles. Sometimes we are reluctant to let them govern themselves. At other times we are too prone to beg others to follow our counsel: "Please, won't you do as I say?" Or as some misdirected missionaries may say, "Please, won't you join my true church?"

Discipleship of truth is demanding, and great responsibility is placed upon the hearers of truth. They must ask in order to receive. They must knock and it will be opened unto them. In order for others to grow, you must be willing to give them the opportunity to learn for themselves. This includes being willing to allow them to make mistakes. Don't be too quick to ask and knock for others—taking away their rights of choice—thus violating irrevocable laws of personal growth. The mistakes of others bother us because they show our own weaknesses. Not allowing others to learn from their mistakes not only stunts their growth, it stunts our growth as well.

Though it may be difficult, especially with those who are very important to you, you must sometimes be willing to let go and allow them to be free so that they can grow. For your happiness and theirs, you must deliberately plan to detach sufficiently to leave their agency and your peace intact. As the well-known saying goes, "Happiness is like a butterfly. The more you chase it, the more it eludes you. But if you turn your attention to other things, it comes and sits softly on your shoulder." So it is with interpersonal relationships. The more you try to force compliance to your wishes, the more you create resistance.

THE PRINCIPLE OF LEAST INTEREST

The one who cares the least has the most power.

Willard Waller coined the expression of "the principle of least interest."[19] This interesting principle is relevant to almost all interpersonal relationships. The person who is least interested has the most power. For example, whoever has the least interest (ego investment, financial investment, time investment, energy investment, identity investment) in maintaining a relationship has the most power and control in that relationship. The person who loves less, cares less, or is attracted less will be in a position to exercise greater control. If a person who is fiercely independent is married to a dependent and submissive mate, the independent mate will probably need the relationship less and hence will be in a position to dominate or control the partner.

A sister visited my office complaining of her boyfriend's lack of respect for her. He was critical of the way she dressed, expressed herself, used makeup. Generally she could do nothing to please him. He made light of her wants and needs for open and safe communication. They could not agree on many issues such as goals and use of time. He was very condescending toward her, and she found herself trying harder and harder to make him happy—all to no avail. When I asked her why she stayed in the relationship, she had no real answer. She seemed to understand when I asked her if she stayed because she was worried she may not find another boyfriend. When I explained to her the principle of least interest, she quickly saw how she had allowed herself to be controlled by her boyfriend. She was caring too much in unhealthy ways. She could see that if she were to stay in the relationship, she would need to plan more indifference and let him take more initiative.

Another of my students complained of a similar problem. She, too, had problems with people intimidating and controlling her. The harder she tried to work at relationships with men, the worse things seemed to get. A boy she had been dating for two years was now backing off and was not showing the same commitment he had earlier. Her nature was to run after him and almost beg him to continue the relationship. Marriage was feverishly on her mind. When I suggested to her that she back off and give him some space, she was threatened, thinking that if she did that, she would certainly lose him. But as I explained to her the logic of vicious cycles and the principle of least interest, she decided to give it a try. Logically, it made sense to her, but emotionally she struggled with her feelings. It is difficult for people who have invested a lifetime in "caring the most" to learn a better balance. Sometimes, in order to establish better relationships, it is important that you choose to be less interested than you have been in the past. This does not mean that you are not sensitive to the needs of others, it just means that you are learning to be more wise.

DON'T COMPARE YOURSELF TO OTHERS

I accept and build on the choices I have made.

Much stress and unneeded anxiety can be avoided when we stop looking back, comparing ourselves to others, and wishing that we had made other choices; therefore, it is important that you avoid choice comparisons. Each of us makes choices as we go through life. Some of us decide to become medical doctors, some choose a business career. Still others choose to be teachers or writers. Some women opt to become wives and choose motherhood as a career. We should not compare ourselves with others who have made different choices. Such comparisons only hurt us. You should not feel remorse that you are not like others who have become great musicians or champion chess players; you have spent your time and energies in other areas and have developed other gifts. Sometimes when you compare yourself to others, you don't look at the decisions you have made as much as you look at the power, position, or prestige that did or did not come as a result of your choices. These comparisons lead to a greater vice—that of competition.

COOPERATION INSTEAD OF COMPETITION

I accomplish more good through cooperation than through competition.

The rewards that contribute most to personal and interpersonal fulfillment are pride in accomplishment, fulfillment in task completion, joy in fine craftsmanship, feelings of contributing to the success of the whole community, harmony with the environment, and communion with the infinite. However, there seems to be an increase in our competitiveness and a decrease in our generosity with one another. Too many of us are struggling and suffering, too many are running faster than we have strength, expecting too much of ourselves. As a result, we are experiencing new and undiagnosed stress-related illnesses. The Epstein-Barr virus, for one, has come into our popular medical jargon as the malady of the times. "The victims are plagued by low-grade fevers, aching joints, and sometimes a sore throat—but they don't have the flu. They're overwhelmingly exhausted, weak, and debilitated—but they don't have AIDS. They're often confused and forgetful—but it isn't Alzheimer's. Many patients feel suicidal, but it isn't clinical depression. . . . Female victims outnumber males about 3 to 1, and a great many are intelligent high achievers with stressful lives."[20] Many of these symptoms result from being immersed in a world saturated with competition.

Be aware of the poison of competition. Life is not an incessant zero-sum game where one person's gain is another person's loss. Competition is one of Satan's most effective tools for destroying relationships and crippling ease between yourself and others. Interpersonal competition is not—nor can it be—related to righteousness. You must not suppose that your righteousness involves climbing some imaginary vertical ladder, thinking you hasten your progress toward perfection by getting above or ahead of others. This is a manifestation of the pride of the world that we are repeatedly warned against. In Alma we are told, "The preacher was no better than the hearer, neither was the teacher any better than the learner; and thus they were all equal, and they did all labor, every man according to his strength" (Alma 1:26).

We are all born with internal motivation, self-esteem, dignity, and eagerness to learn. In almost all social contexts—business, education, politics, and industry—materialistic values have replaced values of the soul and external rewards have replaced internal inducements. In school, too often students study, not to learn anything, but for the grade. Everywhere, people are constantly compared to one another and are encouraged to compete for incentive pay, annual appraisals, and production quotas. Our civilization's afflictions are symptoms of an entire cultural lifestyle that has become increasingly pathological as it has become more competitive.

As Elder Boyd K. Packer of the Quorum of the Twelve has wisely said, "Our competition in life is solely with our old self. We ought to be free of the jealousies and anxieties of the world which go with interpersonal competition."[21] The energies of the Saints should be directed toward the establishment of Zion—a society built upon cooperative relationships, not interpersonal competition. Joseph Smith taught that we should

> not seek to excel one above another, but act for each other's good, and pray for one another, and honor our brother or make honorable mention of his name, and not backbite and devour our brother. . . . Now, in this world, mankind are naturally selfish, ambitious and striving to excel one above another; yet some are willing to build up others as well as themselves. So in the other world there are a variety of spirits. Some seek to excel. And this was the case with Lucifer when he fell. He sought for things which were unlawful. Hence he was sent down, and it is said he drew many away with him.[22]

Members of the Church are particularly warned against the evils of the last days. The Lord has forewarned:

> Darkness covereth the earth, and gross darkness the minds of the people, and all flesh has become corrupt before my face. Behold, vengeance cometh speedily . . . upon all the face of the earth. . . . And upon my house [The Church of Jesus Christ of Latter-day Saints] shall it begin. . . . First among those among you . . . who have professed to know my name and have not known me. (D&C 112:23–26)

The Prophet Joseph Smith stressed the importance of helping instead of competing with one another when he taught, "The nearer we get to our heavenly Father, the more we are disposed to look with compassion on perishing souls; we feel that we want to take them upon our shoulders, and cast their sins behind our backs."[23] Again, "Friendship is one of the grand fundamental principles of 'Mormonism'; [it is designed] to revolutionize and civilize the world, and cause wars and contentions to cease and men to become friends and brothers."[24] In contrast, the Prophet taught that "God had often sealed up the heavens because of covetousness in the Church."[25]

Our performance of acts of service is often motivated by various feelings. For instance, in going to the temple, some people are motivated by fear: "If I do not go to the temple, I will be punished." Some people are motivated by responsibility: "I should go to the temple, because it is my duty." Lastly, some people are motivated by love: "I choose to go to the temple because I love helping those who can't help themselves."

We can choose to let love be the motivating force behind our actions, instead of being motivated by a competitive desire to get ahead or to exalt ourselves above others. We benefit the most in terms of mental and spiritual health when we choose to be motivated by love.

Few people realize that they can *choose* to be motivated by love. When you are motivated by love for yourself and others, you seek to do things that allow you to grow and progress. You set eternal goals and seek to obtain them. At the same time, you recognize that eternal goals take time and consistent righteous effort. While you can anticipate eventual perfection, your expectations for yourself and others should reflect the knowledge that perfection is a line-upon-line process. These expectations allow you to keep your anticipations in perspective and can motivate you as you continue to move forward.

HAVING THE COURAGE TO BE IMPERFECT

Perfection will come in the eternities; for now, I have the courage to be imperfect.

You can wear yourself out trying to always be number one or by trying to be all things to all people. King Benjamin warned, "See that all these things are done in wisdom and order; for it is not requisite that a man should run faster than he has strength" (Mosiah 4:27).

It is important to hold to your long-range expectations, but be careful of short-range anticipations. It is possible to maintain high levels of expectations and still accept imperfect, immediate performance from yourself and others. Have the courage to be imperfect in the present. Give yourself and others some space to grow naturally. There are few perfect immediate answers in our imperfect finite world.

LEARNING TO LAUGH

I know that a "merry heart doeth good like a medicine"
(Prov. 17:22).

Norman Cousins, a pioneer in the work of healing through change in mental imagery, was diagnosed as "terminally ill" and given six months to live. His chance for recovery was one in five hundred. Seeing that his conditions were greatly influenced by worry, depression, and anger, he wondered, "If illness can be caused by negativity, can wellness be created by positivity?"

He decided to conduct an experiment using himself as the subject. Laughter was one of the most positive activities he knew. He rented all of the comedy movies he could find. He read all the funny stories he could find. He asked friends to call him each time they came across a funny anecdote.

He was in so much pain he could not sleep. Laughing for five solid minutes, he found, relieved the pain for several hours, and he could sleep. Norman Cousins fully recovered from his illness; and he lived another twenty happy, healthy, and productive years. He credits visualization, the love of his family and friends, and laughter for his recovery.[26]

You, too, can benefit from laughter. Though some diseases may be contagious, none is as contagious as the cure—laughter. While Latter-day Saints do not endorse levity (light-mindedness), we recognize that light-heartedness is good for the soul. Laughter cleanses the soul and helps keep the adversities of this life in perspective.

THY WILL BE DONE

"Nevertheless not my will, but thine, be done"
(Luke 22:42).

Real and lasting peace comes as we, too, learn to say, "Thy will be done." There is an old Chinese story that illustrates the idea that we cannot always tell what is good and what is bad for us.

There once was an old country farmer who one day was visiting across the fence with his neighbor. The farmer said, "My horse broke out of the barn last night and ran away."

"Oh," said the neighbor. "That is bad!"

"Who knows," said the farmer, "what is good and what is bad?"

The next afternoon, the horse returned and brought with him two other horses. Later, the farmer was talking with his neighbor again and explained that he now had three horses.

The neighbor said, "Oh that is good!"

"Who knows," said the farmer, "what is good and what is bad?"

The next afternoon, while the farmer's son was breaking one of the new horses, he fell off the horse and broke his leg.

Later, while talking to his neighbor again, the farmer explained that his son had broken his leg.

The neighbor responded with, "Oh that is bad!"

"Who knows," said the farmer, "what is good and what is bad?"

Later on in the week, the army recruiters came through the village where the farmer lived and were drafting all the eligible young men into active service. The farmer's son was not able to go because of his broken leg. After the farmer explained to his neighbor what had happened, the neighbor had learned his lesson and did not say, "Oh, that is good!"

He said, "Who knows what is good and what is bad?"

And so it is in your life. Who can say what is good and what is bad? Perhaps those adverse things that have come your way will be a great blessing in the long run. They can have a refining effect in your life. You need not think that the Lord will impose more upon you than is for your good. He is a kind and loving Heavenly Father. Remember that, "There hath no temptation taken you but such as is common to man: but God is faithful, who will not suffer you to be tempted above that ye are able; but will with the temptation also make a way to escape, that ye may be able to bear it" (1 Cor. 10:13).

An example of God's power to bless in times of adversity comes from a friend of mine. She wanted to adopt a child from Romania. When she went there, she found a little girl whom the Spirit confirmed was to be her daughter, but the adoption proceedings and her ability to leave the country with her little girl proved very difficult. She faced many challenges along the way, and her faith was sorely tried. In a journal entry she recorded: "I concluded that I was not going to lose my faith in God. And I decided that faith was jumping again after you have been dropped." And she continued to jump. As things got more and more difficult, she often thought about the subject of sacrifice. She said, "While still accepting 'thy will be done,' I hoped for the sudden deliverance given Abraham and Isaac." After passing through many more challenges, she did receive a sudden deliverance—the adoption cleared the Romanian government, and she was allowed to leave the country.

Looking back, she said, "It is my feeling that the last minute deliverance was no less miraculous than that of Abraham and Isaac. But it is interesting to note that my moments of growth were in the midst of my trial, when my values were challenged, when my faith was tried. The determined conclusion that 'I will not lose my faith' was as great a personal victory as the resolution of the problem. My victories were the lessons learned, the spiritual growth, the depth of prayer required, the commitment to integrity, the reliance upon the Lord. The resolution of the problem was the Lord's victory."

When you are willing to submit your will to the Lord's and trust him, he will open a way for your deliverance. If you continue to trust him even when you've "been dropped," he will bless you with a knowledge of his love for you. But you must trust him and exercise your faith that he knows what is best for you. As you focus your thoughts on him you will see that, though the trials may be difficult, it is the way that you decide to view them that will determine your ability to endure and overcome them.

Sister Marguerite DeLong, who was born with spina bifida, has come to view her condition as a conduit through which the Lord has been able to teach her marvelous truths. She has learned to view the "restrictions" of spina bifida, not as limitations, but as means of spiritual and emotional growth:

> To mortals, things always seem to be limited. There is a beginning and an ending of everything around us—days, seasons, relationships and even life itself. We see people with handicaps as limited. This is another way Satan has tried to block our vision and stop our growth. The world to him is limited, because he is restricted in time and in the power he can use against us. God has set limits to all things—laws and conditions—bounds we cannot pass unless we want to reap sad consequences. But if we are willing to obey these laws and conditions, we will gain infinite power. This power is still controlled by laws, but it is unlimited in that it encompasses all things. My real self is unlimited in power, glory, and beauty. Satan would have me believe that God's limits prevent me from doing things. Only Satan's limits are preventive. The word *handicap* suggests a *cap* on a person's limits or

abilities. But as children of God we are not "capped," we're capable—capable of growing, of being and doing the things that our Father is and does. I think the thing that irritates Satan the most is that his preventive limits always have "an escape hatch" provided by our Heavenly Father. We just have to look to him and as we do we will have life—and that more abundantly. He may not take the limitation out of us—like Paul with his "thorn in the flesh"—but he takes us out of the limitation. His grace is sufficient to make weak things strong, if we will humble ourselves and look upward. I used to feel handicapped. Now I know I am handi*capable*—limited physically, but not spiritually. Someday, when I grow up spiritually, I won't be limited physically either. I am a child of God.[27]

Through Christ, we can overcome our present limitations, the evils of this life, and eventually arrive "at a point of faith where [we are] wrapped in the power and glory of [our] Maker and are caught up to dwell with Him."[28] This faith grows as we submit our will to his and "come unto Christ, who is the Holy One of Israel, and partake of his salvation, and the power of his redemption. Yea, come unto him, and offer your whole souls as an offering unto him, and continue in fasting and praying, and endure to the end; and as the Lord liveth ye will be saved" (Omni 1:26). Here, enduring to the end is not to be thought of as a static, cliff hanging enterprise—rather we should see enduring to the end as a dynamic, progressive, moving thing—climbing the mountain, so to speak.

Not all of the sick are healed—even those who have great faith. The will of the Lord should always be paramount as we call for his healing grace. We don't have the final say on anything; the Lord does. But we can plan, make requests, start things in motion. We must pray with real intent, but we are also to conclude our prayers by saying, "Nevertheless not my will, but thine, be done" (Luke 22:42).

Elder Bruce R. McConkie taught that,

> the law governing faith and signs is eternal and everlasting; it is the same in all ages and among all peoples, and it has been given to us in our day in these words: "It shall come to pass that he that hath faith in me to be healed," saith the Lord, "and is not appointed unto death, shall be healed."[29]

The exercise of faith is always subject to the overriding providences of the Lord. If it is the will of the Lord to take one of his children from this life to the next, then the Lord's will prevails. Faith cannot be exercised contrary to the order and will of heaven.

Nevertheless, "He who hath faith to see shall see. He who hath faith to hear shall hear. The lame who hath faith to leap shall leap. And they who have not faith to do these things, but believe in [the Lord] have power to become my sons; and inasmuch as they break not my laws thou shalt bear their infirmities." (D&C 42:49–52.)

So, not all power is given to us at once—we gain power with the Lord gradually. Though you may want the Lord to bless you and heal you right now, you need to trust that the Lord, in his infinite knowledge and love, will bless you according to his time frame. Again, the Lord may not always answer your prayers when you want, but he will never be late. In our impatience we may want things our way, but we learn to trust the Lord.

From these examples, you can see how I have used the scriptures, statements of the prophets, clinical experience, and general observation to form faith statements. I invite you to join in the quest for correct principles to help you govern your life and manage your pain and suffering in harmony with faith in the Lord and in your own divine nature. Now let us take a look at how *hope* in receiving the sought-for blessings can help in the healing process.

NOTES

1. *Teachings,* 292.
2. *Teachings,* 328.
3. *Teachings,* 160.
4. Joseph F. Smith, *Gospel Doctrine* (Salt Lake City: Deseret Book, 1939), 34.
5. *Teachings,* 151.
6. Richard G. Scott, *Conference Reports,* October 1989, 38.
7. Boyd K. Packer, "The Candle of the Lord," *Ensign,* January 1983, 543.
8. *Mormon Doctrine,* 2d ed. (Salt Lake City: Bookcraft, 1966), 264.
9. "Know This, That Every Soul Is Free," *Hymns of The Church of Jesus Christ of Latter-day Saints* (Salt Lake City: The Church of Jesus Christ of Latter-day Saints, 1985), no. 240.
10. Boyd K. Packer, "Obedience," *Brigham Young University Speeches of the Year* (Provo: Brigham Young University Press, 1972), 1–4, 6–7.
11. *Teachings,* 150.
12. Hugh Nibley, "The Best Possible Test," *Dialogue,* vol. 8, no. 1, p. 75.
13. W. H. Murray as quoted in McWilliams, *Negative Thought,* 154.
14. As quoted in McWilliams, *Negative Thought,* 416.

15. *Hymns*, no. 30.

16. Neal A. Maxwell, "O Divine Redeemer," *Ensign,* November 1981, 8.

17. *Teachings,* 255–56.

18. George Q. Cannon, *Life of Joseph Smith, the Prophet* (Salt Lake City: Deseret Book Co., 1964), 496.

19. Willard Waller, *The Family: A Dynamic Interpretation,* rev. (New York: Dryden Press, 1951), 190–92.

20. *Newsweek*, Oct. 27, 1986, 105.

21. As quoted by Neal A. Maxwell, "Patience," *Ensign*, October 1980, 29.

22. *Teachings,* 155, 297.

23. *Teachings,* 241.

24. *Teachings*, 316.

25. *Teachings,* 9.

26. Cousins, *Anatomy of an Illness.*

27. Marguerite DeLong, personal correspondence with the author.

28. *Teachings*, 51.

29. Bruce R. McConkie, *A New Witness for the Articles of Faith* (Salt Lake City: Deseret Book, 1985), 206.

10

Hope in Christ—
Anticipating the Miracle

For without faith there cannot be any hope.
—MORONI 7:42

Many people who are trained scientifically are taught that "seeing is believing." This process has served us well and has been the basic model used in modern discovery. But wanting to see results before believing is not sufficient to build faith power. When we work by faith, believing is seeing. Believing in the promises of the Lord and working by faith give us a hope that allows us to retain our motivation. Both faith and hope are anticipatory in nature. When you use faith-talk and faith-picturing, you are seeing in your mind's eye the expected blessings and can therefore experience joy in anticipation. By believing truths in the present (that is, by affirming them) you come to know them in the future. This is the principle Moroni had in mind when he described the faith of the Jaredites when they came to "see with their eyes the things which they had beheld with an eye of faith" (Ether 12:19).

The sequence of how information leads to joy is shown in Figure 11.

Information. Before you can have faith in something, you must have information presented to your mind. "[The Lord] imparteth his

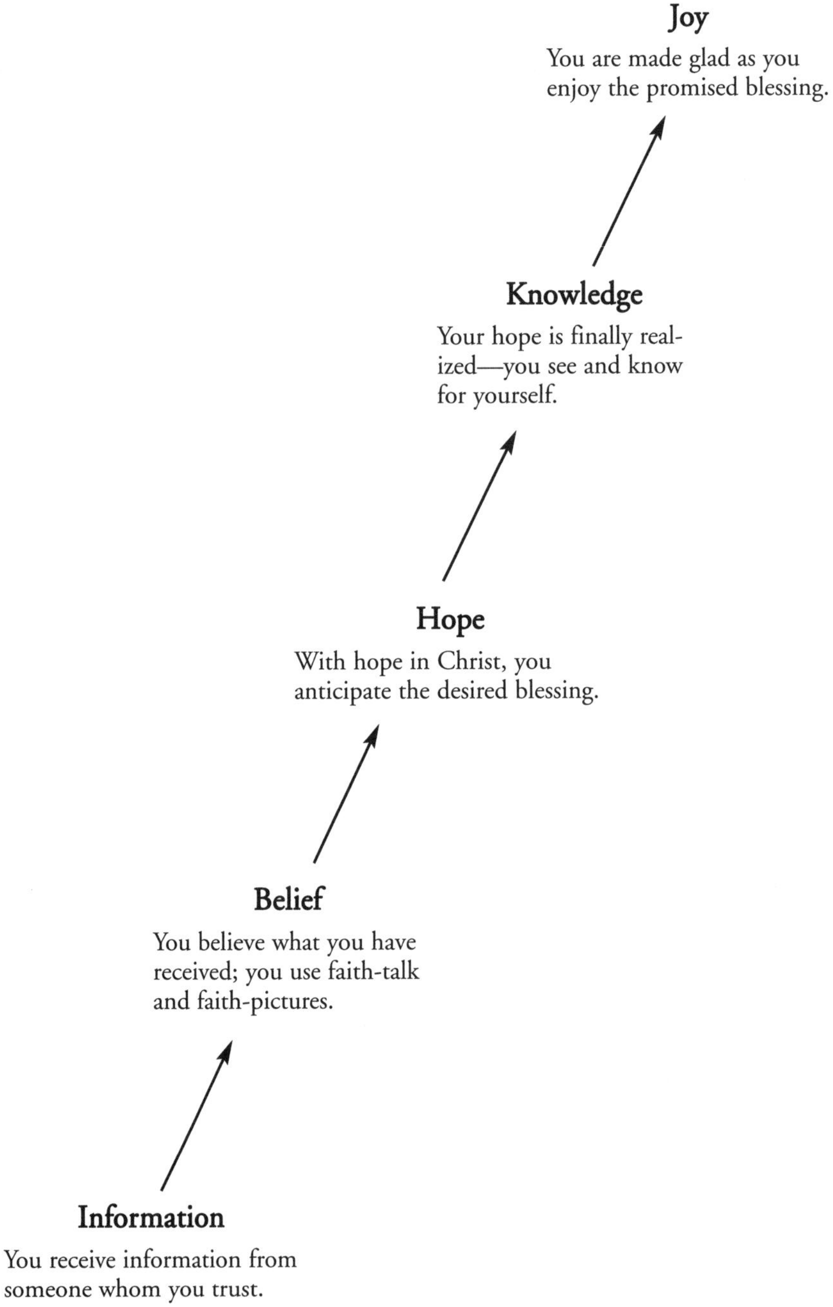

Joy
You are made glad as you
enjoy the promised blessing.

Knowledge
Your hope is finally realized—you see and know
for yourself.

Hope
With hope in Christ, you
anticipate the desired blessing.

Belief
You believe what you have
received; you use faith-talk
and faith-pictures.

Information
You receive information from
someone whom you trust.

Figure 11. How information can lead to joy.

word by angels unto men, yea, not only men but women also. Now this is not all; little children do have words given unto them many times which confound the wise and the learned" (Alma 32:23).

Belief. You conduct an experiment with the information. You do not cast out the word of truth because of unbelief. You nourish the word through affirmations and visualizations—faith-talk and faith-pictures. You anticipate the miracle on the thought level.

Hope. As you anticipate the miracle, your strong belief engenders within you feelings of hope. The healing words of truth "swell within your breast," they enlarge your soul, enlighten your understanding and become delicious unto you (Alma 32:28).

Knowledge. The time finally arrives when, because of your faith, diligence, and patience, your faith grows into a great tree and bears healing fruit. "By and by ye shall pluck the fruit thereof, which is most precious" (Alma 32:42). What you had merely believed is now realized; it is seen and tasted. Thus, your believing is turned to seeing. Now you no longer live by faith regarding the healing power of the Lord, for you know, nothing doubting. (See Ether 3:19.)

Joy. Words that had been suggested to your believing mind have turned to knowledge, and you are made to rejoice. "And there were many whose faith was so exceedingly strong, even before Christ came, who could not be kept from within the veil, but truly saw with their eyes the things which they had beheld with an eye of faith, and they were glad" (Ether 12:19).

THE POWER OF WORDS

Gaining the power to unlock healing faith begins with words. The fire of faith is kindled or snuffed out by words—words that are spoken within our own minds or heard from others. Words from angels, men, women, and even little children trigger in our minds thoughts that stimulate our faith. Words have great power. I remember as a child reading fantasy comic books. By saying the magic word "Shazam," Captain Marvel was empowered with supernatural energy. When I became a man, I put away these childish beliefs about "magical words." But as an adult, I gained a new respect for the power of words.

"The old idea that words possess magical powers is false," Aldous Huxley wrote, "but its falsity is the distortion of a very important truth. Words do have a magical effect, but not in the way that the magicians supposed, and not on the objects that they are trying to influence. Words are magical in the way they affect the minds of those who use them" . . . and those who hear them. It is in using this kind of magic that sloganeers try to plant words in the public mind which produce reflexive generalizations. "A good catch word," the American politician Wendell Wilkie once said, "can obscure analysis for fifty years."

For example, the word "democracy" has cropped up in the names of some of the world's most dictatorial countries, such as the Democratic People's Republic of Korea and the Democratic Republic of Afghanistan. Generations of absolute tyrants have claimed to be defending democracy as they lined up their opponents in front of firing squads.

In his novel *1984*, George Orwell presents a picture of a bizarre society in which the "Ministry of Truth" dispenses words that mean just what the dictator, Big Brother, wants them to mean. The state language, "Newspeak," turns logic inside-out in brazen contempt for the public intelligence; hence the universal slogan, "War is Peace."

Closer to home, Hugh Nibley revealed the power of rhetoric in such expressions as "Zion's Used Car," "Zion's First National Bank," and "Zion's Upholstery." The owners of these businesses attempt to obscure the worldly nature of their enterprises by using the word "Zion" in their names.[1]

Early in my seminary teaching career, I had difficulty understanding why Jesus was called "the Word." I could understand why he was the Light and the Life of the world, but why "the Word"? I think I understand now—in part. Words are wonderful, almost like magic. They have the astonishing power to stir our thoughts and feelings. Hitler obtained such astonishing power with his words that he swayed almost a whole nation toward lunacy. On the other hand, Jesus, through his words, established the everlasting covenant of light, life, and joy. Words form faith-statements and provide cues for faith-pictures. Words are the essence of the healing power of faith.

SATAN—THE DESTROYER OF YOUR HOPE AND HAPPINESS

Satan would have you doubt that God can or will bless you or grant you your desired blessings. Carolyn Pearce Ringger suggests that we often doubt because Satan whispers to us, spirit to spirit, in our own tone of voice that we are not worthy to receive blessings from God. We may even hear vulgar and indecent expressions in our own tone of voice that we think are of our own creation. Some people may even choose to act upon this vulgarity placed in their heads, believing that such is their real nature.[2] To bind Satan we must understand his methods of deception, then erase the evil thoughts and replace them with positive, Christ-centered affirmations.

From an apocryphal source we read these words:[3]

> Again he said unto me; remove from thee all doubting; and question nothing at all, when thou asketh anything of the Lord; saying within thyself: how shall I be able to ask anything of the Lord and receive it, seeing I have so greatly sinned against him?
>
> Do not think thus, but turn unto the Lord with all thy heart, and ask of him without doubting, and thou shalt know the mercy of the Lord; how that he will not forsake thee, but will fulfill the request of thy soul.
>
> For God is not as men, mindful of the injuries he has received; but he forgets injuries, and has compassion upon his creatures.
>
> Wherefore purify thy heart from all the vices of this present world; and observe the commands I have before delivered unto thee from God; and thou shalt receive whatsoever good things thou shalt ask, and nothing shall be wanting unto thee of all thy petitions; if thou shalt ask of the Lord without doubting.
>
> But they that are not such, shall obtain none of those things which they ask. For they that are full of faith ask all things with confidence, and receive from the Lord, because they ask without doubting. But he that doubts, shall hardly live unto God, except he repent.
>
> Wherefore purge thy heart from doubting, and put on faith, and trust in God, and thou shalt receive all that thou shalt ask. But and if thou shouldest chance to ask somewhat and not [immediately] receive it, yet do not therefore doubt, because thou hast not presently received the petition of thy soul.
>
> For it may be thou shalt not presently receive it for thy trial, or else for some sin which thou knowest not. But do not thou leave off to ask, and then thou shalt receive. Else if thou shalt cease to ask, thou must complain of thyself, and not of God, that he has not given unto thee what thou didst desire.
>
> Consider therefore this doubting, how cruel and pernicious it is and how it utterly roots out many from the faith, who were very faithful and firm. For this doubting is the daughter of the devil, and deals very wickedly with the servants of God.
>
> Despise it therefore, and thou shalt rule over it on every occasion. Put on a firm and powerful faith: for faith promises all things and perfects all things. But doubting will not believe, that it shall obtain anything, by all that it can do.

> Thou seest therefore, says he, how faith cometh from above, from God and hath great power. But doubting is an earthly spirit, and proceedeth from the devil, and has no strength.
>
> Do thou therefore keep the virtue of faith, and depart from doubting, in which is no virtue, and thou shalt live unto God. And all shall live unto God, as many as do these things.[4]

As you learn to bind Satan by erasing your negative, world-centered thoughts and replacing them with positive, Christ-centered thoughts, you will find yourself drawing upon the powers of heaven in powerful, magnificent ways, resulting in greater manifestations of the healing gifts of the Spirit.

PATIENCE—CHANGE REQUIRES TIME

When the Lord endows his Saints with the power of heaven associated with the establishment of Zion, abundant gifts of the Spirit will be manifest. In the meantime, we will be more limited in the actual power to be healed in comparison to that glorious day in the Lord. We must be patient in our pain, maximizing the gracious gifts and tools presently available to us.

In our quest to bring the principle of faith into sharp focus in our lives, we must be careful that we do not become discouraged by what we sometimes see as slow progress. Thomas E. and Ann F. Pritt provide the following encouragement:

> Changes . . . are gradual and require time as well as sustained effort in right directions. Individuals may become distracted and discouraged and lose sight of meaningful growth. Three weeks after Michelangelo began sculpting his magnificent David, he was probably joyfully engaged in his work. His vision of the finished creation was indelibly stamped in his mind and heart. Neither in the beginning nor as the work neared completion were the remaining rough edges and unsmoothed curves seen as evidence of failure. He saw and built only on his previous day's progress. Such is the craft of Christian faith, and such must be diligently expressed by those correcting an inappropriate identification. Such an exercise in belief will soon bring recognition of the miraculous. Those who have successfully dealt with all forms of "impossibilities" could joyfully attest to such a reality.[5]

The Lord will bless us as we patiently seek to know and do his will, exercise faith, repent, and serve others. He has promised that he will not leave us alone. We can have faith in him when he says, "I will not leave you comfortless: I will come unto you. . . . In the world ye shall have tribulation: but be of good cheer; I have overcome the world" (John 14:18).

NOTES

1. Hugh Nibley, *Approaching Zion* (Salt Lake City: Deseret Book, 1989).
2. Carolyn Pearce Ringger, *Reaching toward Heaven* (American Fork, Utah: Covenant Communications, 1992), 49–50.
3. See D&C 91 for the Lord's explanation on how we should view apocryphal writings.
4. 2 Hermas 9:1–11, *The Lost Books of the Bible and the Forgotten Books of Eden* (Cleveland: Fontana, 1974). See also 2 Nephi 4:17–26; D&C 91.
5. Thomas Pritt, "Homosexuality: Getting Beyond the Therapeutic Impasse," *Association of Mormon Counselors and Psychotherapists Journal* 13, no. 1 (1987), 57.

11

Charity—Receiving
Grace for Grace

I say unto you, you shall receive grace for grace.
—D&C 93:20

Your faith, power, and grace with the Lord will increase as you reach out to others with a sincere desire to bless their lives. Jesus himself had to grow in this manner. He did not receive a fullness of power and knowledge at first, "but received grace for grace; and he received not of the fulness at first, but continued from grace to grace, until he received a fulness" (D&C 93:12–13). This is given to you about Jesus so that you

> may understand and know *how* to worship, and know *what* you worship, that you may come unto the Father in my name, and in due time receive of his fulness. For if you keep my commandments you shall receive of his fulness, and be glorified in me as I am in the Father; therefore, I say unto you, you shall receive grace for grace. (D&C 93:19–20)

It is through showing grace toward others—mercy, compassion, love, and assistance—that we receive grace from our Father in Heaven. Jesus received a fullness of the Father through his service to others. Before we can receive a fullness of heaven's power, we must grow in our desire to serve others. "It is by grace we are saved, after all we can do" (2 Ne. 25:23). We are saved by God's grace after all we can do to render grace ourselves through service to our fellow men. As Jesus said, "Inasmuch as ye have done it unto one of the least of these my brethren, ye have done it unto me" (Matt. 25:40). We become pure through service. Charity, the quality of our hearts as it is manifest in action through service, unifies and sanctifies us. As we become sanctified in Christ, we become one with him. We receive the blessings associated with being pure in heart: we receive of his power, we know him face to face, and we receive his embrace.

Among the greatest opportunities to serve the Lord and your fellow men is the opportunity we have, in our day and time, to marry in the temple, have children, and rear them in righteousness. The prophets have counseled us that the most important work we will ever do will be within the walls of our own homes. Beyond serving our families, we are expected to reach out and declare the good news of the gospel to every nation, kindred, tongue, and people. An important dimension of the gospel—the good news—has to do with the healing blessings of the Spirit.

I don't know of anything that will bring you more peace and joy than learning the truths and light of the gospel and then finding opportunities to share what you have found. Your faith will be therapeutic in your own behalf in direct proportion to your willingness to gain and share truth. You receive grace for grace. When you bring your thoughts, feelings, and actions in harmony with the mind and will of the Lord, and then seek to bless the lives of others through proper service, you prepare yourself for blessings unimaginable and incomprehensible.

Your faith in the Lord Jesus Christ and in your own divine nature will grow as you commit yourself to serving others. In proper time you will enjoy all the gifts of the Spirit—awesome and superhuman gifts— wisdom, knowledge, healing, miracles, discernment of spirits, speaking in tongues, and interpreting tongues. (See D&C 46:13–25.) Your power with the Lord will grow to the point where, through a fullness of priesthood ordinances, you will someday have a perfect knowledge that Jesus is the Christ.

By learning about and obeying correct principles and then seeking to help and lift others, we are creating the conditions of a Zion society like that of Enoch and the Nephite saints. As we unitedly develop the powers of faith in our lives, we as a people will become united with the Lord and not only enjoy his thoughts and feelings, but also be participants in his actions and powers.

The scriptures provide vivid descriptions of ancient followers of Christ who not only found great healing blessings, but also received marvelous powers to control the elements of the earth and the powers of heaven. The survivors of our generation are promised a society similar to that of the Nephites, one in which there were no contentions or disputations among them and every man dealt justly with his neighbor. All of the sick were healed among them. (See 3 Ne. 17, 19; 4 Ne. 1.) We must not forget the Lord's assurance that as we become united in the gospel and truly seek to serve one another, we will receive these same great blessings. But first we need to learn to be less selfish, more sensitive to the needs of others, and more willing to share ungrudgingly. Our ability to do this is based on our recognition of our own unconditional worth and God's love for us.

Heavenly Father uses people to help people. We are sanctified through charity. If you want to feel good about yourself, do good things for others and treat yourself with the same kind of concern and love. Now that you are beginning to understand how to unlock faith's healing power by using faith-talk and faith-picturing, it is important that you help others who are suffering the pain of loneliness, depression, or physical problems. You will grow in your own faith as you help others acquire trust in the Lord and in their own divine nature.

King Benjamin, the Book of Mormon prophet, counseled his people how they could retain a remission of sins. His message was one of service. (See Mosiah 4: 11–12.) We obtain a remission of sins through baptism, but we *retain* a remission of our sins through service to our fellow men. This process of service helps others and heals us.

Of course, it is important to do good things for yourself, too. Learn something new, focus on the positive, read a good book, exercise, get a massage, practice forgiveness, spend time with a loved one, or see a good movie. At other times, you can do something for someone else such as surprising your spouse or children with an unexpected gift or activity, preparing and teaching a lesson, or participating in a service project. The opportunities for both are limitless.

When your actions are directed at helping someone else, the blessings flow. If you have tendencies toward depression, getting involved in some sort of physical action or service is most healing. Next to controlling your thoughts, the keys here are action, doing, movement, involvement.

In our Heavenly Father's plan for our happiness, he has ordained that we help one another. His plan includes very specific contacts to be made with others. You, for example, may make contacts with others where you may sense a holy relationship. What may appear to be a casual chance encounter with someone will, in reality, be part of the Lord's plan. Each encounter has the potential for becoming a teaching-learning situation.

You and another person may enter into an intense teaching-learning situation and then appear to separate. These meetings are not accidental, nor is what appears to be the end of the relationship a real end. Each of you has learned the most you can at the time. Yet all of us who meet will someday meet again, for it is the destiny of all holy relationships to endure eternally. Good friends, like families, can be forever. These eternal relationships provide innumerable opportunities for us to love and serve each other. You don't have to be a full-time missionary to do missionary work.

HELPING OTHERS WHO ARE HURTING

Every time you lead someone to healing truth, you are doing missionary work, and there is no greater work. "And now, behold, I say unto you, that the thing which will be of the most worth unto you will be to declare repentance unto this people, that you may bring souls unto me, that you may rest with them in the kingdom of my Father" (D&C 15:6. See also D&C 16:6).

The Lord has said that if you have a desire to serve, you are called to the work. (See D&C 4:3.) But he has also counseled that we must obtain his word before we seek to declare his word (D&C 11:21). In order for you to lift others, you must be standing on higher ground; the miracle is, however, that in lifting others you obtain higher ground.

Whenever you are teaching by the correct Spirit, you learn as you are teaching. The teacher and the learner become one and "both are edified and rejoice together" (D&C 50:22). What you have learned about faith, you can share with others; and they in turn give to others. That is why it is so important that you respond when you are called to bless the lives of others.

This life is the time to prepare to meet God (Alma 12:24). It is difficult to think about being prepared to return to our heavenly home if you are just trying to make it through each day. However, when you have begun the process of healing and growing, time becomes a wonderful thing. You may have observed that when you are in your real self time seems to cease, or at least slow down, because you sense you are already in a part of eternity. And yet you have time enough to do all things necessary. However, when you are in your negative self, time seems to move slowly, and yet you never have enough time to get things done.

You must use the time that you have been allotted wisely. Your own preparation must precede your teaching of others. Just as a butterfly cannot fulfill its mission until it has changed from a caterpillar, so you cannot fulfill your role without certain growth experiences. As you come to understand the processes involved in unlocking healing faith, you will be given the gift of healing, not only of yourself, but of others too. You will be able to help them to heal their wounds the way yours were healed. This will bring great joy into your life as this healing process becomes a part of you.

When the student is ready, the teacher will appear. The opposite is also true; once you have chosen to fulfill your role, your pupils will appear. It is only a matter of the proper time and season. As you recognize and take advantage of these opportunities, you will grow.

The Prophet Joseph Smith taught that "God has created man with a mind capable of instruction, and a faculty which may be enlarged in proportion to the heed and diligence given to the light communicated from heaven to the intellect."[1] This information often comes when you are in the service of others. For example, many of the ideas found in this book have come to me while I have been teaching in a classroom or while conducting therapy in my office. "Sudden strokes of ideas"[2] have come to me that have helped others solve problems. I have written them down and they have become mine. However, what has worked for one class or one person does not necessarily work for others because there are so many different levels of learning. One class may be on day three of their spiritual journey and another on day five. As you work with others, you will be guided to know how to proceed.

To suggest that you help others is not to suggest that you will know all the subtleties involved in clinical therapy. You need not be a trained counselor to apply the basic principles discussed in this text, but familiarity with some of the basic principles used in this book can assist you in fulfilling your divine charge to help others.

The Lord has commanded us to teach and thereby bless the lives of others. "And as all have not faith, seek ye diligently and teach one another words of wisdom; yea, seek ye out of the best books words of wisdom; seek learning, even by study and also by faith" (D&C 88:118). Because you use the principles involved in the unlocking process, you will be blessed to share your insight and ability with others.

Before you can effectively help others, a climate of mutual trust must exist. This basic truth holds whether you are a missionary, classroom teacher, parent, or priesthood leader. You can positively influence others only when this high level of trust exists. The Lord has explained the conditions by which you may help others and build relationships of trust: "No power or influence can or ought to be maintained by virtue of the priesthood, only by persuasion, by long-suffering, by gentleness and meekness, and by love unfeigned; By kindness, and pure knowledge, which shall greatly enlarge the soul without hypocrisy, and without guile" (D&C 121:41–42).

What we have read governing the priesthood holds true for all relationships. As we build trust through love, we become more effective in helping others focus their faith in Christ and correct principles, to bring about desired changes.

The following account illustrates how you can help others unlock healing faith, especially as it relates to thought detection and thought selection.

Linda was a thirty-eight-year-old woman who had been hospitalized for attempted suicide. She believed that environmental toxins were the cause of her stress. She sought associations and literature that supported her view that external agents were the sources of her problems. Her husband, Mark, was a very successful businessman, having inherited the family business from his successful but emotionally distant father and mother. Mark was willing to participate in therapy sessions, but had a difficult time involving himself in any depth because he had trouble expressing himself verbally.

The following list represents Linda's negative self-talk:
1. I do not like the thoughts of getting old.
2. I am gaining weight.
3. My brain scan shows there are abnormalities with my myelin sheaths.
4. I have had a hysterectomy. I am not desirable.
5. I have a hormonal imbalance. I have different emotional responses than others.

6. Last June I was rejected while making love. He left me to answer the phone and did not come back. He does this a lot. He has not touched me in weeks.
7. He goes to work all the time to get away from me.
8. I have a fear of Alzheimer's disease. It's in the family.
9. I have high expectations for my marriage which aren't being fulfilled.
10. My husband won't talk to me.
11. My teenage son and I often argue, but when I don't have my husband around, I need someone to talk to.
12. All these things make me so depressed at times.

Linda selected faith-talk statements from her real self as follows:

1. I may be getting older, but the older I get, the closer I get to a resurrected body. While I am here on earth, I can repent, forgive others, and gain knowledge.
2. This is a great chance for me to learn self-discipline and self-control.
3. Even if there are neurological problems, I will take opportunities while I still can.
4. I am more than my body. I may not be able to have children anymore, but I am still a desirable woman.
5. If I have a hormonal imbalance, I will seek competent medical help and do all that I can cheerfully. I will keep a sense of humor.
6. My husband's problems are his and mine are mine. I'll take care of mine first. My husband's indifference is an opportunity for charity from me. I can tell him how I feel in a firm but loving way.
7. I can appreciate my husband for his good qualities.
8. I'll turn it over to the Lord. I will replace fear with trust.
9. High expectations are good, but for today I will be patient.
10. I'll seek ways of making it more safe for my husband to talk with me.
11. I'll learn to do my own therapy, so he will be able to do his.
12. I will remember some of my depression is "divine discontent" turned inward. I will turn it outward and upward.

Ideally, you could help Linda by:

1. Helping her restate her thoughts in faith-talk form: first person, present tense, positive statements.
2. Helping her practice faith-picturing: visualizations, vivid mental pictures in which she sees herself doing and being these positive things.
3. Helping her relax. The process of neurological imprinting or reprinting seems to take place better when the body is relaxed. Faith-talk and faith-pictures when coupled with relaxation exercises, provide a sensation of immediate peace and long-range goal attainment.
4. Helping her to *do it*. Because of the preceding three steps, when the time comes to make the behavioral changes she can say, "Of course I can do it. I have already done it in my mind many times."

When you are able to help someone, as described above, you experience great joy yourself and both you and the receiver are blessed. By extending love, you receive love, grace for grace, and mercy for mercy.

LETTING OTHERS SERVE YOU

One of the greatest forms of service is to allow others to serve you. The principle behind this is, "We love those whom we serve." One of the reasons parents love their children so much is they do so much for them. Mothers sacrifice and bring forth children in pain and much discomfort. Rearing children requires sustained patience on the part of both mother and father. Share the blessings of service. Let someone else give the lesson once in a while. You sit back and let someone else do the work. (This counsel, however, is directed toward those who have a tendency to do all the work all the time. You who sit back and let others serve all the time already—please skip this counsel!)

Giving to others feels good. It strengthens your body and enhances your self-worth. When you allow others to give to you, they experience these same blessings. If you are a parent, once in a while let your children fix your breakfast, wake you up for a meeting, remind you of an important appointment. By letting others help you, you might experience some negative feelings: Your pride might get in the way ("I have always taken care of myself!"), you might feel that you are unworthy of their service ("I really don't deserve all this attention"), or you might mistakenly feel inadequate if you need any help at all ("If I were competent, I could handle all this by myself").

Each time someone does something for you, humble yourself and remind yourself, "I am worthy of this service." You will be blessed as you allow others to serve you and as you strive to serve them.

SUMMARY AND TESTIMONY

This book is an attempt to meet a great need that I have observed. We have many faithful members of the Church who needlessly suffer the pains of depression, sorrow, disease, sin, and loneliness because of mental, social, spiritual, and physical problems.

While I acknowledge that there are Saints whose pains our Heavenly Father allows to continue as a refiner's fire in spite of their strong faith, in many cases, the pain and suffering can be eased, lessened, and often eliminated as one learns and applies the principles involved in working by faith. The Lord's promise is true: "Therefore, dearly beloved brethren, let us cheerfully do all things that lie in our power; and then may we stand still, with the utmost assurance, to see the salvation of God, and for his arm to be revealed" (D&C 123:17).

The key principle in unlocking the healing power of faith is found in the scripture, "And ye shall know the truth, and the truth shall make you free" (John 8:32). Jesus Christ is "the way, the truth, and the light" of the world (John 14:6). By learning of the Lord Jesus Christ and his plan of salvation (including our own divine nature), we are healed and blessed and learn of marvelous powers upon which we can draw.

We are empowered through truth as we learn of Christ and focus our thoughts on him and the healing principles which he has revealed. The steps are these:

1. We must have knowledge, being acquainted with Christ and his teachings.

2. Through faith-talk and faith-pictures, we focus our thoughts on him and on the correct principles he has revealed and is yet revealing.

3. Because of our faith, we experience hope in Christ.

4. A true hope in Christ enables us to exercise charity in our relationships with others.

5. By walking in obedience to the commandments, we eventually receive, according to the promise of our Heavenly Father, "health in [our] navel and marrow to [our] bones; And shall find wisdom and great treasures of knowledge, even hidden treasures; And shall run and not be weary, and shall walk and not faint. And I, the Lord, give unto [you] a promise, that the destroying angel shall pass by [you], as the children of Israel, and not slay [you]" (D&C 89:18–21).

I know that faith in the Lord Jesus Christ can heal us. I know the principles outlined in this book can act as a lullaby to your pain and loneliness. As difficult as it is to describe the workings of faith on paper, I know that the earnest seeker after truth will find many treasures that were heretofore hidden from view. I wish it were possible that I could sit with each of you, my readers, and hear your problems. I know that on a one-to-one basis I could be of more assistance. It is easier to establish a trust relationship when we are eye-to-eye. But our Heavenly Father has not ordained that we all be healed in that manner. It is truth, as testified of by the Holy Ghost, that makes us free. Many truths are presented in this book, truths I am satisfied with and excited about because of the healing power in them. The Spirit of the Lord has borne witness to me many times that these principles are true, and I have seen them bear their fruits in the helping and healing of people.

While I do not believe that I have even scratched the surface of the healing powers of faith in Jesus Christ and in our own divine natures, I do believe that the healing principles presented here will point you in the right direction. I am comfortable with the focus on Jesus Christ, our own agency to choose the power of our thoughts, the interaction between our thoughts, feelings, and actions, and how all this affects our health.

I believe strongly that faith, hope, and charity do indeed lighten our loads and heal our pain. At the same time I know that being carnal, sensual, and devilish ladens us with unnecessary burdens and leads to disease and death.

I am so very grateful for my knowledge of Jesus Christ. I am grateful for parents who introduced me to things of the Spirit, and for brothers and sisters in my own family and throughout the Church who have helped me focus my mind and heart on gospel truths. I know that the nearer we approach perfection, the clearer are our views and the greater are our enjoyments. I trust that there will come a time when I will lose every desire for sin and someday be prepared to return to my Heavenly Father's presence. However, I know that my preparation and your preparation has much to do with receiving the gospel into our lives. We must hunger and thirst after righteousness, and then we will be filled with the Holy Ghost. As we grow in the Spirit, receiving grace for grace, we not only gain control of our personal lives, but we are promised to enjoy both the mind and the power of the Lord—awesome and superhuman powers of which we can scarcely dream.

I have a firm conviction that without a vision of these things, we can grow weary of attending meetings and serving in the kingdom. But with an eye of faith, we can look up with great and hopeful anticipation to not only ridding ourselves of our mortal aches and pains, but also receiving blessings which "eye hath not seen, nor ear heard, neither have entered into the heart of man, the things which God hath prepared for them that love him" (1 Cor. 2:9). We have the Lord's faithful promise: "Unto you that fear my name shall the Son of righteousness arise with healing in his wings" (Mal. 4:2).

May these words and principles find a place in your mind, heart, and actions, that you may find the answers to your most intimate prayers. The answers will come through the "good news" of the gospel of our kind and loving Heavenly Father, and through his Almighty Son, Jesus Christ, our Lord, our God, our Redeemer, and our Savior.

NOTES

1. *Teachings,* 51.
2. *Teachings,* 151.

APPENDIXES

APPENDIX A

Breaking the Grip of the False Self

The lists below contain faith-talk statements that can help you overcome the habits of your false self. Remember that faith-talk statements are to help you get faith-pictures that are effective in helping you shed your false self. By earnestly using faith-talk and faith-pictures, you are inviting the Holy Ghost to intervene in your life and help you make changes. Then you can let go of your false self, and your new commitment eventually becomes reality. When you sincerely select faith-talk statements, you are, in effect, making commitments to the Lord and yourself. You are bearing testimony to the ideals expressed. It is important to remember that you don't have to reach your target in each of these areas to be committed to them. Faith-talk is the seed that becomes sure knowledge.

When you wholly commit yourself to anything, the powers of the eternities combine to assist you beyond your wildest imagination. Ideas, feelings, means, powers, and people will come into your life and empower you to make decisions and take steps that will change your life for the better.

ANGER

The Spirit of God empowers me with righteous energy.
My real self always responds with constructive force.

I lower my sails when others are angry.

I am a free agent. I control my emotions at all times and in all situations.

The Lord gives me the things I really need.

I am very effective in all my relationships because I am empowered by the Spirit.

I always control my emotions.

I become a shadow when others are angry. Their arrows cannot pierce a shadow.

BEING ALONE

I know there is a time and a season for all things.

The Lord in his wisdom whispers to me, "Be patient," and I am patient.

I am remembered by the Lord. He knows my private yearnings and desires. In his own time he will grant me my heart's desire.

I have a witness of God's perfect justice.

In time, all things will be placed in proper order.

I love the Lord. He is mindful of me and is preparing a place for me that will be thrilling and wonderful.

I am comforted by good friends and by the ever-present influence of the Holy Ghost.

CONTROLLING MY THOUGHTS

My real self controls the thoughts I think about. No thought, at any time, can dwell in my mind without my real self's approval or permission.

I become tomorrow what I think today, so I choose thoughts that will bring me a brighter tomorrow.

I shape my character by the thoughts I think and the way I spend my time.

I let virtue garnish my thoughts unceasingly.

Rocks and stones are not free to act. I am! I am constantly and earnestly involved in erasing the negative and replacing it with the positive. As a result, my real self is becoming stronger and stronger.

DEALING WITH DEPRESSION

I know that happiness is the object and design of my existence.

I was created that I might know joy. Any sadness I experience now prepares me for more joy.

I know that God is with me every step of the way.

I am committed to the Christlike way of life that always brings happiness.

Since happiness is a choice, I choose to be happy, cheerful, and optimistic.

My feelings come from my thoughts; I select happy thoughts; I feel happy.

I am a different person now.

GAINING SELF CONTROL

God has given me the power to control how I think, feel, and act about everything.

I have less need for "things" as I draw closer to the Lord.

I have made covenants with the Lord. I follow his teachings because I trust that the greatest amount of good will come out of it.

I live the teachings of the gospel, knowing they are for my happiness.

I live the commandments and experience the promised blessings.

My false self wants complete control, but my real self is much stronger.

My real self is self-existent. I choose to let it rise through the sludge of my false self's old, worn-out habits.

My real self is growing stronger every day. It feels good to have my real self gain control again.

I know with God all things are possible.

LOSING WEIGHT

I eat the right foods and the right amount to stay healthy and at my correct weight.

I like myself thin. I feel better thin.

Eating is fleeting; fasting is lasting.

My real self weighs _____ pounds. Every day I get closer to my real self's weight because I eat less and exercise more.

I eat a balanced diet that includes high-fiber, high-protein, low-fat foods, and I enjoy their natural taste.

I know that my weight is a reflection of how I see myself. I have learned to focus on my real self who is slim, trim, healthy, energetic, feels good, and is very happy.

I am willing and able to pay the price to look and feel better.

I like matching my physical appearance with my real self.

When I want a snack, it will be food that is light, nutritious, and healthy.

OVERCOMING ADVERSITY

I know that all these things will give me experience and will be for my good.

I let adversity teach me with God's blessings.

I know that all things work together for my good.

I know God loves me enough to prune me.

I know that life at its worst is a very fascinating experience.

I know that through trials come blessings. I have experienced this many times.

I recognize growth potential in everything that happens.

I reach my targets although there are surprises along the way.

I accept my present condition and make the best of it; it is what I agreed to do.

I know that God's delays are not God's denials.

God may not always rescue me when I want him to, but I know that he will never be late.

OVERCOMING BAD HABITS

It feels good to be in control.

Because I know what it is like not to be in control, I know I want to always be in control.

I know I can serve only one master. I choose to serve the Lord.

Even as a helium-filled balloon rises when the string is cut, so do I rise as I let go of my bad habits.

OVERCOMING FEARS

Where there is faith, there can be no fear. I choose faith.

I fear the face of no man, but rather I fear (respect and love) God.

Although I show respect for authority figures, I am full of confidence that my real self can handle any situation.

I am as important in the eyes of God as any other person.

I stand tall.

I always have the courage to try something new.

While I listen to the advice of others, I always make my own choices and accept their consequences.

OVERCOMING SELF-DOUBT

I know in whom I trust. Jesus is my Savior, my Redeemer, my Deliverer.

I am of good cheer; I am loved and respected.

I spread good cheer to others; I radiate happiness.

I am always true to the best that is inside of me.

OVERCOMING SHYNESS

I am very confident. I speak with a strong, firm voice, and my facial expressions and my body language reflect my strong voice.

Even when I mispronounce a word, I do it with deliberation. I can correct it later.

In any group I sit near the front and make at least one comment or ask at least one question.

I know that it is not enough to just be a nice person. To be balanced, I am also a strong person.

I balance my strength with kindness and warmth.

RESOLVING CONFLICTS WITH OTHERS

Because I choose to allow my real self to be in control, I respond to others in constructive, loving ways.

Since a soft answer turneth away wrath, I always give a soft answer.

I am both soft and firm, as the situation warrants it.

I always communicate kindness in my tone of voice, facial expressions, and choice of words.

I am firm, fair, friendly, and flexible in all my relationships.

When others are upset, I respond with "you" statements: I say, "So you are saying that . . . " "What are you feeling?" "What is it that you want?" or "What is it that you are afraid of?"

When I need to confront others, I use "I" statements like "I feel frustrated when you leave your dirty clothes around, because I get the feeling you want me to pick them up."

When others do not respond to my bid for cooperation ("I" statements), I give them choices: "Do you want to cooperate with me, or do you want me to . . . (create some kind of distance, withdraw emotionally, withdraw physically)?"

STOPPING HEADACHES

I am wise enough to know when a headache is caused by a physical problem and when it is caused by stress. When it is caused by stress, I am able to deal with the stress through appropriate faith-talk and faith-pictures, relaxation, and rubbing it away.

I have inner peace because I let my real self control my thoughts, feelings, and actions.

I am calm and confident. I have the quiet self-assurance of being at peace with myself because my real self is in control.

I watch my long-range expectations and short-range anticipations. Although I keep my expectations high for myself and others, I am able to be relaxed about my present anticipations.

I have the courage to be imperfect for now.

STOPPING UNNECESSARY WORRY

I know the difference between problem dwelling and problem solving. I spend my mental energies in solving problems, not just dwelling on them.

All of my thoughts create healthiness within me. My mind dwells only on those thoughts that create more harmony, balance, and well-being within me and in the world around me.

My mind focuses its attention only on those things that I can do something about. If I cannot affect it or direct it, I accept it.

I keep my mind too busy thinking good, healthy, positive, constructive, and productive thoughts to have any time for worry, doubt, or uncertainty.

I know that when I accept a situation, suffering ceases.

APPENDIX B

Empowering Your Real Self

As you repeat the following faith-statements, you will be inviting the Holy Ghost to empower you with the blessings mentioned. It is important that you associate with people who are committed to the same ideals. Try to avoid negative situations or persons who would tear you down or would lessen your commitment to the light and truth expressed in these affirmations.

ACQUIRING KNOWLEDGE

I am hungry for knowledge.

I am enthralled by, and love to feed on, light and truth.

I know that my exaltation is related to my gaining knowledge, therefore I rejoice in gaining understanding and insight.

I enjoy seeing patterns and cycles, extracting principles to live by, seeing contrasting principles, making connections in my own life and, as a result, being empowered to make wise decisions enabling me to experience the abundant life.

I am committed to the idea that I can learn something from everyone.

I search for further light and knowledge and experience joy with each discovery.

I make decisions based upon correct principles.

ACQUIRING TEMPERANCE

I know that the temperate life is the balanced life. I follow a steady course that leads to eternal life.

I always try to help people who go "overboard" in things.

I recognize in others a balance in spiritual and temporal affairs, and I learn from their successes.

Christ was perfectly balanced in his courage and his humility; every day and in every way, I am becoming more Christlike.

I balance my energies between things spiritual and temporal. I read and ponder the scriptures and pray fervently; I exercise regularly; I eat low-calorie, high-fiber foods.

I know the Lord knows better than I what I need to experience to return to him.

BEING CHARITABLE

I am full of charity, the pure love of Christ.

I love others in a Christlike way. I love as he loves.

I am wise in my expressions of affection for others.

I am Christlike: merciful, kind, unselfish, loving, listening, caring, empathetic, and thoughtful.

I know that true charity is a balance between firmness and tenderness. I am Christlike in my balance.

BEING DILIGENT

I follow the whisperings of the Spirit moment by moment.

I am diligent in all good works.

I stay with worthwhile tasks until they are finished.

I cheerfully do all I can with all diligence, and then I stand still and watch the Lord's arm come to my rescue in accomplishing important tasks.

I dwell in the spirit of prayer at all times, in times of gratitude as well as in times of pleading. I constantly pour out my heart to him who knows me better than I know myself.

GAINING COURAGE

I demonstrate courage and strength in my voice, my eyes, and even in the confident way I walk.

My real self has a perfect balance of courage and warmth that is true charity.

I temper my strength through the love of all humanity.

I am strong when I need to be. I am tender when I need to be. I am balanced always.

I can handle any situation that comes my way because I am strong and kind.

GAINING HUMILITY

I have a good balance between humility and courage.

I willingly offer to the Lord my sacrifice of a broken heart and a contrite spirit.

Because I am humble and searching, the Lord is able to empower me with his Spirit that teaches me all things.

Humility prepares my heart for the promptings of the Spirit. I am open and eager to learn the lessons I need in my eternal progress.

I enjoy humility in other people and respond to such people with kindness.

INCREASING IN FAITH

Every day I am growing in my faith in Christ and faith in my real self. I use faith-talk and faith-pictures to create the world I live in.

Because I have faith in Christ and in my real self, my mind prospers and so do the works that follow.

I ask in faith, so all things are possible for me.

I have a growing faith in Christ and in my real self.

My faith is strong. I have great trust, belief, assurance, dependence, confidence, hope, reliance, certainty, and expectation that things will work out well for me.

Because I allow the Holy Ghost to empower my real self, I am able to unlock doors that lead to blessings incomprehensible and unimaginable.

I have boundless wealth, joy, and peace in this world. I expect eternal life in the world to come.

IMPROVING INTERPERSONAL RELATIONSHIPS

In my relationships with others, I am firm and friendly as the occasion requires.

When others are upset, I remain calm and collected.

When others are on the attack, I become a shadow that their arrows cannot pierce.

When I speak in public, I start slowly and build momentum.

In communicating with others, I ask about the other person's feelings, goals, and plans.

I am able to ask others the three listening questions: "What are you feeling?" "What is it that you want?" and "What are you afraid of?"

LEARNING KINDNESS

When I am kind, I feel a sweetness.

I make eye contact with and smile at every person I pass or meet.

I reach out and give a mental blessing to every person I meet.

I have a deep respect for all life.

I am increasing in my kindness every day.

I am wise in how I express my kindness and affection for others.

RECEIVING REVELATION

I gain new insights with deeper understanding guided by the Spirit.

I am full of light and knowledge.

I know repentance is a change of attitude. I heed the precious promptings of the Spirit.

Because I am true and faithful in all things, the Holy Ghost is my constant companion, and I receive revelation that settles on my mind and heart like dew from heaven.

I unlock the powers of heaven through my faith and my knowledge.

I draw on the powers of heaven.

I know a spiritual immersion is greater than all the wealth of the world.

I know that struggling for the Spirit is one of the most challenging and worthwhile things I can do.

I know that understanding things of the Spirit becomes easier with patience.

I plead with the Lord, so my prayers are sincere and with real intent.

STRENGTHENING MY REAL SELF

My real self is intelligent. I can figure things out. I can make good, healthy decisions.

My real self is not hindered by worrying about what others might think.

When I have to make decisions, I give my real self a reasonable amount of data and my answers come to me as "sudden strokes of intelligence." I recognize these as gifts of the Spirit and express gratitude for them.

My real self says "I can" instead of "I can't."

I experience pure intelligence flowing into me.

My real self knows when to say, "This is as far as I go. This is my limit. I won't tolerate any more. It is not right!"

When others are upset, my real self says things like, "Sounds like you're having a problem. What can I do to help you?"

If others want to blame me, I can simply say something like, "I'm sorry you're having that problem." I can let go. I do not have to fix their problem. To do so would deny them the learning experience that comes from taking personal responsibility for decision making.

My real self recognizes that some things cannot be changed yet. My false self will try to force change in an untimely way. I let my real self take charge. It will lead me right.

APPENDIX C

Your Personal Thought Profile

Answer the following questions on a scale from +2 to -2 according to the following measurement.

Always	(+2)
Usually	(+1)
Sometimes	(0)
Rarely	(-1)
Never	(-2)

Record your answers on the answer sheet provided at the end of the questions.

QUESTIONS

A. 1. Can you keep your mind focused on what you are doing when you are reading or studying?
    2. Can you keep calm when you are with noisy, active children?
    3. Are you free from nervous habits like nail biting, foot tapping, or scratching?
    4. Is it easy for you to relax without having to keep busy all the time?

5. Do you feel relaxed and calm most of the time?

B. 1. Do you feel accepted and loved by others?
   2. Do you feel happy and encouraged because you are making good progress in life?
   3. Are you free from sadness and feelings that might bring tears?
   4. Do you feel that people appreciate, love, and respect you?
   5. Are you free from feelings of sadness or depression that might last for days at a time without good reason?

C. 1. Do you enjoy going to social activities?
   2. Do you move quickly and with energy?
   3. Do you like to keep busy and have plenty of things to do?
   4. Do people think you are a hard worker?
   5. Do you like people and enjoy making new friends?

D. 1. Can you show love and affection without feeling silly or embarrassed?
   2. Do you express pleasure when looking at beautiful things?
   3. When you talk, do you speak with animation, enthusiasm, and expression?
   4. Do you like to talk a lot?
   5. Do you feel free to talk about your personal problems with close friends?

E. 1. Is it easy for you to forgive others?
   2. Are you sympathetic and understanding when others in your family are ill?
   3. Are you a good listener when others need to talk about their troubles?
   4. Do people come to you when they are in trouble or in need of a good friend?
   5. Would you do everything you could to protect an animal from neglect or cruelty?

F. 1. Do people compliment you for thinking clearly and logically?
    2. Are you usually in control of your emotions?
    3. Do you understand others and get the right meaning out of what they say and do?
    4. Are you thought of as being a rational thinker?
    5. Are you free from worrying about what other people might think of you?

G. 1. Do people listen to what you have to say?
    2. Do you take the lead in making plans for activities and programs?
    3. Do you stand up for your rights?
    4. Do you let people know where you stand on issues?
    5. Are you strong enough that people do not take advantage of you?

H. 1. Do you refrain from thoughtless remarks that might hurt people's feelings?
    2. Do you have a deep respect for all people?
    3. Do people compliment you on your patience and sympathy?
    4. Do you refrain from sarcastic and cutting remarks when people are rude to you?
    5. Do you think most people would be willing to help others in need?

I. 1. Do you think things through before you get involved?
    2. Do you plan ahead and then carry out your plans?
    3. Do you have places for everything and keep things in their places?
    4. Do you like to stay with a job until it is finished?
    5. Do you think it is important to always be working for some future goal?

ANSWER SHEET

	A	B	C	D	E	F	G	H	I
1	—	—	—	—	—	—	—	—	—
2	—	—	—	—	—	—	—	—	—
3	—	—	—	—	—	—	—	—	—
4	—	—	—	—	—	—	—	—	—
5	—	—	—	—	—	—	—	—	—
Total	—	—	—	—	—	—	—	—	—
Grade	—	—	—	—	—	—	—	—	—

GRADE YOURSELF

Total your scores in each column, and then grade your scores in each of the nine areas according to the following scale:

+10 to +7	= (A)	Excellent
+6 to +3	= (B)	Acceptable
+2 to -2	= (C)	Improvement Recommended
-3 to -6	= (D)	Improvement Necessary
-7 to -10	= (F)	Improvement Urgent

PLOT YOUR SCORES

Plot the total from each column on the graph by making a point on each lettered line. Connect each point with a line.

Your Personal Thought Profile

Positive Self Traits

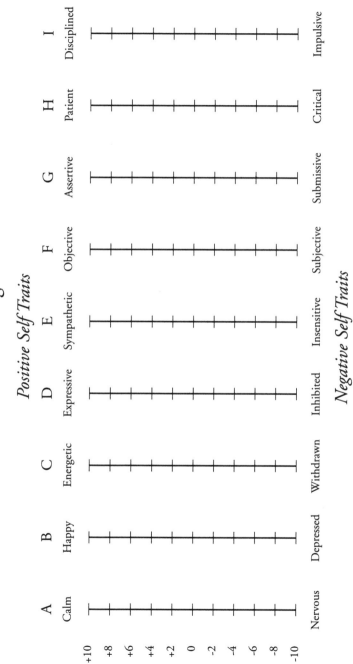

Negative Self Traits

APPENDIX D

Relaxation Exercise

This relaxation exercise will help you learn to relax and to become sensitive to tension in your body when it is present. Stress awareness is one of the most important factors in reducing stress.

Record the following exercise in your own voice (or if you would prefer, have a friend with a pleasing voice record it for you). Read slowly and pause between sentences. Play the tape back and follow the suggestions as they are presented. Repeat each suggestion slowly and be sure you have given yourself time to execute each direction.

Play the tape several times a day for a period of one week until you have done at least twenty exercises. By playing the tape that many times, you will learn the habit of relaxation. After you are familiar with the process of relaxation, you may want to write out your own script for a relaxation exercise.

Lie down and concentrate on the muscles around your eyes. You are completely relaxed. Your eyes are closed, and you create a feeling of relaxation in the muscles around your eyes. You cause this relaxation in your eyes with your mind. Your body is a perfect reactor to your mind, and right now your mind is commanding your eyes to completely relax.

Now that feeling of relaxation gradually spreads across your face. Wave after wave of relaxation extends across your face, down through your neck, and across your shoulders. This relaxation all begins in your eye muscles. Your entire body is comfortable: there is no tension anywhere in your body. You are completely calm, relaxed, and tranquil. Now is the time for relaxation. Now is the time for complete relaxation. It feels good just to relax for a few minutes. Check your eye muscles again; make sure they are very relaxed. The feeling of relaxation continues to spread from your face to the back of your head, down through your neck, and across your shoulders. Wave after wave of calmness, like ripples on a pond. Visualize these ripples in your mind. See them start as if from a pebble dropped into a lake. My voice is the cue for relaxation. When you hear my voice, it becomes the pebble in the lake, and wave after wave of relaxation spreads out from your eye muscles, across your face, down your neck, and over the placid lake of your body. There is no tension anywhere in your body, just complete and total relaxation and calmness.

These feelings of calmness spread down through your body and extend to the end of your very fingertips. Your whole body is completely limp. You are causing this to happen with your mind. Your mind completely controls your body, and your spirit controls your mind. Now sense the feeling of relaxation in your chest, your stomach, across your back, your legs, your feet, even your toes. You are completely relaxed and calm.

Now with your left hand, make a tight fist. Make a fist and hold it very tightly. Clench your fist. The feeling of tension in your fist affects your whole arm. You feel the tension in your fist, your arm, and your shoulder.

Now relax your hand. Let your hand go very limp. Your fingers are very relaxed. Your hand and your arm are loose and slack. The whole left side of your body is much more relaxed now. There is opposition in all things. Notice the difference between the tension in your hand and arm when your fist was clenched and the feeling you have now that it is relaxed. When you have experienced tension, you can know and appreciate the feeling of relaxation. You appreciate relaxation more and more each day. Every day you gain more and more control over your body through faith-power. You are calm, relaxed, and tranquil, and you accomplish this state of relaxation through your mind.

Clench your right fist and make it tight. Hold it for a few moments. Feel it. Sense it. Label that feeling tension. Feel the tension in your fingers. Your arm. Your whole arm and shoulder. The whole right side of your body is very tense.

Okay, let go now. Let go of the tension. Your right hand is limp and relaxed. Contrast the feelings of tension and relaxation. Relaxation exercises help you relax and become aware of tension in your body, even when this tape is not playing. The sound of your own voice is the cue for relaxation; your voice commanding your body to relax. When you hear yourself say, "relax," you relax on cue. When you sense tension in your eyes, neck, shoulders, back, legs—anywhere in your body, any time of the day or night—you will say, "relax" and your body will obey your command.

Your whole right hand is relaxed now. You feel the calmness in your arm, shoulder, and whole body. Enjoy the feeling of relaxation for a few moments . . . [let the tape record silence for a few moments].

From your eyes you are still experiencing those ripples, those waves of relaxation and calmness. Wave after wave of relaxation spreads down through your body.

Now squint your eyes as hard as you can. Close them as tightly as you can. Hold it. Sense the tension. Label that feeling in your mind tension. Now relax your eyes. Again, contrast the feelings of tension and relaxation. Allow the feelings of relaxation in your eye muscles to continue in wave after wave of relaxation. These feelings of relaxation, that you are creating with your mind, encompass your entire body. Your whole body is becoming more and more relaxed. As you get more and more relaxed, your whole body seems to be getting heavier and heavier. It is sinking deeper and deeper into relaxation.

Now raise your left leg about two inches from its resting place. Hold it in this position for a few moments. Sense the tension. Label it as tension. Hold it. Now let it go back down and relax. Again, concentrate on the difference between tension and relaxation. Continued tension in your body is like poison. Relaxation is the desired feeling. Now raise your right leg about two inches from its resting place. Hold it. Sense the tension. Label the feeling as tension. Hold it a few seconds longer. Now let it relax. This feeling of relaxation is what you want to achieve throughout your entire body. No tension anywhere. Your whole body is like a limp dishcloth.

While you are relaxed, all of your bodily processes work better and more efficiently. Your mind is free to visualize scenes of calmness and tranquility. Your mental pictures are vivid and clear. In your mind, picture someone you love giving you a foot massage. Few things help to relax more than a foot massage. Someone you love has your foot in their lap and is spreading your toes. One by one your toes are pushed in the down position. One by one your toes are pushed in the up position, gently extending them to the pleasurable limit. You do all of this in your mind. Picture in your mind a cat being stroked on its head and down its back. As it arches its back in anticipation of the petting, you anticipate in your mind each of your toes being stretched and pulled. Firm but gentle hands rub and massage your toes, and the arch of your right foot . . . and then your left.

Your brain cannot tell the difference between a vividly imagined experience and a real one. The imprinting is the same. Your mind programs your brain with relaxation cues, and your body responds to your brain's commands.

When your body is relaxed you can create vivid, mental pictures. With visualizations you can take some wonderful trips. You can travel to far-off places. You can go to your favorite mountain retreat. Perhaps you prefer the beach. Anywhere you choose, you can create a mental picture and go there and enjoy its relaxation. Take a moment now and create a mental picture of a place you find very peaceful and relaxing. Notice the colors, feel textures, smell fragrances . . . make the experience as vivid as you can. Now let your mind caress the images you see in your mind. Each time you play this tape, visualize a different setting. Enjoy the power of your mind to create places of calmness and beauty . . . [Let the tape record silence for a few moments].

Carry these feelings of relaxation with you wherever you go. When you are faced with what have been stressful situations in the past, remember your visualizations of peace, quiet, and relaxation and take these images with you. Your body will relax on cue as you picture peaceful settings. It feels good to relax right now. You feel secure, happy, and in control. Enjoy the feelings of relaxation now. You are completely composed, calm, relaxed, and tranquil. [Let the tape play out to the end.]

If you are preparing the tape for night relaxation, you might suggest, "You will sleep soundly all night and awaken refreshed and invigorated in the morning." If playing the tape in the morning, say, "You now feel rested and energetic, and you will be able to accomplish the things you need to do today." You can also make similar suggestions for relaxation any time of the day.

INDEX

ABOUT THE AUTHOR

Garth L. Allred was born in Cardston, Alberta, and grew up in Provo, Utah. After completing a two-year mission in the Eastern States, he obtained his bachelor's and master's degrees from Brigham Young University and his doctorate degree in Marriage and Family Therapy from Florida State University.

He was employed by the Church Educational System of The Church of Jesus Christ of Latter-day Saints. Within the system, he taught seminary and institute classes, and wrote and coordinated programs. He also served on a priesthood correlation task committee, writing lessons for Primary and Sunday School.

In 1986, he joined the religion faculty at BYU–Hawaii, where he was named Teacher of the Year. In 1992–93 he taught at the BYU Jerusalem Center for Near Eastern Studies. Subsequently he has led several private tours to the Holy Land. He also has been a featured speaker at Know Your Religion and Education Week.

Brother Allred has served in such Church callings as: Sunday School teacher, bishop, stake president, temple ordinance worker, and as a member of the Tabernacle Choir. He currently teaches Gospel Essentials in his ward.

Brother Allred has published several articles in professional journals and in the *Ensign*. His book *The Eternal Plan of Happiness* features many important but not well known teachings of the Prophet Joseph Smith regarding the plan of salvation.

Brother Allred and his late wife Mary Best raised eight children and two foster children. He now resides in Utah with his wife, Noriko, and maintains a marriage and family therapy practice in the Provo/Orem area.